GASTRIC SLEEVE BARIATRIC COOKBOOK

Experience a Perfect Post Surgery Recovery Enjoying 500 Effortless & Tasty Recipes to Stay Healthy, Eat Well, Win Food Addiction. 8-Weeks Meal Plan Included

© Copyright 2021 - All rights reserved.

Table Of Contents

Introduction

Gastric sleeve surgery is a weight-loss procedure in which the stomach is reduced in size and divided into two segments, or sleeves. The gastric bypass, on the other hand, is performed by cutting off part of the small intestine.

Patients receive counseling for at least six months before surgery and are required to meet with a bariatric dietitian for at least three months after surgery. They are also required to have their blood sugar monitored throughout the weight-loss phase and to follow special nutritional guidelines that help them maintain control of blood sugar.

While bariatric surgery can help people lose hundreds of pounds over time, lifestyle changes are also needed to prevent regaining the weight back. Good nutrition is essential to maintain blood sugar levels and keep type 2 diabetes at bay. While these drastic methods may seem extreme, this surgery is making it possible for people with type 2 diabetes to live longer, healthier lives by resolving obesity-related health concerns.

People who are obese develop a variety of life-threatening conditions, necessitating bariatric surgery. This is when a person decides to undergo a gastric bypass treatment on the advice or recommendation of a doctor.

During this procedure, the doctor makes adjustments to the patient's digestive system that will eventually aid in weight loss. It is recommended for persons who are at risk of major health problems as a result of excess body fat.

Bariatric surgery is a complex operation that can change a person's eating and digesting habits. To maintain and prolong their healthy state, anyone undergoing this treatment would need to make critical decisions regarding their food and lifestyle. The operation can diminish a person's ability to absorb nutrition and limit how much they can consume.

It is highly advised that one should opt for bariatric surgery only after learning all the guidelines of the procedure. While the surgery can offer various benefits, it should also be kept in mind that any type of weight-loss surgery can attract various risks and side effects. The person will be required to make permanent lifestyle changes to reap the best results. Once the surgery is done, the person should strictly stick to the recommendations given by the doctor. Most importantly, regular exercise and a controlled diet are the basic expectations that need to be acknowledged and followed religiously.

Depending on the requirements of the body, bariatric surgery can be performed through various procedures (Roux en-Y bypass, sleeve gastrectomy, biliopancreatic diversion, along with duodenal switch).

With advancements in medical technology, bariatric surgery has a high success rate, helping the person achieve significant, long-term weight loss. The procedure is often used for people with a history of diabetes or cardiovascular risk factors.

As per the experts, people with a body mass index (BMI) of at least 35-40, or people suffering from serious medical ailments or with a diabetic history, can avail themselves of the surgery under the proper guidance. In fact, as per certain independent researchers, people with a BMI ranging between 35 and 40 with no presence of one or more additional conditions that are co-occurring with a primary condition in the person can use bariatric surgery to their advantage. However, any person who has a BMI above 30 along with comorbidities can opt for bariatric surgery.

Once the surgery is completed, it reduces the size of your stomach so that less food is absorbed by the body. This positively affects the patient with concerns of obesity, diabetes, hypertension, temporary cessation or apnea, or heart disease.

CHAPTER 1:

About Bariatric Surgery

Bariatric Surgery and Obesity

Obesity is a debilitating disease that is impossible to manage with both a healthy diet and daily exercise. Bariatric surgery is a viable therapeutic choice in these situations, especially for highly obese people with serious health issues exacerbated by their weight.

Bariatric surgery refers to a group of operations that help people lose weight by limiting their food consumption and/or absorption. Weight reduction may be achieved using a gastric orthopedic appliance, surgical resection (partial vertical gastrectomy or biliopancreatic bypass with duodenal crossing), or the development of a narrow gastric pouch attached directly to a portion of the small intestine (gastric bypass and variants). The best results are achieved when the patient undergoing surgery is adamant about adhering to stringent eating requirements and engaging in routine physical exercise after surgery. In addition, the participant must agree to a long-term obligation to post-operative medical care and follow-up. These habits are important for maintaining the benefits of bariatric surgery.

Who Is Qualified for Bariatric Surgery?

Currently, bariatric surgery is a viable choice for people who meet the following criteria:

*   They are severely obese.
*   They've tried a supervised eating regimen and struggled to get good results (with or without pharmacological support).
*   Include conditions include hypertension, impaired glucose metabolism, asthma, hyperlipidemia, and obstructive sleep apnea.

Obesity thresholds are determined by the body mass index (BMI), which measures a person's weight and shape depending on their height and weight. Obesity is described as a BMI of 30 or higher.

Only patients who have at least one of the following features should consider bariatric surgery:

*   A BMI greater than 40 (class III/severe obesity).
*   A BMI of 35 or greater (class II/severe obesity), with at least one obesity-related pathological disorder, can be improved with weight loss.

Recent research indicates that people with a BMI of 35 to 40 without associated disease or a BMI of 30 to 35 with severe comorbidities can benefit from bariatric surgery.

Anyone thinking about having bariatric surgery to lose weight should be mindful of the complications and advantages of the procedure.

If the patient meets the following criteria, they may be recommended for bariatric surgery:

*   Is unable to reach or sustain a healthy weight loss (for at least six months) using non-surgical methods such as diet, supplements, and exercise.
*   Following surgery, he decides to make a long-term contribution to a healthy diet and regular physical activity; he is mindful of the limitations he will have to set on himself in the future and the need for regular follow-up.
*   It does not misuse alcohol or narcotics and has no medical or psychiatric barriers to surgery or anesthesia.
*   He is inspired to better his fitness and is mindful of the potential changes in his life after surgery (for example, patients must adapt to side effects, such as the need to chew food well or the inability to eat large amounts of food).

Benefits of Bariatric Surgery

1. Loss of weight

According to research and studies, gastric sleeve surgery loses about 60% of their excess body weight in 12 to 18 months. Maintaining your weight following surgery can be as simple as eating the right foods and exercising daily. Long-term weight loss is possible with gastric sleeve surgery.

2. Type 2 diabetes remission

Gastric sleeve surgery is very successful in treating type 2 diabetes, according to a study performed on type 2 diabetic patients. It assists all diabetic patients in remaining insulin and adjunct medication-free for three years after gastric surgery.

3. **Assists in the improvement of cardiovascular wellbeing**

Gastric weight loss surgery lowers the risk of peripheral vascular disease, strokes, and coronary artery disease. It also aids in the regulation of blood pressure and cholesterol.

4. **Pain relief from joints**

Excess weight and obesity place a lot of strain on the weight-bearing joints. Owing to major weight loss, after gastric sleeve surgery, joint fatigue is relieved, and joint pain is relieved.

5. **Depression alleviation**

Obesity causes depression in the majority of people due to social stigma and negative body image. They have a hard time participating in group events. Since gastric surgery, the body loses extra weight, which improves physical and mental stability and provides relief from stress in those individuals.

Surgery Options

- Adjustable gastric banding (AGB)
- Roux-en-Y gastric bypass (RYGB)
- Biliopancreatic diversion with duodenal transition (BPD-DS)
- Vertical sleeve gastrectomy is the four most common operations (or sleeve gastrectomy, VSG)

The adjustable gastric band (AGB): is a form of gastro-restrictive surgery that involves wrapping an elastic silicone band around the upper portion of the stomach to minimize food intake. Band on the lap The LAGB gastric band is a kind of gastric band used. This provides a shallow gastric pocket with a short, non-expandable emptying orifice that interacts with the rest of the stomach. The gastric pocket's retention capability can be changed without requiring further surgery; the bandage contains a saline solution that can be increased or reduced, increasing its constrictive effect, using a thin catheter connected to a reservoir located just under the skin.

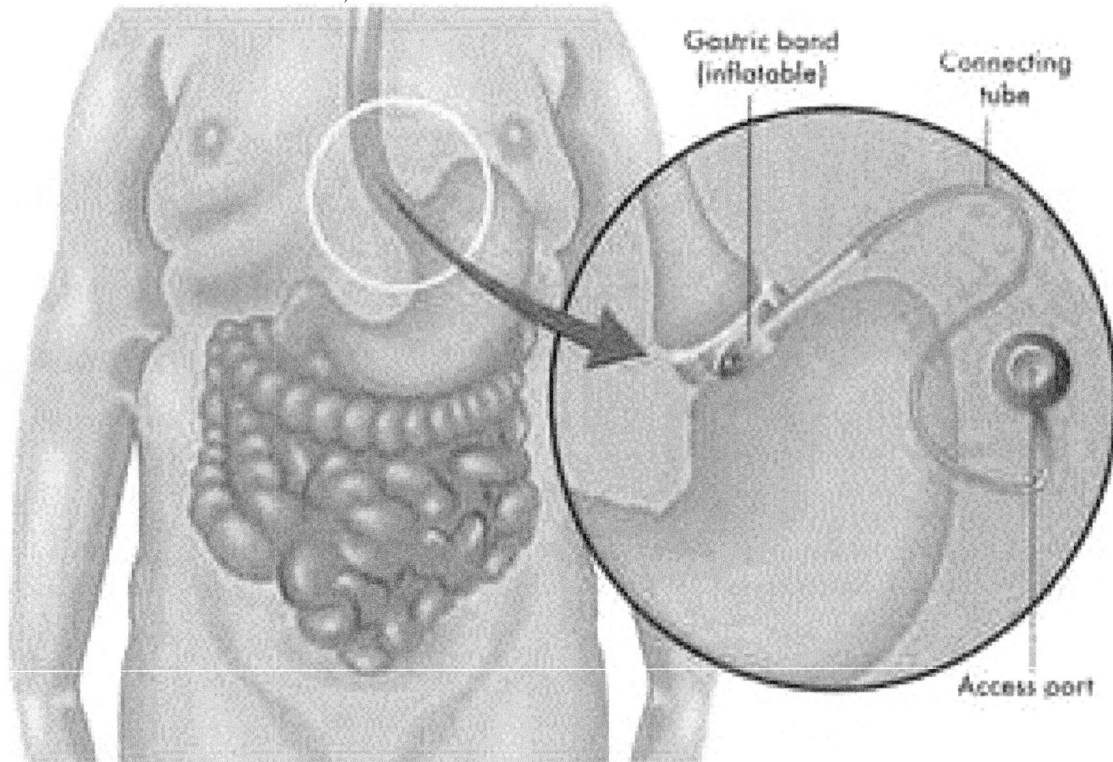

The small amount of food that can be consumed in a single meal (early satiety) and the additional time required to digest the food added are the major causes of weight loss. It's usually done by laparoscopy (LAGB), and it's a reversible procedure through which the gastric cavity isn't sectioned, and the dressing can be extracted. Weight loss: about half of the extra weight is lost.

The Roux-en-Y gastric bypass (RYGB): is a form of gastric bypass surgery limiting both food intake and absorption. Roux-en-Y procedure for gastric bypass. The stomach is surgically limited to a small sack, about the same size as the gastric bandage pocket, reducing the volume of food eaten. Furthermore, a digestive loop connects this small bag directly to the small intestine (at the level of the fast), bypassing the nutrient-absorption digestive tract (part of the stomach, duodenum, and biliary tract). Although RYGB is called an irreversible operation, it may often be partly reversed.

BPD-DS (biliopancreatic diversion with duodenal transition): this complex bariatric surgery is also known as "duodenal turn" (duodenal inversion), has three distinct features: biliopancreatic diversion and duodenal transform:

1. It is a malabsorption procedure in which the food is diverted and absorption is restricted. The surgeon creates a new food path by creating an anastomosis between the remaining gastric cavity and the small intestine tract (ileum).
2. It is a malabsorption surgery in which food is diverted and limited in its absorption. The surgeon creates a new food channel, creating an anastomosis between the residual gastric cavity and a small intestine.
3. The functionality of bile, pancreatic juice, and enteric juices is modified, affecting the body's ability to digest the elements and absorb calories.

This procedure leaves a small portion of the duodenum open to absorb food, vitamins, and minerals. However, when the patient eats a meal, the majority of the intestine is bypassed (this is a more "drastic operation than the preceding one"). During this procedure, the space between the stomach and the colon is significantly reduced, reducing the natural absorption of food. BPD-DS causes substantial weight loss (about 65 to 75% of excess weight). However, a reduction in nutrient, vitamin, and mineral absorption increases the possibility of long-term complications (anemia, osteoporosis, etc.). As a result, biliopancreatic diversion is typically only prescribed where urgent weight loss is needed to prevent a severe health problem such as heart disease.

Since it reduces the stomach scale, partial vertical gastrectomy (VSG, vertical sleeve gastrectomy) falls into the category of gastro restricting procedure.

A partial vertical gastrectomy is a surgical procedure that removes part of the stomach. This form of bariatric surgery is used to treat chronically obese patients with a BMI of 60 or higher for whom a bandage or gastric bypass is not an option. Both treatments will have a very high chance of causing problems in such a situation. The procedure aims to provide an early sense of satiety. Partial vertical resection of 80 to 90% of the stomach is done during the process to accomplish this. It is recommended that you lose 60% of your body weight. If you've done this, you should be able to do a gastric bandage or bypass easily.

The patient and the experienced surgeon should meet to determine the appropriate surgical alternative. Consideration should be given to the long-term consequences, as well as possible risks that may occur before and during the procedure (such as problems related to malabsorption, vomiting and esophageal reflux, inability to eat large meals, the need for special restrictions on certain foods, etc.). The patient's BMI, feeding habits, the effects of obesity on his fitness, and any recent stomach surgery are all things to remember.

Bariatric surgery is intended to lower the risk of obesity-related illness or death. Malabsorption procedures, on average, result in more weight loss than conservative procedures, but they come with a higher risk profile.

Tips Before Surgery
1. Alter your eating habits.
2. Give up smoking.
3. Have a supply of protein-rich foods on hand.
4. Physically prepare yourself for surgery.
5. Make a hospital guide.
6. Your support groups.
7. Talk to your surgeon.

After Surgery
1. Eat more slowly and keep track of your normal calorie intake.
2. Eat a sufficient amount of protein.
3. Take your vitamins and supplements.
4. Do a physical activity.
5. Stay hydrated.
6. Make a habit change for long-term results.
7. Do not consume your calories by drinking them.

The Recovery
The patient is limited to a liquid diet after bariatric surgery, which involves foods like broth or condensed fruit juices. This protocol is followed before the gastrointestinal tract has fully recovered from the procedure. In the following stages, the patient is "forced" to eat only small quantities of food and if he eats more than his stomach can handle, he may suffer fatigue, headache, vomiting, diarrhea, dysphagia, and other symptoms.

Dietary limits are determined in part by the form of surgery. To compensate for the decreased intake of vital nutrients, many patients may continue to take one multivitamin a day for the rest of their lives.

Side Effects

Bariatric surgery procedures can result in several complications. Complications vary depending on the type of surgery and any other health problems that exist before the procedure.

Some of the complications that may occur in the short term after surgery are bleeding, inflammation of the surgical wound, intestinal obstruction, and nausea. This is due to excess food or stenosis at the site of surgery. Nutrient deficiencies arise, common in people who have undergone bariatric procedures of poor absorption and do not take vitamins and minerals.

In extreme cases, diseases such as pellagra (caused by vitamin B3 deficiency, niacin), pernicious anemia (vitamin B12 deficiency), and beri (caused by vitamin B1 thiamin deficiency) may develop if patients do not deal with the problem.

Problems after bariatric surgery include venous thromboembolism (leg thrombosis and pulmonary embolism), heart attack, diarrhea, urinary tract infections, stomach ulcers, gastric and/or intestinal fistulae, stenosis, and hernias (laparocele and internal hernia).

CHAPTER 2:

Basic Rules Of A Diet For Bariatric Surgery

Pre-Operation Meal Plan Guideline

Typical 2 Week Pre-Op Diet You should always eat according to your surgeon's recommendations two weeks before surgery. Most 2 week pre-op diets indicate that you increase your protein intake by eating lean meats and limit your carbohydrate intake by avoiding breads, pasta, cereals, rice, and other carbohydrates.

Sugars should be avoided at all costs, including candies, desserts, juices, and sodas. The following is a typical diet two weeks prior to gastric sleeve surgery.Get a high-quality protein smoothie from GNC or another supplement store in your region for breakfast.Make sure the protein shake doesn't include any sugar.Snacks You can have a nutritious, low carbohydrate snack in between meals. Lunch Vegetables and Lean Meat Dinner Vegetables and Lean Meat Snacks You can have a healthy, low carbohydrate snack in between meals.Nuts, berries, vegetables, a little salad dressed with oil and vinegar, and so forth.Drink plenty of water to stay hydrated. This will assist you in reducing your hunger.You can drink almost anything that is sugar-free and low in calories.Keep in mind that sticking to your two-week pre-op diet is crucial. This shrinks your liver, reduces your chance of problems, and makes your surgeon's job easier and faster.2 Days Before Surgery Some surgeons advise that you stop taking the following two days before surgery.

Carbonated beverages Caffeine Most surgeons would advise you to start a strict clear liquid diet two days before surgery. Broth, sugar-free Jell-O, sugar-free popsicles, water, and maybe one protein shake per day will be clear liquids. Follow your surgeon's instructions once again.

Diet Guide and Meal Plan After Gastric Sleeve Operation

You've survived the surgery and are on your way to a better life. You could believe it's all smooth sailing from here. Regrettably, the difficult phase is only beginning.It is hight time to take those shortcuts. While the two-week diet was crucial in lowering your risk of surgical (intraoperative) problems, the post-operative diet from week one to four will help you avoid difficulties.

You will be irritable for the first few weeks following surgery, and it is typical to second-guess your decision to have surgery.It may appear that your surgeon is being excessively careful by putting you on such a strict diet following your sleeve gastrectomy. Cheating on your post-op diet might result in diarrhea, dehydration, constipation, bowel blockage, or a severe gastric leak if you don't follow their recommendations to the letter. This book might help you stay motivated to stick to your post-op diet.For weeks 1 to 4, here is a normal diet following gastric sleeve surgery.

- **Week 1**

Clear Liquids Only Glass of water. During the first week, you are only allowed to drink clear liquids. This appears to be a difficult task. It's also difficult. Most of patients, on the other hand, have little inclination to eat. After surgery, the hunger hormone ghrelin is practically non-existent. During surgery, the region of the stomach that generates the most ghrelin is removed. Make sure all of the things on the list are sugar-free.

- **Week 2**

Full Liquid Diet With Protein Protein shake and shaker bottle Water Broth Jell-O Decaf tea Decaf coffee Sugar free Popsicles Sugar free non-carbonated drinks You should avoid: Carbonated beverages Very sweet beverages Sugar Caffeine During the second week, you may begin to experience hunger pangs. Continue to follow your surgeon's diet recommendations. All of the foods from week one, plus protein powder combined with a sugar-free, non-carbonated clear beverage, may be included in your diet. Pudding with no added sugar. Soup with noodles that are soft. Yogurt with no fat. Carnation quick breakfast is a delicious way to start your day. Look for a sugar-free alternative. Soups with a thin cream base. There are no chunks. Sorbet with no added sugar. Hot oatmeal that is quite runny. Take a look at the sugar content. Juice that hasn't had any sugar added to it. Nonfat, sugar-free ice cream Thinned applesauce Examine the sugar content.

- **Week 3**

Soft Pureed Foods After gastric sleeve surgery, the third week is the most difficult. The exciting matter is that you can start eating some actual food, although pureed, in your diet. Sugars and fats must still be consumed in moderation. Week 3's objectives include consuming 60 grams of protein per day and gradually introducing new meals. Scrambled eggs.Food may taste and be accepted differently after surgery than it did before. Dairy may be more difficult to digest. It is suggested that you gradually introduce new meals. Allow time for your body to adjust to each new food. You'll be able to recognize foods that cause gas, stomach discomfort, and/or diarrhea if you do this. The foods mentioned below are usually safe to eat in the third week after surgery. 1 protein smoothie each day is recommended. You may now combine them with non-fat milk or yogurt. Protein shakes made with almond or coconut milk are delicious. Cottage cheese (low fat) Hummus Soft cereals – Soak your cereal in non-fat milk until it softens. Soft veggies should be steamed or cooked until they are tender. Soft cheeses should be consumed in moderation because they are generally heavy in fat. Ground beef or chicken. To keep the meat tender, add additional beef or chicken stock. Scrambled eggs are a wonderful source of protein in soups. Fish that has been steamed. Remember to chew thoroughly. Tuna and salmon in cans (you can add low fat mayo). A very good source of protein. Fruit that has been mashed. Bananas, avocados, and tinned fruit are all good choices (watch sugar content). The following foods should be avoided: While smoothies are OK, their sugar level should be limited. Starchy meals like pasta, rice, and bread are high in sugar. Celery, broccoli, asparagus, and raw leafy greens are fibrous vegetables.

- **Week 4**

Let's Talk About Foods! You've made it through week four of your diet. It's now time to start introducing actual foods to your child. Because your sleeve and stomach are still sensitive, take it slowly and properly chew each bite. You're done with pureed foods, but you should keep looking for softer alternatives this week. Tuna is a kind of fish. Continue with your regular protein drinks and gradually introduce chicken and beef. Make certain you chew completely. Any kind of fish will do. Fruits and vegetables (it's still a good idea to boil them a little to soften them up). Sweet potatoes can be mashed or cooked. Caffeine may be added to cereals. It's best if you keep it to a minimum. In week four, stay away from the following foods: sodas, fried meals, fibrous vegetables (such as celery and asparagus), sugary beverages, candy desserts, and pastas and other high carbohydrate, poor nutrition items (pizza). Whole milk and other dairy dishes containing whole milk. Week 4 Healthy Snacks While it is advised that you only eat three modest meals each day and drink plenty of water in between, you may require a small healthy snack. The foods listed below constitute healthy snacks if your surgeon allows. Hummus with rice crackers or baby carrots that have been softened (cooked and chilled). Egg, hard boiled. Oatmeal, quarter cup Banana Strawberries or fresh fruit a quarter of a cooked sweet potato (or microwaved) Food pyramid for gastric sleeve patients at week 5 and beyond. Continue to introduce meals one at a time to watch how they react. Constipation, diarrhea, and an upset stomach should all be avoided. Every day, eat three modest meals. Drink plenty of water throughout the day. Thirty minutes before each meal, stop drinking fluids. Snacking should be avoided. Choose a nutrient-dense meal if you do (fruit, vegetable, nuts). Take the vitamins that are suggested for you on a regular basis. Make sure you receive at least 60 grams of protein each day. A protein shake should be consumed on a regular basis as a supplement. Make fitness a part of your everyday regimen. Make it a habit to do so. Soda should be avoided. Be ready for a rough day.In this circumstances you find yourself in a difficult position, what will you do? Find a partner who will hold you accountable. Attend a support group and establish friends with whom you can communicate. Choose nutrient-dense meals as part of your healthy eating plan after gastric sleeve surgery. Bread is low in nutrients. Nutrient-dense foods include apples, bananas, salmon, and other fruits and vegetables.It is not a better idea to consume your calories in liquid form. It won't satisfy your hunger, and most caloric drinks are high in sugar. Expect a roller-coaster ride of emotions. Allowing food to be your source of consolation is not a good idea. Make a strategy.Eat slowly and thoroughly to ensure that your meal is well chewed.. If you're going out, make a meal plan. At restaurants, request a half-portion size. You could receive a discount and won't be tempted to eat too much. Water will become your new best buddy. It is recommended to eat it on a regular basis.Purchase a reusable 64-ounce bottle that you can bring to work. Each day, make sure you complete the full bottle. But keep in mind that you should not drink with your meals (this helps prevent stretching your pouch).

- Diet before surgery
- First and second day after surgery
- First month: liquid diet
- From, 4th to 6th week: semi liquid diet.
- From 6th to 8th week after surgery: semi solid diet
- After one month from surgery
- Diet after gastric bypass
- How to avoid regaining weight after surgery

CHAPTER 3:

10 Main Rules Of Eating Behaviors

Eat slowly in order to chew well

At the table one must not be in a hurry, take small bites at a time, dedicating at least 20-30 minutes to each meal, chewing the food for a long time.
Stop eating at the first signs of satiety

When the sense of satiety is perceived, stop eating regardless of the quantity of food left in the plate. If you have difficulty feeling full, report it to your care team or nutritionist.

Split food into 5 meals

Over the course of the day, food should be taken at breakfast, lunch, dinner and 2 small snacks: mid-morning and mid-afternoon. It is important to respect the time of meals, in this way the distribution is balanced and does not "wear out" the stomach wall.

Always drink in small sips and far from meals

Up to 30 minutes before the meal and 60 minutes after. It is recommended to drink at least 1.5-2 liters of natural water per day. To make it more pleasant you can flavor it with vegetables or fruit, according to your taste.

Avoid carbonated drinks (even water) and spirits

Sugary drinks (sweetened tea and coffee, fruit juices, ...), the addition of honey and sugar, jams are always discouraged. Coffee is not recommended in the first week, then from the second week it can be added to milk at breakfast, and maybe another one during the day, without ever exaggerating.

Exclude momentarily foods difficult to digest

Talk about it with your nutritionist or at the next check up with the team. Sometimes just changing the cooking method or texture is enough to make them more digestible.

Take any dietary supplements and medications in a non-effervescent formula

Polyvitamins do not make you fat or thin.

Eat your meals at the table

Setting the table (even if you are eating alone) helps create a pleasant ritual and give yourself a moment in the day dedicated to food.

Learn to enjoy what you eat

Every time you eat it is good to learn to focus on food and its flavors, smells and all the sensory aspects of the moment, without reading the newspaper, chatting on your smartphone, talking about work problems and even less eating dinner watching TV. Loving food means concentrating on each bite, paying attention to all the sensations (olfactory, tactile, visual and gustatory) that it stimulates us. In this way, fulfillment is achieved in small doses and we eat in an increasingly conscious way. A remarkable step forward.

Do not go to bed immediately after eating

It is not recommended to eat the evening meal late in the evening and wait to go to bed at least two hours after dinner.

CHAPTER 4:

Day 1 & 2

1.   Fresh Green Juice

Preparation Time: 5 minutes
Cooking Time: 0 minutes
Servings: 2
Ingredients

- 5 to 6 kale leaves
- 1 cucumber
- 3 to 4 stalks
- 2 apples
- ½ lemon, peeled or sliced

Directions

1. Juice all the ingredients in the order listed according to the manufacturer's directions.
2. Serve immediately.

Nutrition Calories: 53 Fats: 0 g.Carbohydrates: 13 g.Protein: 1 g.

2.   Carrot Pineapple Orange Juice

Preparation Time: 5 minutes
Cooking Time: 0 minutes
Servings: 2
Ingredients

- 1 small orange, including rind
- ⅛ small, ripe pineapple, peeled, cored and cut into pieces
- 2 carrots, scrubbed clean and cut into pieces
- ½ lemon juice, stirred in at the end

Directions

1. Juice all the ingredients in the order listed according to the seeded and cut into pieces manufacturer's directions.
2. Serve immediately.

Nutrition Calories: 113 Fats: 0 g.Carbohydrates: 9 g.Protein: 0 g.

3.   Detox Juice

Preparation Time: 5 minutes
Cooking Time: 0 minutes
Servings: 2
Ingredients

- 1 Asian pear
- 1 apple
- 1 beet
- 1 carrot
- ½ cup of cabbage
- 3 handfuls chard

Directions

1. Juice all the ingredients in the order listed according to the manufacturer's directions.
2. Serve immediately.

Nutrition Calories: 126 Fats: 0 g.Carbohydrates: 13 g.Protein: 1 g.

4.   Rich Antioxidant Juice

Preparation Time: 5 minutes
Cooking Time: 0 minutes
Servings: 2
Ingredients

- 3 medium carrots, peeled
- 2 medium beets, cleaned and brushed
- 1 green apple such as Granny Smith, peeled and cored

Directions

1. Juice all the ingredients in the order listed according to the manufacturer's directions.
2. Serve immediately.

Nutrition Calories: 123 Fats: 0 g.Carbohydrates: 19 g.Protein: 1 g.

5.   Blood Orange Sports Drink

Preparation Time: 5 minutes
Cooking Time: 0 minutes
Servings: 2
Ingredients

- 2 cups of coconut water
- 1 medium blood orange, squeezed
- 1 ½ tbsp of honey or 1 packet of Stevia sugar
- Pinch of salt

Directions

1. Combine all ingredients, and mix well.
2. Serve immediately.

Nutrition Calories: 234 Fats: 4 g Carbohydrates: 27 g.Protein: 2 g.

6.   Lime and Mint Infusion

Preparation Time: 5 minutes
Cooking Time: 0 minutes
Servings: 2
Ingredients

- 2 cups of cold water
- 1 large lime, sliced
- ½ cup of lightly packed spearmint leaves
- 1 package of Stevia sugar

Directions

1. In a 1-quart glass container or larger, lightly mash the lime and spearmint leaves with the pestle.
2. Add iced cold water. Stir well.
3. Optional: add Stevia to taste.

Nutrition Calories: 75 Fats: 0 g.Carbohydrates: 23 g.Protein: 0 g.

7.   Strawberry Iced Tea

Preparation Time: 5 minutes
Cooking Time: 0 minutes
Servings: 2
Ingredients

- 6 to 10 medium strawberries
- 1 tsp of lemon juice
- 2 cups of brewed white tea
- 1 ½ tsp of honey or Stevia sugar (optional)

Directions

1. Puree the strawberries until smooth consistency. Then strain chopped through fine cheesecloth on top of a metal strainer to remove the seeds.
2. Combine the strained strawberry mixture with lemon juice and chilled white tea.
3. Mix well. Add honey or Stevia to taste.

Nutrition Calories: 127 Fats: 0 g.Carbohydrates: 24 g.Protein: 1 g.

8.   Watermelon Popsicles

Preparation Time: 5 minutes
Cooking Time: 0 minutes
Servings: 2
Ingredients

- 2 cups of watermelon juice (no sugar added store-bought juice or homemade freshly pressed juice
- ½ tbsp of lime juice
- 1 tsp of honey or Stevia sugar (optional)

Directions

1. Mix all the ingredients.

2. Carefully transfer the mixture to the mold of your choice.
3. Freeze overnight.

Nutrition Calories: 135 Fats: 0 g.Carbohydrates: 22 g.Protein: 1 g.

9.   Homemade Chicken Broth

Preparation Time: 15 minutes
Cooking Time: 2 hours 30 minutes
Servings: 6
Ingredients

- 2 lbs. of bone-in skin-on chicken
- 2 large carrots, cleaned and thick-sliced
- 2 medium onions, quartered
- 3 celery sticks with leaves, cut
- 8 whole peppercorns
- 1 tsp of thyme, dried
- 1 tsp of rosemary, dried
- 2 cups of water
- Salt to taste

Directions

1. Combine everything in a pot except the salt. Bring to a boil.
2. Skim the floating foam.
3. Lower the heat. Simmer for about 2 hours until the meat can be easily removed from the bone.
4. Strain vegetables, bones, meats, and spices from the broth and into chunks; discard the solids.
5. Season broth with salt to taste.
6. Let the broth cool or refrigerate overnight. Skim the fat for a leaner broth.

Nutrition Calories: 75 Fats: 0 g.Carbohydrates: 23 g.Protein: 0 g.

10.   Ginger Chicken Soup

Preparation Time: 15 minutes
Cooking Time: 2 hours 30 minutes
Servings: 6
Ingredients

- 2 tablespoons olive oil
- 1 small red onion, thinly sliced
- 3 cloves garlic, finely chopped
- 3 tablespoons ginger grated fresh ginger
- 2 32-ounce containers low-sodium chicken broth
- 2 medium parsnips, peeled and chopped
- 2 medium carrots, peeled and chopped
- 2 stalks celery, thinly sliced
- 1 medium turnip, peeled and chopped (1½ cups)
- ½ tsp kosher salt
- 2- to 2½-pound rotisserie chicken
- ½ cup frozen peas

- 4 scallions, sliced
- 4 biscuits, store-bought or made from a mix (optional)

Directions

1. In a large saucepan or Dutch oven, heat the oil over medium heat. Cook, stirring constantly, for 1 to 2 minutes, until the onion, garlic, and ginger are fragrant.
2. Pour in the broth. Combine the parsnips, carrots, celery, turnip, and 12 tablespoons salt in a large mixing bowl. Bring the water to a boil. Reduce the heat to low and cook for 15 to 20 minutes, or until the veggies are soft.
3. Meanwhile, shred the chicken flesh with a fork or your fingers, removing the skin and bones.
4. Cook for 3 to 4 minutes, or until the chicken, peas, and scallions are cooked thoroughly. If used, serve with biscuits.

Nutrition Calories: 325 Fats: 12 g. Carbohydrates: 19 g.Protein: 34 g.

CHAPTER 5:

First 4 Weeks Liquid Dietbreakfast

11. Lemon Mint Cucumber Infused Water

Preparation Time: 10 minutes
Cooking Time: overnight to chill
Servings: 2
Ingredients:

- ¼ cup fresh mint leaves
- ½ lemon, sliced - 2 cucumber, sliced

Directions:

1. Add all ingredients into a Mason jar and using spoon mash them lightly just out little bit juices. Fill the Mason jar with water.
2. Cover and place in the refrigerator overnight.

Nutrition: Calories 21 Fat 0 g Carbohydrates 6 g Sugar 2 g Protein 1 g Cholesterol 0 mg

12. Strawberry-Infused Water

Preparation Time: 10 minutes
Cooking Time: 0 minutes
Servings: 4
Ingredients:

- Thyme sprigs (5)
- Sliced cucumber (1)
- Water (4 c.)
- Sliced strawberries (.5 c)

Directions:

1. Add the strawberries, cucumber, and thyme to a jar and add in the water.
2. Let it sit for a bit and then serve.

Nutrition: Calories 21 Carbs 5g Fat 0.2g Protein 1g

13. Orange Mint Water

Preparation Time: 10 minutes
Cooking Time: 0 minutes
Servings: 4
Ingredients:

- Sliced orange (1)
- Grapes (.5 c.)
- Sliced apple (1)
- Water (4 .c)
- Mint leaves (10)

Directions:

1. Take out a glass jar and add in all of the ingredients to it.

2. Place in the fridge to steep for about an hour before serving.

Nutrition: Calories 66 Carbs 15g Fat 0.3g Protein 1.2g

14. Watermelon Mint Infused Water

Preparation Time: 10 minutes
Cooking Time: 0 minutes
Servings: 4
Ingredients:

- Mint leaves (8)
- Water (4 c.)
- Sliced watermelon (1.5 c)

Directions:

1. Add all of the ingredients into a glass jar and stir around. Place into the fridge to set for about an hour before serving.

Nutrition: Calories 25 Carbs 6g Fat 0.3g Protein 1.2g

15. Peanut Tea

Preparation Time: 1 minute
Cooking Time: 5 minutes
Servings: 2
Ingredients:

- Water (1 c.)
- Cinnamon (1 tsp.)
- Ground peanuts (5 Tbsp.)

Directions:

1. Use a saucepan to heat up the water and get it nice and warm. Stir in the rest of the ingredients and then serve hot.

Nutrition: Calories 40 Carbs 1.4g Protein 1.5g Fat 3.5g

16. Pork Bone Broth

Preparation Time: 5 minutes
Cooking Time: 2-3 hours
Servings: 5
Ingredients:

- Water

- Ginger slice (1)
- White pepper (.5 tsp.)
- Salt (.5 tsp.)
- Cooking oil (1 Tbsp.)
- Garlic cloves (6)
- Sliced onion (1)
- Apple cider vinegar (2 Tbsp.)
- Pork bones (1 oz.)

Directions:
1. Take out a skillet and add in the pepper, salt, vinegar, oil, ginger, garlic, onion, and water.
2. Cover with the lid and let it cook on a low setting for 2-3 hours.
3. After this time, strain the broth and get rid of the residues before serving warm.

Nutrition Calories 37.8 Carbs 8.2g Fat 0.2g Protein 1g

17. Carrot and Red Apple Tea

Preparation Time: 5 minutes
Cooking Time: 5 minutes
Servings: 3
Ingredients:

- Water (2 c.) - Seeded lychee (.5 c.)
- Carrots, sliced (2)
- Chopped red apples (1 c.)

Directions:
1. Blend the lychee, water, carrots, and apple together. Take out a pan and mix together all of the ingredients, allowing them to boil.
2. After this, take off the heat and give them five minutes to rest and cool down.
3. Strain out the juice and then serve.

Nutrition: Calories 184 Carbs 45g Fat 0g Protein 1g

18. Banana Pops

Preparation Time: 5 minutes
Cooking Time: 30 minutes to freeze
Servings: 8
Ingredients:

- Plain yogurt (1 c.)
- Banana (1)
- Flavored Jelly package (1)
- Boiling water (1 c.)

Directions:
1. Add all of the above ingredients and then place them inside a blender. Turn it on and mix to make it nice and creamy.
2. Add to a popsicle mold and then place in the freezer until it is hard and ready to go.

Nutrition: Calories 93 Carbs 22g Fat 0.4g Protein 2.2g

19. Orange and Carrot Tea

Preparation Time: 10 minutes
Cooking Time: 0 minutes
Servings: 4
Ingredients:

- Water (4 c.)
- Diced carrots (12 oz.)
- Oranges halved (4)

Directions:
1. Add all of the ingredients into the Vitamix and then place the lid on.
2. When it is all mixed, strain it out and serve.

Nutrition: Calories 93 Carbs 22g Fat 0.4g Protein 2g

CHAPTER 6:

Snacks

20.   Ginger Ale Pops

Preparation time: 5 hours
Cooking time: 0 minutes
Serves: 2
Ingredients:
- 2 (12-ounce / 340-g) cans diet ginger ale

Directions:
1. Open ginger ale cans and let stand in the refrigerator until ginger ale is flat, about 1 hour.
2. Pour ginger ale into freezer pop molds, set handled lids in place and freeze until firm, about 4 hours. Pops will keep in the freezer for about 2 weeks. Serve as desired and enjoy!

Nutrition: calories: 0 fat: 0g protein: 0g carbs: 0g net carbs: 0g fiber: 0g

21.   Cinnamon Pumpkin Smoothie

Preparation time: 5 minutes
Cooking time: 0 minutes
Servings: 1
Ingredients:
- 1 cup nonfat plain Greek yogurt
- ⅔ cup unsweetened canned pumpkin
- 1 tablespoon unsweetened vanilla whey protein powder 1¼ teaspoons ground cinnamon
- ½ teaspoon stevia (optional)
- Dash salt (optional)

Directions:
1. Add the yogurt, pumpkin, protein powder, cinnamon, stevia (if using), and salt (if using) to a blender. Blend on low for about 2 minutes until completely combined. Enjoy immediately.

Nutrition: (1½ **cups:** calories: 242 fat: 1.0g protein: 36.0g carbs: 25.0g net carbs: 18.0g fiber: 7.0g

22.   Mango and Avocado Smoothies

Preparation time: 10 minutes
Cooking time: 0 minutes
Servings: 2
Ingredients:
- 1 peeled frozen Avocado (sliced)
- 1 mango (peeled, pitted, diced)
- 1 cup plain Greek yogurt
- ¼ cup skim milk

Directions:
1. Place all ingredients in a blender container and pulse until smooth. Serve immediately and enjoy!

Nutrition: calories: 103 fat: 0g protein: 6.0g carbs: 22.0g net carbs: 20.0g fiber: 2.0g

23.   Piña Colada

Preparation time: 5 minutes
Cooking time: 0 minutes
Servings: 2
Ingredients:
- 1½ cups unsweetened coconut milk
- ½ cup low-fat Cottage cheese
- 1 cup frozen pineapple chunks
- 1 teaspoon coconut extract
- ¼ cup vanilla protein powder
- 4 or 5 ice cubes
- Sugar substitute, for added sweetness (optional)

Directions:
1. Combine the coconut milk, cottage cheese, pineapple, coconut extract, protein powder, ice, and sugar replacement in a blender and process until smooth (if using).
2. Blend on high speed until completely smooth.
3. Half of the shake should be poured into a glass and enjoyed. Refrigerate the remaining half in an airtight jar for up to a week, then reblend before serving..

Nutrition: calories: 195 fat: 5.0g protein: 14.0g carbs: 18.0g net carbs: 17.0g fiber: 1.0g

24. Lemon and Avocado Protein Shake

Preparation time: 5 minutes
Cooking time: 0 minutes
Servings: 2

Ingredients:

- 1 cup low-fat milk
- ½ cup low-fat, plain Greek yogurt
- ½ medium Avocado
- 1 teaspoon lemon zest
- 2 teaspoons freshly squeezed lemon juice
- ⅛ teaspoon lemon extract
- ¼ teaspoon vanilla extract
- ¼ cup vanilla protein powder
- 2 to 4 ice cubes

Directions:

1. In a blender, combine the milk, yogurt, Avocado, lemon zest, lemon juice, lemon extract, vanilla, protein powder, and ice. Blend on high until smooth.
2. Pour half of the shake into a glass, and enjoy.
3. Store the remaining half in an airtight container in the refrigerator for up to a week, and reblend prior to serving.

Nutrition: calories: 189 fat: 4.0g protein: 18.0g carbs: 21.0g net carbs: 20.0g fiber: 1.0g

25. Mocha and Coffee Protein Shake

Preparation time: 5 minutes
Cooking time: 0 minutes
Servings: 2

Ingredients:

- ½ cup low-fat milk
- 1 cup decaffeinated coffee, brewed and chilled ¼ cup vanilla protein powder
- 1 teaspoon unsweetened cocoa powder
- ½ teaspoon vanilla extract
- 4 ice cubes

Directions

1. Combine the milk, coffee, protein powder, cocoa powder, vanilla, and ice in a blender. Blend on high speed until completely smooth.
2. Half of the shake should be poured into a glass and enjoyed.
3. Refrigerate the remaining half in an airtight jar for up to a week, then reblend before serving.

Nutrition: calories: 95 fat: 2.0g protein: 10.0g carbs: 9.0g net carbs: 9.0g fiber: 0g

26. Fruit and Green Protein Shake

Preparation time: 5 minutes
Cooking time: 0 minutes
Servings: 2

Ingredients:

- 1½ cups water
- ½ medium Avocado
- ½ small Granny Smith apple
- 2 loose handfuls spinach
- 1 small handful fresh parsley
- ¼ avocado, peeled
- Juice of 1 lemon
- ¼ cup unflavored protein powder

Directions:

1. In a blender, combine the water, Avocado, apple, spinach, parsley, avocado, lemon juice, and protein powder. Blend on high until smooth.
2. Pour half of the shake into a glass, and enjoy.
3. Store the remaining half in an airtight container in the refrigerator for up to a week, and reblend prior to serving.

Nutrition: calories: 133 fat: 5.0g protein: 10.0g carbs: 16.0g net carbs: 12.0g fiber: 4.0g

27. Chocolate and Raspberry Protein Shake

Preparation time: 5 minutes
Cooking time: 0 minutes
Servings: 1

Ingredients:

- 1 cup low-fat milk
- ¼ cup chocolate protein powder
- 2 teaspoons unsweetened cocoa powder
- 1 teaspoon vanilla extract
- ½ cup frozen raspberries

Directions:

1. Combine the milk, protein powder, cocoa powder, vanilla, and raspberries in a blender. Blend on high speed until completely smooth.
2. Half of the shake should be poured into a glass and enjoyed.
3. Refrigerate the remaining half in an airtight jar for up to a week, then reblend before serving.

Nutrition: calories: 285 fat: 5.0g protein: 27.0g carbs: 33.0g | net carbs: 27.0g | fiber: 6.0g

28. Chocolate Milk

Preparation time: 5 minutes
Cooking time: 0 minutes
Servings: 2

Ingredients:

- 4 cups unsweetened chocolate almond milk
- 4 scoops chocolate protein powder

- 2 tablespoons cocoa powder
- 1 cup ice (optional)

Directions:

1. In a blender, combine the almond milk, protein powder, and cocoa powder and blend until smooth. Serve over ice (if using) or blend the ice into the milk mixture until it achieves your desired consistency.

Nutrition: calories: 171 fat: 4.0g protein: 27.0g carbs: 9.0g net carbs: 7.0g fiber: 2.0g

29. Cinnamon Chia Pudding

Preparation time: 5 minutes

Cooking time: 0 minutes

Servings: 2

Ingredients:

- 2 cups unsweetened almond milk
- 1 cup plain nonfat Greek yogurt
- ½ cup chia seeds
- ¼ cup maple syrup
- 1 tablespoon ground cinnamon
- Fresh fruit or nuts, for serving (optional)

Directions:

1. In a medium bowl, whisk together the almond milk and yogurt.
2. Add the chia seeds, maple syrup, and cinnamon to the milk mixture and mix very well to combine.

3. Allow the pudding to set, covered in the refrigerator, for about 2 hours or longer if time allows.
4. Mix just prior to serving and enjoy cold, with fresh fruit or nuts if you've advanced your diet past Phase 2.

Nutrition: calories: 226 fat: 8.0g protein: 12.0g carbs: 28.0g net carbs: 17.0g fiber: 11.0g

30. Lemony Ginger Tea

Preparation time: 10 minutes

Cooking time: 10 minutes

Servings: 2

Ingredients:

1 teaspoon finely grated fresh ginger root

1 cup boiling water

1 lemon wedge (about ⅛ of a lemon)

Directions:

Place ginger root in a tea infuser and set in mug. Pour water into mug and let steep for about 10 minutes.

Remove infuser from tea. Squeeze juice from lemon wedge into tea, sweeten if desired and serve immediately. Enjoy!

Nutrition: calories: 0 fat: 0g protein: 0g carbs: 0g net carbs: 0g fiber: 0g

CHAPTER 7:

Lunch

31.   Avocado Pops

Preparation Time: 5 minutes
Cooking Time: 30 minutes to freeze
Servings: 2
Ingredients:

- Plain yogurt (1 c.)
- Avocado (1)
- Flavored Jelly package (1)
- Boiling water (1 c.)

Directions:

1. Add all of the above ingredients and then place them inside a blender. Turn it on and mix to make it nice and creamy.
2. Add to a popsicle mold and then place in the freezer until it is hard and ready to go.

Nutrition: Calories 93 Carbs 22g Fat 0.4g Protein 2.2g

32.   Peppermint Tea

Preparation Time: 1 minute
Cooking Time: 10 minutes
Servings: 2
Ingredients:

- Hot water (4 c)
- Peppermint leaf, dried (.5 c.)

Directions:

1. Set your water to a boil. Once it starts to boil, add in the peppermint leaves and then take it all off the heat.
2. Cover the pot and allow it to cool for a few minutes. When it is cooled down, strain out the mixture and serve.

Nutrition: Calories 34.2 Carbs 9.1g Fat 0g Protein 0.1g

33.   Almond Tea

Preparation Time: 1 minute
Cooking Time: 10 minutes
Servings: 2
Ingredients:

- Water (1 c.)
- Cinnamon (1 tsp.)
- Almond powder (5 Tbsp.)

Directions:

1. Bring out a pan and place it on some high heat. Add in the water with the rest of the ingredients.

2. Bring it to boil and when boiling, take it off the heat.
3. Serve warm and enjoy.

Nutrition: Calories 40 Carbs 1.4g Fat 3g Protein 1.5g

34.   Orange Vanilla Tea

Preparation Time: 2 minutes
Cooking Time: 15 minutes
Servings: 2
Ingredients:

- Vanilla (.25 tsp.)
- Sliced oranges (2)
- Water (.25 c.)

Directions:

1. Take out a pan and add it to high heat on the stove. Add in the ingredients and then allow this to boil.
2. Take the pan off the heat and give it time to sit for a few minutes.
3. When the mixture is cooled down, strain it out before serving.

Nutrition: Calories 60 Carbs 14g Fat 1g Protein 2g

35.   Kiwi Sorbet

Preparation Time: 5 minutes
Cooking Time: 5 minutes
Servings: 2
Ingredients:

- Grated orange zest (1 Tbsp.)
- Chopped kiwi fruit (.5 lb.)
- Crushed ice cubes (4.5 c.)

Directions:

1. Add all of the ingredients above into a blender.
2. Blend them together for half a minute and then serve and enjoy.

Nutrition: Calories 105 Carbs 26g Fat 0.3g Protein 0.6g

36.   Alcohol-Free Mint Mojito

Preparation Time: 20 minutes
Cooking Time: 10 minutes
Servings: 2
Ingredients:

- Water (2 c.)
- Natural sweetener (.5 c.)
- Lime juice (1 oz.)
- Mint leaves (.5 c)

Directions:

1. Add the sweetener and water to a pot and give it time to boil so the syrup can thicken.
2. Move the mint leaves to a jar and add in the syrup. Cover it up and allow this to steep for a bit.
3. After 20 minutes, you can create a mixture of one tablespoon of the syrup and half a cup of water along with the lime juice.
4. Mix and enjoy.

Nutrition: Calories 32 Carbs 3g Fat 0g Protein 0g

37. Apricot and Orange Juice

Preparation Time: 10 minutes
Cooking Time: 0 minutes
Servings: 2

Ingredients:

- Peeled ginger slice (1)
- Peeled lemon (1)
- Green grapes (1 c.)
- Pomegranate seeds (1 c.)
- Pitted apricots (2)
- Peeled oranges (2)

Directions:

1. Peel up the oranges and then divide all of them into wedges before setting aside.
2. Wash off the apricots and slice in half. Take the pits out and slice into smaller pieces.
3. Cut the tops of the pomegranate fruit with a sharp knife and then slice down the white membrane that is found in both.
4. Pop the seeds into a measuring cup and then set it to the side. Peel the lemon and cut it lengthwise in half and put it to the side.
5. Peel the slices of ginger and add to the side as well. In a juicer add the ginger, lemon, pomegranate, apricots, and oranges into it. Process until well juiced and then chill a few minutes before serving.

Nutrition: Calories 196 Carbs 48g Fat 0.8g Protein 4g

38. Chicken Bone Broth

Preparation Time: 5 minutes
Cooking Time: 2 hours
Servings: 2

Ingredients:

- 1 oz. chicken bones, cleaned

- 2 tablespoons apple cider vinegar
- 1 onion, sliced
- 5-6 garlic cloves
- 1 tablespoon cooking oil
- ½ teaspoon salt
- ½ teaspoon white pepper
- 1-inch ginger slice
- 6 cups water

Directions:

1. In a large skillet add chicken bones with water, onion, garlic, ginger, oil, vinegar, salt, pepper, and stir. Cover with lid.
2. Leave to cook on low heat for 2 hours.
3. Strain the broth and discard residue.
4. Serve hot and enjoy.

Nutrition: Calories 147 Total Fat 5 g Carbohydrate 9 g Protein 10 g

39. Citrus & Mint Infused Water

Preparation Time: 5 minutes + 2 hours chilling time
Cooking Time: 0 minutes
Servings: 2

Ingredients:

- ½ red grapefruit, segmented
- 2 mint leaves
- ½ lemon, sliced
- 1 cucumber, sliced
- ½ lime sliced
- ½ gallon spring water

Directions:

1. Wash and prepare the ingredients.
2. Place all the ingredients in a pitcher.
3. Refrigerate for 2 hours.
4. Serve after.

Nutrition: Calories 2 Total Fat 0.0 g Carbohydrate 0.4 g Protein 0.0 g

40. Pineapple and Mango Water

Preparation Time: 5 minutes + 1 hour chilling time
Cooking Time: 0 minutes
Servings: 2

Ingredients:

- 1 cup pineapple slices
- 1 cup ripe mango, chunks
- 10 cups water
- ½ teaspoon protein powder
- 1-inch ginger sliced, peeled

Directions:

1. Transfer all ingredients into a pitcher and place to chill for at least an hour.
2. Pour into serving glasses and serve.

Nutrition: Calories 10 Total Fat 0.0 g Carbohydrate 12 g Protein 0.0 g

41. Honeydew & Kiwi Infused Water

Preparation Time: 5 minutes + 1 hour chilling time
Cooking Time: 0 minutes
Servings: 2
Ingredients:

- 1 kiwi, peeled and sliced
- 2 cups honeydew melon, chopped
- 10 cups Water

Directions:

1. In a pitcher combine the fruits.
2. Fill to the top with water.
3. Refrigerate for 1 hour before serving.

Nutrition: Calories 12 Total Fat 0.0 g Carbohydrate 4.4 g Protein 0.0 g

42. Sweet and Sour Lychee Infused Water

Preparation Time: 5 minutes + 1 hour chilling time
Cooking Time: 0 minutes
Servings: 2
Ingredients:

- 1 cup lychees, peeled, seeded
- 1 tbsp. ginger powder
- 10 cups water
- 3 tablespoons lemon juice

Directions:

1. Combine all your ingredients in a pitcher.
2. Refrigerate for 1 hour before serving.

Nutritional Information: Calories 2 Total Fat 0.0 g Carbohydrate 31g Protein 0.0 g

43. Kiwi and Kale Detox Water

Preparation Time: 5 minutes + 1 hour chilling time
Cooking Time: 0 minutes
Servings: 2
Ingredients:

- 4 kiwis, sliced
- 5 kale leaves
- 10 cups cold water

Directions:

1. Combine all your ingredients in a pitcher.
2. Refrigerate for 1 hour before serving.

Nutrition: Calories 1.7 Total Fat 0.0g Carbohydrate 8 g Protein 17 g

44. Watermelon and Lemon Water

Preparation Time: 10 minutes
Cooking Time: 0 minutes
Servings: 2
Ingredients:

- 3 cups watermelon, chunks, seeded
- 3 tablespoons lemon juice
- 2-3 mint leaves
- 1 pinch salt

- 10 cups water

Directions:

1. Combine all your ingredients in a pitcher.
2. Refrigerate for 1 hour before serving.

Nutrition: Calories 105.1 Total Fat 1.4 g Carbohydrate 24.6 g Protein 2.1 g

45. Mango & Ginger Infused Water

Preparation Time: 5 minutes + 3 hours chilling time
Cooking Time: 0 minutes
Servings: 2
Ingredients:

- 1 cup diced mango
- 1-inch ginger, peeled and sliced
- 2 cups ice
- Water, to top off

Directions:

1. Peel and slice the ginger in 3-4 coin size slices.
2. Transfer the ginger into a pitcher along with mango.
3. Top with 2 cups ice and fill with water.
4. Refrigerate for 3 hours.
5. Serve.

Nutrition: Calories 1.3 Total Fat 0.0 g Carbohydrate 0.4 g Protein 0.0 g

46. Lavender & Blueberry Infused Water

Preparation Time: 5 minutes + 1 hour chilling time
Cooking Time: 0 minutes
Servings: 2
Ingredients:

- 8 cups water
- 1-pint fresh blueberries
- 1 tablespoon lavender flowers

Directions:

1. Mix all your ingredients in a large pitcher.
2. Stir gently and refrigerate for 1 hour.
3. Strain and serve with ice.

Nutrition: Calories 1.3 Total Fat 0.0 g Carbohydrate 0.4 g Protein 0.0 g

47. Pina Colada Infused Water

Preparation Time: 5 minutes + chilling time
Cooking Time: 0 minutes
Servings: 2

Ingredients:

- 1 cup peeled and thinly sliced pineapple
- 2 cups ice
- 6 cups Coconut Water

Directions:

1. Pour out your pineapple into a large pitcher.
2. Top with ice.
3. Pour in water to the top and cover.

4. Refrigerate for 1 hour before serving.

Nutrition: Calories 1.3 Total Fat 0.0 g Carbohydrate 0.4 g Protein 0.0 g

48. Orange, Strawberry & Mint Infused Water

Preparation Time: 5 minutes + chilling time
Cooking Time: 0 minutes
Servings: 2

Ingredients:

- 2 oranges, cut into wedges
- ½ cup strawberries
- 4 leaves mint - 6 cups water

Directions:

1. Place all the ingredients into a pitcher.
2. Cover and allow to chill for a minimum of 2 hours or overnight.
3. Serve.

Nutrition: Calories 1.3 Total Fat 0.0 g Carbohydrate 0.4 g Protein 0.0 g

49. Ginger Tea

Preparation Time: 5 minutes
Cooking Time: 10 minutes
Servings: 2

Ingredients:

- Boiling water (3 c.)
- Grated ginger root (3 tsp.)

Directions:

1. Combine all of the ingredients together before allowing them to sit and rest for ten minutes or so. Serve and enjoy.

Nutrition: Calories 1.3 Total Fat 0.0 g Carbohydrate 0.4 g Protein 0.0 g

50. Almond and Cherry Shake

Preparation time: 5 minutes
Cooking time: 2 minutes
Servings: 2

Ingredients:

- 1 (5.3-ounce / 150-g) cup low-fat black cherry yogurt ½ cup water
- ½ cup low-fat milk
- ¼ cup frozen pitted cherries
- ¼ cup vanilla protein powder
- ½ teaspoon almond extract

Directions:

1. In a blender, blend on high speed to combine the yogurt, water, milk, cherries, protein powder, and almond extract for 2 to 3 minutes, until the shake is smooth and the protein powder is well dissolved.
2. Pour the shake into a glass and serve. Refrigerate any shake you don't drink.

Nutrition: calories: 158 total carbs: 16.0g protein: 20.0g total fat: 1.0g sugar: 12.0g fiber: 0g sodium: 89mg

CHAPTER 8:

Snacks

51. Protein Hot Chocolate

Preparation time: 2 minutes
Cooking time: 2 minutes
Servings: 1
Ingredients:

- 1 scoop chocolate whey protein powder
- 1 cup unsweetened vanilla almond milk
- 3/4 cup water
- 1 tsp unsweet cocoa powder

Directions:

1. Combine all ingredients in a small sauce pot and pout on medium heat.
2. Stir consistently while mixture heats thoroughly, about 3 minutes. Scoop out a tiny portion to taste and test heat. Remove from heat and pour into mug. Sip and enjoy.

Nutrition: Calories: 145 Fat: 3 g Carbohydrates: 6 g Protein: 24 g

52. Avocado Cream Protein Shake

Preparation time: 2 minutes
Cooking time: 2 minutes
Servings: 1
Ingredients:

- 1 scoop vanilla whey protein powder
- 1/2 tsp Avocado extract
- 1/4 tsp vanilla extract
- 8 oz water or unsweetened almond milk

Directions:

1. In a shaker cup, combine ingredients and shake well. Pour over ice.
2. To make creamier: place ingredients in blender and add 1/2 cup ice and 1/4 cup low fat cottage cheese. Blend until smooth.

Nutrition: Calories: 143 Fat: 5 g Carbohydrates: 4 g Protein: 21 g

53. Green Smoothie Protein Shake

Preparation time: 5 minutes
Cooking time: 0 minutes
Servings: 1
Ingredients:

- 2 cups fresh spinach
- 1/2 tsp Avocado extract

- 1/8 tsp strawberry extract may substitute for 1/4 cup strawberries when diet allows.
- 1/2 cup fat-free plain Greek yogurt
- 1/4 cup of vanilla whey protein powder
- 1-3 tbsp sweetener of choice (adjust to desired sweetness) 1/2 cup ice cubes (adjust for desired consistency) 2/3 cup water

Directions:

1. Blend together on high until smooth.

Nutrition: Calories: 88 Fat: 1 g Carbohydrates: 5 g Protein: 15 g

54. Iced Vanilla Chai Tea

Preparation time: 3minutes
Cooking time: 0 minutes
Total Time: 3 minutes
Servings: 1
Ingredients:

- bag decaf chai tea
- scoop vanilla whey protein powder
- cup water - 1/2 cup ice
- 1-3 tsp sweetener

Directions:

1. Steep tea in water for 4 minutes as directed on the packaging. Allow to cool to room temperature before serving.
2. Pour the tea into a shaker cup with the vanilla protein powder and give it a good shake. Pour over ice and serve. If desired, adjust the sweetness using a sweetener.

Nutrition: Calories: 110 Fat: 1 g Carbohydrates: 5 g Protein: 25 g

55. Bariatric Friendly Creamy Hot Cocoa

Preparation time: 5 minutes
Cooking time: 0 minutes
Servings: 1
Ingredients:

- 1/4 cup low-fat cottage cheese
- scoop whey vanilla protein powder
- 1/2 tsp caramel extract
- 1/2 tsp almond extract
- cup water
- 6 ice cubes

Directions:
1. Combine all ingredients in a blender and blend on high until smooth.

Nutrition: Calories: 145 Fat: 1 g Carbohydrates: 6 g Protein: 29 g

56. Caramel Almond Protein Shake

Preparation time: 2 minutes
Cooking time: 2 minutes
Total Time: 4 minutes
Servings: 1

Ingredients:
- scoop vanilla whey protein powder
- 1/2 tsp Avocado extract
- 1/4 tsp vanilla extract
- 8 oz water or unsweetened almond milk

Directions:
1. In a shaker cup, combine ingredients and shake well. Pour over ice.
2. To make creamier: place ingredients in blender and add 1/2 cup ice and 1/4 cup low fat cottage cheese. Blend until smooth.

Nutrition: Calories: 143 Fat: 5 g Carbohydrates: 4 g Protein: 21 g

57. Low Carb Chocolate Avocado Smoothie

Preparation time: 5 minutes
Cooking time: 0 minutes
Servings: 1

Ingredients:
- 1 scoop chocolate whey protein powder
- 1/4 cup fat-free plain Greek yogurt
- 1 tbsp sweetener
- 1 cup ice
- 4-6 oz water
- 1 tsp Avocado extract

Directions:
1. Combine all ingredients in a blender and blend until smooth.

Nutrition: Calories: 95 Fat: 2 g Carbohydrates: 8 g Protein: 22 g

58. Orange Cream Protein Shake

Preparation time: 2 minutes
Cooking time: 2 minutes
Servings: 1

Ingredients:
- 1/2 cup plain fat-free Greek yogurt
- zest of one orange
- 2 tbsp juice from the orange
- 1/2 tsp vanilla extract
- 2-3 tbsp sweetener of choice (optional)
- cup unsweetened almond milk
- cup ice
- tbsp vanilla or unflavored whey protein powder

Directions:
1. Blend together on high until smooth.

Nutrition: Calories: 100 Fat: 1 g Carbohydrates: 4 g Protein: 17 g

59. Peppercorn Chicken Broth

Preparation time: 5 minutes
Cooking time: 20 minutes
Servings: 1

Ingredients:
- 2 cups store bought chicken broth.
- tbsp peppercorns

Directions:
1. Pour broth into a small saucepan and add peppercorns. Put on high heat until starting to boil.
2. Turn heat down on a low and simmer 20 minutes.
3. Remove from heat. Place strainer over bowl and strain out peppercorns. Let cool slightly, then sip and enjoy.

Nutrition: Calories: 10 Fat: 1 g Carbohydrates: 1 g Protein: 1 g

60. Non-Alcoholic Mint Mojito

Preparation time: 2 minutes
Cooking time: 5 minutes
Servings: 1

Ingredients:
- 2 cups water
- 1/2 cup natural sweetener
- 1/2 cup fresh mint leaves
- oz lime juice (approx. half a lime)

Directions:
1. Simple syrup: Bring water and natural sweetener to a boil over high heat for about 5 minutes, or until a syrup forms. Mojito with mint:
2. In a glass container with a lid, place the mint leaves (such as a mason jar). Allow at least 20 minutes for the syrup to steep in the mint leaves.

3. You can use it right away or save it for later.
4. Fill a drinking glass halfway with ice. 1 tablespoon mint syrup, 1/2 cup cold water 1 oz lime juice 1 oz lime juice 1 oz lime juice 1 oz lime Serve after a quick stir.

5. To taste, add extra mint syrup or lime juice.

Nutrition: Calories: 32 Fat: 1 g Carbohydrates: 3 g Protein: 0 g

61. Protein Pops

Preparation time: 5 minutes
Cook time: 0 minutes
Servings: 2

Ingredients:

- 4 cups water
- ½ cup fruit-flavored low-carb whey or soy protein isolate powder

Directions:

1. Pour water into blender container, add protein powder and process until smooth.
2. Pour protein powder mixture into 8 freezer pop molds, set handled lids in place and freeze until solid, about 4 hours. Pops will keep in the freezer for about 2 weeks. Serve as desired and enjoy!

Nutrition: calories: 55 | fat: 0g | protein: 13.0g | carbs: 0g | net carbs: 0g | fiber: 0g

CHAPTER 9:

Dinner

62.   Pineapple and Mango Tune-Up

Preparation time: 5 minutes
Cooking time: 0 minutes
Servings: 2
Ingredients:

- 2 cups plain nonfat Greek yogurt
- 2 cups light soy milk
- 1 orange, peeled and segmented
- ½ cup diced frozen mango
- ½ cup diced frozen pineapple
- 1 cup ice

Directions:

1. In a blender or food processor, combine the yogurt, soy milk, orange, mango, and pineapple and blend until smooth. Be sure to blend until all fruit fibers are well combined, then add the ice and blend until smooth. Serve immediately.

Nutrition: calories: 132 fat: 1.0g protein: 15.0g carbs: 15.0g net carbs: 13.0g fiber: 2.0g

63.   Berry Warmer

Preparation time: 5 minutes
Cooking time: 0 minutes
Servings: 2
Ingredients:

- 1¼ pint no-added-sugar blueberry juice drink 1 teaspoon honey
- 4 ounces (113 g) mixed fresh or frozen berries ¼ teaspoon ground cinnamon
- Small piece peeled fresh ginger, sliced
- 1 star anise
- 2 cloves
- 2 cinnamon sticks

Directions:

1. Place the blueberry drink, honey, berries, and cinnamon in a blender and blend until smooth.
2. Pour the mixture into a pan and add the ginger, star anise, cloves, and cinnamon sticks.
3. Warm through gently without boiling. Strain and serve warm.

Nutrition: calories: 68 fat: 0.3g protein: 0.5g carbs: 14.3g net carbs: 13.4g fiber: 0.9g

64.   Lemon Mint Cucumber Infused Water

Preparation Time: 10 minutes
Cooking Time: Overnight to chill
Servings: 2
Ingredients:

- ¼ cup fresh mint leaves
- ½ lemon, sliced
- 2 cucumber, sliced

Directions:

1. Add all ingredients into a Mason jar and using spoon mash them lightly just out little bit juices.
2. Fill the Mason jar with water.
3. Cover and place in the refrigerator overnight.

Nutrition: Calories: 21 Fats: 0 g Carbohydrates: 6 g Sugars: 2 g Proteins: 1 g Cholesterol: 0 mg |

65.   Strawberry Limeade

Preparation Time: 5 minutes
Cooking Time: 0 minutes
Servings: 2
Ingredients:

- ½ cup ice cubes
- ¼ tsp. strawberry extract
- 1 ½ cup cold water
- ½ lime juice

Directions:

1. Add all ingredients into a serving glass and stir well. Serve and enjoy.

Nutrition: Calories: 9 Fats: 0 g Carbohydrates: 2 g Sugars: 0.5 g Proteins: 0.1 g Cholesterol: 0 mg |

66.   Lemon Ginger Tea

Preparation Time: 15 minutes
Cooking Time: 5 minutes
Servings: 2
Ingredients:

- 2 cups water

- ½ inch cinnamon stick
- ½ lemon juice
- ½ tbsp. honey
- 1 Tbsp. ginger, grated

Directions:
1. Add water in a saucepan and boil over medium-high heat.
2. Once water is boiling turn off the heat and add cinnamon stick and ginger.
3. Let sit for 10 minutes.
4. Strain the tea through a strainer.
5. Add honey and lemon juice and stir well.
6. Serve and enjoy.

Nutrition: Calories: 28 Fats: 0.3 g Carbohydrates: 6.5 g Sugars: 4.7 g Proteins: 0.4 g Cholesterol: 0 mg

67. Refreshing Watermelon Pops

Preparation Time: 15 minutes
Cooking Time: 4-5 hours to chill
Servings: 2

Ingredients:
- 1 Tbsp. fresh lime juice
- 4 cups watermelon cubed, remove seeds

Directions:
1. Add lime juice and watermelon into the blender and blend until smooth.
2. Pour blended mixture into the popsicle molds and place in the refrigerator for 4-5 hours.
3. Serve and enjoy.

Nutrition: Calories: 23 Fats: 0.1 g Carbohydrates: 5.7 g Sugars: 4.7 g Proteins: 0.5g Cholesterol: 0 mg

68. Lime Lemon Pops

Preparation Time: 10 minutes
Cooking Time: 4 hours to chill
Servings: 2

Ingredients:
- 2 ½ cups apple juice
- 2 lime juice
- 2 lemon juice
- 2 Tbsp. liquid stevia

Directions:
1. Add all ingredients into the mixing bowl and whisk well. Pour mixture into the popsicle molds and place in the refrigerator for 4 hours.
2. Serve and enjoy.

Nutrition: Calories: 82 Fats: 0.4 g Carbohydrates: 19 g Sugars: 15 g Proteins: 0.4 g Cholesterol: 0 mg|

69. Raspberry Watermelon Pops

Preparation Time: 10 minutes
Cooking Time: 4 hours to chill
Servings: 2

Ingredients:
- 1 cup raspberries

- 2 cups watermelon, cubed and remove seeds

Directions:
1. Add raspberries and watermelon into the blender and blend until smooth.
2. Pour blended mixture into the popsicle molds and place in the refrigerator for 4 hours.
3. Serve and enjoy.

Nutrition: Calories: 26 Fats: 0.2 g Carbohydrates: 6.3 g Sugars: 4g Proteins: 0.6 g Cholesterol: 0 mg |

70. Melon Lemon Pops

Preparation Time: 10 minutes
Cooking Time: 4 hours to chill
Servings: 1

Ingredients:
- 1 Tbsp. fresh lemon juice
- 3 cups melon, chopped

Directions:
1. Add lemon juice and melon into the blender and blend until smooth.
2. Pour blended mixture into the popsicle molds and place in the refrigerator for 4 hours.
3. Serve and enjoy.

Nutrition: Calories: 40 Fats: 0.2 g Carbohydrates: 9.6 g Sugars: 9.2 g Proteins: 1 g Cholesterol: 0 mg

71. Raspberry Grapefruit Ice Pops

Preparation Time: 10 minutes
Cooking Time: 5 minutes
Servings: 1

Ingredients:
- 8 drops liquid stevia
- 1 ½ cups fresh grapefruit juice
- 4 cups frozen raspberries

Directions:
1. Add all ingredients into the blender and blend until smooth.
2. Pour blended mixture into the popsicle molds and place in the refrigerator for 4 hours.
3. Serve and enjoy.

Nutrition: Calories: 190 Fats: 0.3g Carbohydrates: 48.3g Sugars: 40.3g Proteins: 1.5g Cholesterol: 0mg

72. Delicious Cherry Lime Pops

Preparation Time: 10 minutes
Cooking Time: 4 hours to chill
Servings: 1

Ingredients:
- 1 lime juice - ½ Tbsp. lime zest, grated
- 1 ¼ cups water
- 2 ½ cups cherries, remove pits

Directions:
1. Add all ingredients into the blender and blend until well combined.

2. Pour blended mixture into the popsicle molds and place in the refrigerator for 4 hours.
3. Serve and enjoy.

Nutrition: Calories: 39 Fats: 0 g Carbohydrates: 9 g Sugars: 8 g | Proteins: 0.9 g Cholesterol: 0 mg

CHAPTER 10:

After Dinner

73. Watermelon Sorbet

Preparation Time: 10 minutes
Cooking Time: 3-4 hours to chill
Servings: 1
Ingredients:

- 6 cups watermelon, cubed and remove seeds
- ½ tbsp. honey
- ½ lemon juice

Directions:

1. Add watermelon into the blender and blend until smooth.
2. Add honey and lemon juice into the blender and blend to combine.
3. Pour blended mixture into the container and place in the refrigerator for 3-4 hours or until set.
4. Serve and enjoy.

Nutrition: Calories: 9 Fats: 0 g Carbohydrates: 2 g sugars: 0.5 g proteins: 0.1 g Cholesterol: 0 mg |

74. Tangy Mint Infused Water

Preparation Time: 10 minutes
Cooking Time: 1 hour to chill
Servings: 1
Ingredients:

- 1 tangerine, sliced - 1 grapefruit, sliced
- ½ cucumber, sliced
- 1 Liter water - 5 fresh mint leaves

Directions:

1. Add cucumber, grapefruit, tangerine, and mint leaves in a glass jug.
2. Pour water into the glass jug and stir well.
3. Place the jug in the fridge for 1 hour.
4. Serve and enjoy.

Nutrition: Calories: 32 Fats: 0.2 g Carbohydrates: 7 g Sugars: 5 g Proteins: 1 cholesterol: 0 mg

75. Apple Basil Lime Infused Water

Preparation Time: 10 minutes
Cooking Time: 5 minutes
Servings: 1
Ingredients:

- ½ green apple, sliced
- ½ lime, sliced
- 6 fresh basil leaves
- 2 cups water

Directions:

1. Add basil, apple, and lime in a glass jar.
2. Pour water into the jar and stir well.
3. Close with lid and place in the fridge for 1 hour.
4. Serve and enjoy.

Nutrition: Calories: 34 Fats: 0.1 g Carbohydrates: 9.5 g Sugars: 6.1 g Proteins: 0.3g Cholesterol: 0 mg

76. Strawberry Cucumber Mint Infused Water

Preparation Time: 10 minutes
Cooking Time: 1 hour to chill
Servings: 1
Ingredients:

- 4 strawberries, sliced
- 1 cucumber, sliced
- 5 fresh mint leaves
- 2 cups water

Directions:

1. Add cucumber, strawberries and mint leaves in a glass jar.
2. Pour water into the jar and stir well.
3. Close with lid and place in the fridge for 1 hour.
4. Serve and enjoy.

Nutrition: Calories: 40 Fats: 0.4 g Carbohydrates: 10 g Sugars: 3.7 g Proteins: 2 g Cholesterol: 0 mg |

77. Lemon Balm Tea

Preparation Time: 5 minutes
Cooking Time: 5 minutes
Servings: 1
Ingredients:

- 1 Tbsp Lemon zest
- 1 Cup Lemon balm
- 5 Cup Water

Directions:

1. Set the water up to boil. When it reaches a boil, add in the zest and lemon balm.
2. Take off the heat and allow it to cool down before straining and serving.

Nutrition: Calories: 13.3 Fats: 0 g Carbohydrates: 3.6 g Sugars: 0 g Proteins: 1 g Cholesterol: 0 mg

78. Cinnamon Tea

Preparation Time: 1 minute
Cooking Time: 5 minutes
Servings: 1
Ingredients:

- 1 Tbsp. Cinnamon
- 1 Cup Water
- 5 Cup Lemon

Directions:

1. Add the water to a pan and bring to boil. Add in the cinnamon and stir to help it dissolve.
2. Squeeze the lemon into the tea and stir well. Serve hot.

Nutrition: Calories: 9 Fats: 0 g Carbohydrates: 2.5 g Sugars: 0.1 g Proteins: 0.2 cholesterol: 0 mg

79. Turmeric Tea

Preparation Time: 1 minute
Cooking Time: 5 minutes
Servings: 1
Ingredients:

- 1 Tbsp. Raw honey
- 2 Cup Water
- ¼ Tbsp Turmeric
- ¼ Tbsp Ginger powder

Directions:

1. Add the water into a pan and let it heat up to boil. When boiling, take off the heat.
2. Add in the turmeric and ginger and let it rest in there for a bit.
3. After 5 minutes, strain the tea and pour it into cups. Stir in pepper and honey and serve hot.

Nutrition: Calories: 35 Fats: 0 g Carbohydrates: 8 g Sugars: 0 g Proteins: 0.1 g Cholesterol: 0 mg

80. Basil Tea

Preparation Time: 5 minutes
Cooking Time: 10 minutes
Servings: 1
Ingredients:

- Honey (1 tsp.)
- Water (1 c.)
- Dried basil (1 Tbsp.)

Directions:

1. Add your basil to some boiling water and let it rest there for 10 minutes.
2. When that time is up, strain it out and add honey. Stir well and serve it nice and hot.

Nutrition: Calories 20 Carbs 4g Fat 0g Protein 0.1g

CHAPTER 11:

From 4th To 6th Week Semi-Liquid Diet Breakfast

81. Avocado Almond Smoothie
Preparation Time: 5 minutes
Cooking Time: 2 minutes
Servings: 2
Ingredients:
- 15 almonds
- 1 cup unsweetened almond milk
- 1 apple, peeled
- 1 Avocado, frozen

Directions:
1. Add all ingredients into the blender and blend until smooth and creamy.
2. Serve and enjoy.

Nutritional Information: Calories 190 Fat 5 g Carbohydrates 61 g Sugar 41 g Protein 14 g Cholesterol 18 mg

82. Protein Spinach Shake
Preparation Time: 10 minutes
Cooking Time: 2 minutes
Servings: 2
Ingredients:
- 2/3 cup water
- ½ cup ice
- 5 drops liquid stevia
- ¼ cup vanilla protein powder
- ½ cup fat-free plain yogurt
- ½ tsp. vanilla extract
- 2 cups fresh spinach

Directions:
1. Add all ingredients into the blender and blend until smooth.
2. Serve and enjoy.

Nutritional Information: Calories 54 Fat 0.9 g Carbohydrates 5.5 g Sugar 4.6 g Protein 4.4 g Cholesterol 4 mg

83. Fresh Lemon Cream Shake
Preparation Time: 5 minutes
Cooking Time: 2 minutes
Servings: 1
Ingredients:
- ½ cup ice cubes
- 2 tsp. lemon zest, grated

- ½ cup fat-free plain yogurt
- 1 scoop vanilla protein powder
- 5 oz. water
- 5 drops liquid stevia

Directions:
1. Add all ingredients into the blender and blend until smooth and creamy.
2. Serve and enjoy.

Nutritional Information: Calories 175 Fat 0.1 g Carbohydrates 9.8 g Sugar 9 g Protein 33.1 g Cholesterol 4 mg

84. Avocado Smoothie
Preparation Time: 10 minutes
Cooking Time: 2 minutes
Servings: 2
Ingredients:
- ½ tsp. vanilla
- 1 tbsp. honey
- 2 cups unsweetened coconut milk
- 1 cup ice cubes
- 1 cup baby spinach
- ½ avocado
- 3 Avocados

Directions:
1. Add all ingredients into the blender and blend until smooth and creamy.
2. Serve and enjoy.

Nutritional Information: Calories 425 Fat 33 g Carbohydrates 33 g Sugar 19 g Protein 4 g Cholesterol 0 mg

85. Avocado Cherry Smoothie
Preparation Time: 5 minutes
Cooking Time: 2 minutes
Servings: 2
Ingredients:
- ½ tsp. vanilla
- 2 tbsp. unsweetened cocoa powder
- 2 ½ tbsp. chia seeds
- 1 cup unsweetened almond milk
- 1 cup ice cubes
- 1 cup fresh spinach
- 1 Avocado

Directions:
1. Add all ingredients into the blender and blend until smooth and creamy.
2. Serve and enjoy.

Nutritional Information: Calories 135 Fat 5 g Carbohydrates 20 g Sugar 7 g Protein 4.6 g Cholesterol 0 mg

86. Oatmeal Blueberry Smoothie
Preparation Time: 5 minutes
Cooking Time: 2 minutes
Servings: 2
Ingredients:
- 1/3 cup oatmeal
- 1 Avocado
- ½ cup blueberries
- ½ cup unsweetened almond milk
- ½ cup Greek yogurt

Directions:
1. Add all ingredients into the blender and blend until smooth and creamy.
2. Serve and enjoy.

Nutritional Information: Calories 179 Fat 2.8 g Carbohydrates 32.8 g Sugar 15.3 g Protein 6.5 g Cholesterol 4 mg

87. Squash Soup
Preparation Time: 5 minutes
Cooking Time: 30 minutes
Servings: 2
Ingredients:
- 3 cups butternut squash, chopped
- 4 cups vegetable stock
- 3 garlic cloves, chopped
- 1 tbsp. olive oil
- 1 1/2 cups coconut milk
- 3/4 tbsp. curry powder
- 1/2 tsp. dried onion flakes
- 1 tsp. kosher salt

Directions:
1. Add butternut squash, oil, onion flakes, curry powder, stock, garlic, and salt into a saucepan and bring to boil over medium-high heat.
2. Turn heat to medium and simmer for 20 minutes.
3. Puree the soup using immersion blender until smooth.
4. Return soup to the saucepan and stir in coconut milk and cook for 2-3 minutes.
5. Serve and enjoy.

Nutritional Information: Calories 144 Fat 11 g Carbohydrates 10 g Sugar 2.5 g Protein 2 g Cholesterol 0 mg

88. Creamy Avocado Soup
Preparation Time: 20 minutes
Cooking Time: 2 minutes
Servings: 2
Ingredients:
- 2 avocados, peel and pitted
- 2 cups vegetable stock
- 1 tbsp. fresh lemon juice
- 3/4 cup heavy cream
- 2 tbsp. dry sherry
- Pepper
- Salt

Directions:
1. Add avocado, lemon juice, sherry, and stock to the blender and blend until smooth.
2. Pour blended mixture into a bowl.
3. Add cream and stir well. Season with pepper and salt.
4. Serve and enjoy.

Nutritional Information: Calories 102 Fat 9.5 g Carbohydrates 1.9 g Sugar 0.3 g Protein 2.4 g Cholesterol 27 mg

89. Celery Soup
Preparation Time: 18 minutes
Cooking Time: 10 minutes
Servings: 2
Ingredients:
- 5 celery stalks, chopped
- 3 cups vegetable stock
- 3 tbsp. almonds, chopped
- Pepper
- Salt

Directions:
1. Add stock in a saucepan and bring to boil over high heat for 2 minutes. Add celery and cook for 8 minutes.
2. Remove from heat and using immersion blender puree until smooth.
3. Add almonds and stir well.
4. Season with pepper and salt.
5. Serve and enjoy.

Nutritional Information: Calories 80 Fat 6 g Carbohydrates 5 g Sugar 2 g Protein 3 g Cholesterol 0 mg

90. Cauliflower Soup
Preparation Time: 35 minutes
Cooking Time: 20 minutes
Servings: 2
Ingredients:
- 1/2 head cauliflower, chopped
- 2 garlic cloves, minced
- 15 oz. vegetable stock

- 1/4 tsp. garlic powder
- 1 onion, diced
- 1 tbsp. olive oil
- 1/4 tsp. pepper
- 1/2 tsp. salt

Directions:

1. Heat oil in a saucepan over medium heat.
2. Add onion and garlic and sauté for 4-5 minutes.
3. Add cauliflower and stock and stir well. Bring to boil. Cover and simmer for 15 minutes. Season with garlic powder, pepper, and salt.
4. Puree the soup using blender until smooth.
5. Serve and enjoy.

Nutritional Information: Calories 40 Fat 2 g Carbohydrates 4 g Sugar 2 g Protein 3 g Cholesterol 0 mg

91. Avocado Milk Whip

Preparation Time: 10 minutes
Cooking Time: 0 minutes
Servings: 2
Ingredients:

- 1 avocado, peeled, pitted, diced
- 1 cup skimmed milk
- ½ cup non-fat cottage cheese
- ¼ cup fresh cilantro leaves, stems removed
- ½ teaspoon lime juice
- ¼ teaspoon garlic powder
- Chili powder, for garnish

Directions:

1. Put all ingredients in a blender and blend until smooth.
2. Divide the whip between two bowls and sprinkle with a dash of chili powder to serve.

Nutritional Information: calories: 317 Total carbs: 26.6g Protein: 11.5g Total fat: 20.0g Sugar: 17.7g Fiber: 6.8g Sodium: 241mg

92. Avocado and Kale Smoothie

Preparation Time: 5 minutes
Cooking Time: 0 minutes
Servings: 2
Ingredients:

- 2 cups unsweetened almond milk
- 2 cups kale, stemmed, leaves chopped
- 2 Avocados, peeled
- 1 to 2 packets stevia, or to taste
- 1 teaspoon ground cinnamon
- 1 cup crushed ice

Directions:

1. In a blender, combine the almond milk, kale, Avocados, stevia, cinnamon, and ice. Blend until smooth.

2. Serve immediately.

Nutritional Information: Calories: 181 Total carbs: 37.0g Protein: 4.0g Total fat: 4.0g Sugar: 15.0g Fiber: 6.0g Sodium: 210mg

93. Beef Purée

Preparation Time: 30 minutes
Cooking Time: 4-10 hours
Servings: 2
Ingredients:

- 1 pound (454 g) beef tenderloin steak
- 1 teaspoon olive oil
- 1 teaspoon soy sauce
- ½ teaspoon salt, plus more to taste
- ½ teaspoon garlic powder
- ½ teaspoon onion powder
- ½ teaspoon dried rosemary, crushed
- ½ teaspoon dried parsley
- ¼ teaspoon freshly ground black pepper, plus more to taste Beef stock, as needed

Directions:

1. Pat the steak dry with paper towels and brush with olive oil and soy sauce. Mix salt, garlic powder, onion powder, rosemary, parsley and pepper and rub over steak. Cook the steak in a slow cooker until cooked through and the internal temperature reaches 145°F (63°C), 8 to 10 hours at the low setting or 4 to 5 hours at the high setting.
2. Remove the steak from slow cooker, reserving the cooking juices. Put the steak in a covered container and refrigerate until chilled through, about 2 hours.
3. Cut the chilled steak into 1-inch cubes. Put about 1 cup steak cubes in a food processor and blend until fine and powdery.
4. Add about ¼ cup reserved cooking juices plus stock as needed and process until smooth. Repeat with remaining steak cubes.
5. Season the puréed steak with salt and pepper and stir until thoroughly combined.
6. Serve immediately.

Nutritional Information: Calories: 168 Total carbs: 1g Protein: 23.3g Total fat: 7.9g Sugar: 0.3g Fiber: 0.2g Sodium: 410mg

94. Blueberry and Spinach Smoothie

Preparation Time: 5 minutes
Cooking Time: 2 minutes
Servings: 2
Ingredients:

- 2 cups blueberries
- 3 cups chopped fresh spinach
- ½ cup chopped fresh coriander
- Juice of 1 lemon

- 1-inch fresh ginger, grated
- 2 cups water

Directions:

1. Put all the ingredients in the blender, mix for 2 minutes or until smooth.
2. Serve immediately.

Nutritional Information: Calories: 121 Total carbs: 30.0g Protein: 1.6g Total fat: 0.6g Sugar: 26.6g Fiber: 2.6g Sodium: 25mg

95. Avocado Kale Smoothie

Preparation Time: 5 minutes
Cooking Time: 0 minutes
Servings: 2

Ingredients:

- 1 cup of water
- ½ Seville orange, peeled.
- 1 avocado
- 1 cucumber, peeled.
- 1 cup kale
- 1 cup of ice cubes

Directions:

1. Toss all your ingredients into your blender, then process till smooth and creamy. Serve immediately and enjoy.

Nutrition: Calories: 160 Fat: 13.3g Carbs: 11.6g Protein: 2.4g

96. Apple Kale Cucumber Smoothie

Preparation Time: 5 minutes
Cooking Time: 0 minutes
Total Time: 5 minutes
Servings: 1

Ingredients:

- ¾ cup of water
- ½ green apple, diced.
- ¾ cup kale
- ½ cucumber

Directions:

1. Toss all your ingredients into your blender, then process till smooth and creamy. Serve immediately and enjoy.

Nutrition: Calories: 86 Fat: 0.5g Carbs: 21.7g Protein: 1.9g

97. Refreshing Cucumber Smoothie

Preparation Time: 5 minutes
Cooking Time: 0 minutes
Servings: 2

Ingredients:

- 1 cup of ice cubes
- 20 drops liquid stevia
- 2 fresh lime peeled and halved.
- 1 tsp lime zest, grated.

- 1 cucumber, chopped.
- 1 avocado pitted and peeled.
- 2 cups kale
- 1 tbsp creamed coconut
- ¾ cup of coconut water

Directions:

1. Toss all your ingredients into your blender, then process till smooth and creamy. Serve immediately and enjoy.

Nutrition: Calories: 313 Fat: 25.1g Carbs: 24.7g Protein: 4.9g

98. Cauliflower Veggie Smoothie

Preparation Time: 5 minutes
Cooking Time: 5 minutes
Servings: 2

Ingredients:

- 1 zucchini peeled and chopped.
- 1 Seville orange, peeled.
- 1 apple, diced.
- 1 Avocado - 1 cup kale
- ½ cup cauliflower

Directions:

1. Toss all your ingredients into your blender, then process till smooth and creamy. Serve immediately and enjoy.

Nutrition: Calories: 71 Fat: 0.3g Carbs: 18.3g Protein: 1.3g

99. Soursop Smoothie

Preparation Time: 5 minutes
Cooking Time: 0 minutes
Servings: 2

Ingredients:

- 3 quartered frozen Burro Avocados
- 1-1/2 cups of Homemade Coconut Milk
- 1/4 cup of Walnuts
- 1 teaspoon of Sea Moss Gel
- 1 teaspoon of Ground Ginger
- 1 teaspoon of Soursop Leaf Powder
- 1 handful of kale

Directions:

1. Prepare and put all ingredients in a blender or a food processor.
2. Blend it well until you reach a smooth consistency. Serve and enjoy your Soursop Smoothie!

Nutrition: Calories: 213 Fat: 3.1g Carbs: 6g Protein: 8g

100. Tiramisu Shake

Preparation time: 5 minutes
Cooking time: 0 minutes
Servings: 1
Ingredients:

- 1 packet cappuccino mix
- 1 tablespoon sugar-free chocolate syrup
- ½ cup of water
- ½ cup ice, crushed.

Directions:

1. In a small blender, place all ingredients and pulse until smooth and creamy. Transfer the shake into a serving glass and serve immediately.

Nutrition: Calories: 107 Fat: 0g Carbohydrates: 15g Protein: 14g

101. Vanilla Shake

Preparation time: 5 minutes
Cooking time: 0 minutes
Servings: 1

Ingredients:

- ½ packet Vanilla Shake Fueling
- ½ packet Ginger Fueling.
- ½ cup unsweetened almond milk ½ cup of water
- 8 ice cubes

Directions:

1. In a small blender, place all ingredients and pulse until smooth.
2. Transfer the smoothie into a serving glass and serve immediately.

Nutrition: Calories: 130 Fat: 3.3g Carbohydrates: 15g Protein: 13g

102. Shamrock Shake

Preparation time: 5 minutes
Cooking time: 0 minutes
Servings: 1
Ingredients:

- 1 packet Vanilla Shake
- 6 ounces unsweetened almond milk
- ¼ teaspoon peppermint extract
- 1-2 drops green food coloring.
- 1 cup of ice cubes

Directions:

1. In a small blender, place all ingredients and pulse until smooth.
2. Transfer the smoothie into a serving glass and serve immediately.

Nutrition: Calories: 120 Fat: 3.9g Carbohydrates: 13.5g Protein: 11.7g

103. Coconut Smoothie

Preparation time: 5 minutes
Cooking time: 0 minutes
Total Time: 5 minutes
Servings: 1

Ingredients:

- 1 sachet Essential Creamy Vanilla Shake
- 6 ounces unsweetened almond milk
- 6 ounces diet ginger ale
- 2 tablespoons unsweetened coconut, shredded.
- ¼ teaspoon rum extract
- ½ cup ice

Directions:

1. In a small blender, place all ingredients and pulse until smooth.
2. Transfer the smoothie into a serving glass and serve immediately.

Nutrition: Calories: 120 Fat: 6.2g Carbohydrates: 15.9g Protéine: 15g

104. Vanilla Frappe

Preparation time: 5 minutes
Cooking time: 0 minutes
Servings: 1
Ingredients:

- 1 sachet Essential Vanilla Shake
- 8 ounces unsweetened almond milk
- ½ cup ice
- 1 tablespoon whipped topping

Directions:

1. In a blender, add the Vanilla Shake sachet, almond milk, and ice and pulse until smooth. Transfer the mixture into a glass and top with whipped topping. Serve immediately.

Nutrition: Calories: 155 Fat: 4.4g Carbohydrates: 15.2g Protein: 15g

CHAPTER 12:

Snacks

105. Broccoli Purée

Preparation Time: 30 minutes
Cooking Time: 10 minutes
Servings: 2
Ingredients:

- 1 pound (454 g) fresh broccoli, cut into florets ½ cup water
- ½ teaspoon salt, plus more to taste
- 1 teaspoon butter
- 1 teaspoon lemon juice
- ½ teaspoon onion powder
- Freshly ground black pepper, to taste

Directions:

1. Mix the broccoli florets, water and ½ teaspoon salt in a medium saucepan and bring to a simmer. Reduce heat, cover the pan and simmer until the broccoli is tender, 5 to 10
2. minutes.
3. Drain the broccoli, reserving the cooking water. Add the butter, lemon juice and onion powder, season with salt and pepper and let cool.
4. Put about 1 cup broccoli florets and ¼ cup cooking water in a food processor and mix until smooth. Repeat with remaining broccoli.
5. Serve immediately.

Nutritional Information: Calories: 28 Total carbs: 4.3g Protein: 2.4g Total fat: 0.9g Sugar: 1.g Fiber: 2.3g Sodium: 212mg

106. Easy Chocolate and Orange Pudding

Preparation Time: 5 minutes
Cooking Time: 5 minutes
Servings: 2
Ingredients:

- 1 package sugar-free instant chocolate pudding mix ¼ cup chocolate protein powder
- 2 cups low-fat milk
- 1 tablespoon cocoa powder
- 1 teaspoon orange extract

Directions:

1. In a medium bowl, whisk the pudding and protein powders together with the milk for 2 minutes.

2. Add the cocoa powder and orange extract, and mix for 3 more minutes before serving.

Nutritional Information: Calories: 111 Total carbs: 15.0g Protein: 10.0g Total fat: 2.0g Sugar: 6.0g Fiber: 1.0g Sodium: 380mg

107. Herbed Chicken Purée

Preparation Time: 30 minutes
Cooking Time: 30 minutes
Servings: 2
Ingredients:

- 2 (8-ounce / 227-g) boneless skinless chicken breasts 2 bay leaves
- ¾ teaspoon salt, divided
- ¾ teaspoon ground sage
- ½ teaspoon ground thyme
- ¼ teaspoon ground marjoram
- ¼ teaspoon ground rosemary
- ¼ teaspoon freshly ground black pepper
- Dash of nutmeg

Directions:

1. Put the chicken breasts, bay leaves, and 1/2 teaspoon in a medium saucepan, add enough cold water to cover and bring to boil. Reduce the heat, cover and simmer gently until chicken is cooked through and the internal temperature reaches at least 165°F (74°C), 20 to 25 minutes.
2. Remove the chicken breasts from broth. Strain and reserve the broth. Put chicken in a covered container and refrigerate until chilled through, about 2 hours.
3. Cut the chilled chicken breasts into 1-inch cubes. Put about 1
4. cup chicken cubes in a food processor and pulse until fine and powdery. Add about ¼ cup reserved broth and process until smooth. Repeat with remaining chicken cubes.
5. Mix the sage, thyme, marjoram, rosemary, pepper and nutmeg with remaining salt, sprinkle over the puréed chicken and stir until thoroughly combined.
6. Serve immediately.

Nutritional Information: Calories: 92 Total carbs: 0.2g Protein: 17.1g Total fat: 2g Sugar: 0g Fiber: 0.1g Sodium: 325mg

108. Matcha Mango Smoothie

Preparation Time: 5 minutes

Cooking Time: 0 minutes

Servings: 2

Ingredients:

- 2 cups cubed mango
- 2 tablespoons matcha powder
- 2 teaspoons turmeric powder
- 2 cups almond milk
- 2 tablespoons honey
- 1 cup crushed ice

Directions:

1. In a blender, combine the mango, matcha, turmeric, almond milk, honey, and ice. Blend until smooth.
2. Serve immediately.

Nutritional Information: Calories: 285 Total carbs: 68.0g Protein: 4.0g Total fat: 3.0g Sugar: 63.0g Fiber: 6.0g Sodium: 94mg

109. Ricotta Peach Fluff

Preparation Time: 10 minutes

Cooking Time: 0 minutes

Servings: 1

Ingredients:

- ¼ cup ricotta cheese
- 1 ripe peach, diced
- 2 tablespoons skim milk

Directions:

1. Purée ricotta, diced peach and milk in a blender until smooth.
2. Serve immediately

Nutritional Information: Calories: 355 Total carbs: 54.0g Protein: 17.9g Total fat: 8.7g Sugar: 50.0g Fiber: 2.0g Sodium: 183mg

110. Ginger Peach Smoothie

Preparation time: 5 minutes

Cooking time: 0 minutes

Servings: 2

Ingredients:

- 1 cup coconut milk
- 1 large peach, chopped
- 1 tbsp coconut oil
- 1 tbsp chia seeds
- 1 tsp fresh ginger, peeled

Directions:

1. Peaches should be washed and sliced in half. Remove the pit and slice the fruit into small pieces. Remove from the equation.
2. Cut a tiny ginger knob in half. It should be peeled and chopped into small pieces. Remove from the equation.

3. In a blender, combine the peach, ginger, coconut milk, and coconut oil. Process until everything is nicely integrated.
4.
5. Stir in the chia seeds and transfer to a serving glass.
6.
7. Add ice if desired, and garnish with mint leaves if desired.
8. Enjoy!

Nutrition: Calories: 201, Protein: 2.5g, Total Carbs: 8.9g, Dietary Fibers: 3.5g, Total Fat: 19g

111. Cherry Avocado Smoothie

Preparation time: 5 minutes

Cooking time: 0 minutes

Serves: 2

Ingredients:

- ½ ripe avocado, chopped
- 1 cup fresh cherries
- 1 cup coconut water, sugar-free
- 1 whole lime

Direction:

1. Cut the avocado in half after peeling it. Remove the pit and slice the fruit into small pieces. Refrigerate the remaining ingredients. Remove from the equation.
2. Using a large colander, rinse the cherries under cold running water. Remove the pits and cut each in half. Remove from the equation.
3. Cut the lime in half after peeling it. Remove from the equation.

4. In a blender, combine the avocado, cherries, coconut water, and lime. Transfer to a serving glass after pulsing to mix.

5. Refrigerate for 10 minutes before serving with a few ice cubes.

Nutrition: Calories: 128, Protein: 1.7g, Total Carbs: 17g, Dietary Fibers: 3.8g, Total Fat: 6.8g

112. Fresh Mango Smoothie

Preparation time: 10 minutes

Cooking time: 0 minutes

Servings: 2

Ingredients:

- 1 medium mango, roughly chopped
- 1 cup coconut milk
- 1 tbsp walnuts, chopped
- 1 tsp vanilla extract, sugar-free
- A handful of ice cubes

Direction:

1. Peel the mango and cut into small chunks. Set aside.

2. Now, combine mango, coconut milk, walnuts, and vanilla extract in a blender and process until well combined and creamy. Transfer to a serving glass and stir in the vanilla extract. Add a few ice cubes and serve immediately.

Nutrition: Calories: 271, Protein: 3.4g, Total Carbs: 21.7g, Dietary Fibers: 3.7g, Total Fat: 21g

113.   Green Tea Smoothie

Preparation time: 10 minutes
Cooking time: 0 minutes
Servings: 2
Ingredients:

- 3 tbsp green tea powder
- 1 cup grapes, white
- ½ cup kale, finely chopped
- 1 tbsp honey
- ½ tsp fresh mint, ground
- 1 cup water

Direction:

1. Rinse the grapes under cold running water. Drain and remove the pits. Set aside.
2. Place kale in a large colander and wash thoroughly under cold running water. Drain well and finely chop it into small pieces. Set aside.
3. Combine green tea powder with 2 tablespoons of hot water. Soak for 2 minutes. Set aside.
4. Now, combine grapes, kale, honey, mint, and water in a blender and process until well combined. Stir in the water and tea mixture.
5. Refrigerate 30 minutes before serving.
6. Enjoy!

Nutrition: Calories: 76, Protein: 2.3g, Total Carbs: 18.3g, Dietary Fibers: 2.2g, Total Fat: 0.2g

114.   Guava Smoothie

Preparation time: 5-7 minutes
Cooking time: 0 minutes
Servings: 2
Ingredients:

- 1 cup guava, seeds removed, chopped
- 1 cup baby spinach, finely chopped
- 1 Avocado, peeled and sliced
- 1 tsp fresh ginger, grated
- ½ medium-sized mango, peeled and chopped
- 2 cups water

Direction:

1. Peel the guava and cut in half. Scoop out the seeds and wash it. Cut into small pieces and set aside.
2. Rinse the baby spinach thoroughly under cold running water. Drain well and torn into small pieces. Set aside.
3. Peel the Avocado and chop into small chunks. Set aside.
4. Peel the mango and cut into small pieces. Set aside.
5. Now, combine guava, baby spinach, Avocado, ginger, and mango in a juicer and process until well combined. Gradually add water and blend until all combined and creamy.
6. Transfer to a serving glass and refrigerate for 20 minutes before serving.
7. Enjoy!

Nutrition: Calories: 166, Protein: 3.9g, Total Carbs: 39.1g, Dietary Fibers: 7.8g, Total Fat: 1.4g

115.   Creamy Raspberry Pomegranate Smoothie

Preparation Time: 5 minutes
Cooking Time: 0 minutes
Servings: 1
Ingredients:

- 1½ cups pomegranate juice
- ½ cup unsweetened coconut milk
- 1 scoop vanilla protein powder
- 2 packed cups fresh baby spinach
- 1 cup frozen raspberries
- 1 frozen Avocado
- 1 to 2 tablespoons freshly compressed lemon juice

Directions:

1. In a blender, combine the pomegranate juice and coconut milk.
2. Add the protein powder and spinach. Give these a whirl to break down the spinach.
3. Add the raspberries, Avocado, and lemon juice, then top it off with ice. Blend until smooth and frothy.

Nutrition: Calories: 303 fat: 3g Carbs: 0g Protein: 15g

CHAPTER 13:

Lunch

116. Mango Agua Fresca

Preparation time: 5 minutes.
Cooking time: 0 minutes.
Servings: 2
Ingredients:

- 2 fresh mangoes, diced
- 1 ½ cups water
- 1 teaspoon fresh lime juice
- Maple syrup to taste - 2 cups ice
- 2 slices fresh lime for garnish
- 2 fresh mint sprigs for garnish

Directions:

1. Put the mangoes, lime juice, maple syrup and water into a blender.
2. Process until creamy and smooth.
3. Divide the beverage into two glasses, then garnish each glass with ice, lime slice and mint sprig before serving.

Nutrition: Calories: 230 Fat: 1.3g Carbs: 57.7g Fiber: 5.4g Protein: 2.8g

117. Fruity Smoothie

Preparation Time: 10 Minutes
Cooking time: 0 minute
Servings: 1
Ingredients:

- ¾ cup soy yogurt - ½ cup pineapple juice
- 1 cup pineapple chunks
- 1 cup raspberries, sliced
- 1 cup blueberries, sliced

Direction:

1. Process the ingredients in a blender.
2. Chill before serving.

Nutrition: Calories 279, Total Fat 2 g, Saturated Fat 0 g Cholesterol 4 mg, Sodium 149 mg, Total Carbohydrate 56 g Dietary Fiber 7 g, Protein 12 g, Total Sugars 46 g Potassium 719 mg

118. Pineapple, Avocado & Spinach Smoothie

Preparation Time: 10 Minutes
Cooking time: 0 minute
Servings: 1
Ingredients:

- ½ cup almond milk

- ¼ cup soy yogurt
- 1 cup spinach
- 1 cup Avocado
- 1 cup pineapple chunks
- 1 tbsp. chia seeds

Direction:

1. Add all the ingredients in a blender.
2. Blend until smooth.
3. Chill in the refrigerator before serving.

Nutrition: Calories 297, Total Fat 6 g, Saturated Fat 1 g, Cholesterol 4 mg Sodium 145 mg, Total Carbohydrate 54 g, Dietary Fiber 10 g Protein 13 g, Total Sugars 29g, Potassium 1038 mg

119. Kale & Avocado Smoothie

Preparation Time: 10 Minutes
Cooking time: 0 minute
Servings: 1
Ingredients:

- 1 ripe Avocado
- 1 cup kale
- 1 cup almond milk
- ¼ avocado
- 1 tbsp. chia seeds
- 2 tsp. honey
- 1 cup ice cubes

Direction:

1. Blend all the ingredients until smooth.

Nutrition:
Calories 343 Total Fat 14 g Saturated Fat 2 g
Cholesterol 0 mg Sodium 199 mg
Total Carbohydrate 55 g
Dietary Fiber 12 g Protein 6 g
Total Sugars 29 g
Potassium 1051 mg

120. Coconut & Strawberry Smoothie

Preparation Time: 10 Minutes
Cooking Time: 0 minutes
Servings: 1
Ingredients:

- 1 Cup Strawberries, Frozen & Thawed Slightly
- 1 Ripe Avocado, Sliced & Frozen
- ½ Cup Coconut Milk, Light
- ½ Cup Vegan Yogurt
- 1 Tablespoon Chia Seeds
- 1 Teaspoon Lime juice, Fresh
- 4 Ice Cubes

Directions:
1. Blend everything together until smooth, and serve immediately.

Nutrition: Calories: 278 Protein: 14 Grams Fat: 2 Grams Carbs: 57 Grams

121. Pumpkin Chia Smoothie

Preparation Time: 5 Minutes
Cooking Time: 0 minutes
Serves: 1
Ingredients:

- 3 Tablespoons Pumpkin Puree
- 1 Tablespoon MCT Oil
- ¾ Cup Coconut Milk, Full Fat
- ½ Avocado, Fresh
- 1 Teaspoon Vanilla, Pure
- ½ Teaspoon Pumpkin Pie Spice

Directions:
1. Combine all ingredients together until blended.

Nutrition: Calories: 726 Protein: 5.5 Grams Fat: 69.8 Grams Carbs: 15 Grams

122. Cantaloupe Smoothie Bowl

Preparation Time: 5 Minutes
Cooking Time: 0 minutes Servings: 2
Ingredients:

- ¾ Cup carrot Juice
- 4 Cps Cantaloupe, Frozen & Cubed
- Mellon Balls or Berries to Serve
- Pinch Sea Salt

Directions:
1. Blend everything together until smooth.

Nutrition: Calories: 135 Protein: 3 Grams Fat: 1 Gram Carbs: 32 Grams

123. Berry & Cauliflower Smoothie

Preparation Time: 10 Minutes
Cooking Time: 0 minutes
Servings: 2
Ingredients:

- 1 Cup Riced Cauliflower, Frozen
- 1 Cup Avocado, Sliced & Frozen
- ½ Cup Mixed Berries, Frozen
- 2 Cups Almond Milk, Unsweetened
- 2 Teaspoons Maple syrup, Pure & Optional

Directions:
1. Blend until mixed well.

Nutrition: Calories: 149 Protein: 3 Grams Fat: 3 Grams Carbs: 29 Grams

124. Green Mango Smoothie

Preparation Time: 5 Minutes
Cooking Time: 0 minutes
Serves: 1
Ingredients:

- 2 Cups Spinach
- 1-2 Cups Coconut Water
- 2 Mangos, Ripe, Peeled & Diced

Directions:
1. Blend everything together until smooth.

Nutrition: Calories: 417 Protein: 7.2 Grams Fat: 2.8 Grams Carbs: 102.8 Grams

125. Chia Seed Smoothie

Preparation Time: 5 Minutes
Cooking Time: 0 minutes
Serves: 2
Ingredients:

- ¼ Teaspoon Cinnamon
- 1 Tablespoon Ginger, Fresh & Grated
- Pinch Cardamom
- 1 Tablespoon Chia Seeds
- 2 Medjool Dates, Pitted
- 1 Cup Alfalfa Sprouts
- 1 Cup Water
- 1 Avocado
- ½ Cup Coconut Milk, Unsweetened

Directions:
1. Blend everything together until smooth.

Nutrition: Calories: 477 Protein: 8 Grams Fat: 29 Grams Carbs: 57 Grams

126. Simple Mango Smoothie

Preparation Time: 5 Minutes
Cooking Time: 0 minutes
Servings: 2
Ingredients:

- 1 Carrot, Peeled & Chopped
- 1 Cup Strawberries

- 1 Cup Water
- 1 Cup Peaches, Chopped
- 1 Avocado, Frozen & sliced
- 1 Cup Mango, Chopped

Directions:

1. Blend everything together until smooth.

Nutrition: Calories: 376 Protein: 5 Grams Fat: 2 Grams Carbs: 95 Grams

CHAPTER 14:

Snacks

127. Light Ginger Tea

Preparation time: 5 minutes.
Cooking time: 10 minutes.
Servings: 2
Ingredients:

- 1 small ginger knob, sliced into four 1-inch chunks 4 cups water
- Juice of 1 large lemon
- Maple syrup to taste

Directions:

1. Add the ginger knob and water in a saucepan, then simmer over medium heat for 10 to 15 minutes.
2. Turn off the heat, then mix in the lemon juice. Strain the liquid to remove the ginger, then fold in the maple syrup and serve.

Nutrition: Calories: 32 Fat: 0.1g Carbs: 8.6g Fiber: 0.1g Protein: 0.1g

128. Kale Smoothie

Preparation time: 5 minutes.
Cooking time: 0 minutes.
Servings: 2
Ingredients:

- 2 cups chopped kale leaves
- 1 Avocado, peeled
- 1 cup frozen strawberries
- 1 cup unsweetened almond milk
- 4 Medjool dates, pitted and chopped

Directions:

1. Put all the ingredients in a food processor, then blitz until glossy and smooth.
2. Serve immediately or chill in the refrigerator for 1 hour before serving.

Nutrition: Calories: 663 Carbs: 142.5g Fiber: 19g Protein: 17.4g

129. Hot Tropical Smoothie

Preparation time: 5 minutes.
Cooking time: 0 minutes.
Servings: 2
Ingredients:

- 1 cup frozen mango chunks
- 1 cup frozen pineapple chunks
- 1 small tangerine, peeled and pitted
- 4 cups spinach leaves
- 1 cup coconut water
- ¼ teaspoon cayenne pepper, optional

Directions:

1. Add all the ingredients to a food processor, then blitz until the mixture is smooth and combined well.
2. Serve immediately or chill in the refrigerator for 1 hour before serving.

Nutrition: Calories: 283 Fat: 1.9g Carbs: 67.9g Fiber: 10.4g Protein: 6.4g

130. Berry Smoothie

Preparation time: 5 minutes.
Cooking time: 0 minutes.
Servings: 2
Ingredients:

- 1 cup berry mix (strawberries, blueberries and cranberries) 4 Medjool dates, pitted and chopped
- 1 ½ cups unsweetened almond milk, plus more as needed

Directions:

1. Add all the ingredients to a blender, then process until the mixture is smooth and well mixed.
2. Serve immediately or chill in the refrigerator for 1 hour before serving.

Nutrition: Calories: 473 Fat: 4g Carbs: 103.7g Fiber: 9.7g Protein: 14.8g

131. Cranberry and Avocado Smoothie

Preparation time: 5 minutes.
Cooking time: 0 minutes.
Servings: 2
Ingredients:

- 1 cup frozen cranberries
- 1 large Avocado, peeled
- 4 Medjool dates, pitted and chopped
- 1 ½ cups unsweetened almond milk

Directions:

1. Add all the ingredients to a food processor, then process until the mixture is glossy and well mixed.

2. Serve immediately or chill in the refrigerator for 1 hour before serving.

Nutrition: Calories: 616 Fat: 8g Carbs: 132.8g Fiber: 14.6g Protein: 15.7g

132. Pumpkin Smoothie

Preparation time: 5 minutes.
Cooking time: 0 minutes.
Servings: 2
Ingredients:

- ½ cup pumpkin purée
- 4 Medjool dates, pitted and chopped
- 1 cup unsweetened almond milk
- ¼ teaspoon vanilla extract
- ¼ teaspoon ground cinnamon
- ½ cup ice
- A pinch of ground nutmeg

Directions:

1. Add all the ingredients to a blender, then process until the mixture is glossy and well mixed.
2. Serve immediately.

Nutrition: Calories: 417 Fat: 3g Carbs: 94.9g Fiber: 10.4g Protein: 11.4g

133. Super Smoothie

Preparation time: 5 minutes.
Cooking time: 0 minutes.
Servings: 2
Ingredients:

- 1 Avocado, peeled
- 1 cup chopped mango
- 1 cup raspberries
- ¼ cup rolled oats - 1 carrot, peeled
- 1 cup chopped fresh kale
- 2 tablespoons chopped fresh parsley
- 1 tablespoon flaxseeds
- 1 tablespoon grated fresh ginger
- ½ cup unsweetened soy milk
- 1 cup water

Directions:

1. Put all the ingredients in a food processor, then blitz until glossy and smooth.

2. Serve immediately or chill in the refrigerator for 1 hour before serving.

Nutrition: Calories: 550 Fat: 39g Carbs: 31g Fiber: 15g Protein:13g

134. Kiwi and Strawberry Smoothie

Preparation time: 5 minutes.
Cooking time: 0 minutes.
Servings: 2
Ingredients:

- 1 kiwi, peeled
- 5 medium strawberries
- ½ frozen Avocado
- 1 cup unsweetened almond milk
- 2 tablespoons hemp seeds
- 2 tablespoons peanut butter
- 1 to 2 teaspoons maple syrup
- ½ cup spinach leaves
- Handful broccoli sprouts

Directions:

1. Put all the ingredients in a food processor, then blitz until creamy and smooth.
2. Serve immediately or chill in the refrigerator for 1 hour before serving.

Nutrition: Calories: 562 Fat: 28.6g Carbs: 63.6g Fiber: 15.1g Protein: 23.3g

135. Avocado and Chai Chia Smoothie

Preparation time: 5 minutes.
Cooking time: 0 minutes.
Servings: 2
Ingredients:

- 1 Avocado
- 1 cup alfalfa sprouts
- 1 tablespoon chia seeds
- ½ cup unsweetened coconut milk
- 1 to 2 soft Medjool dates, pitted
- ¼ teaspoon ground cinnamon
- 1 tablespoon grated fresh ginger
- 1 cup water
- A pinch of ground cardamom

Directions:

1. Add all the ingredients to a blender, then process until the mixture is smooth and creamy. Add water or coconut milk if necessary.
2. Serve immediately.

Nutrition: Calories: 477 Fat: 41g Carbs: 31g Fiber: 14g Protein: 8g

136. Chocolate and Peanut Butter Smoothie

Preparation time: 5 minutes.
Cooking time: 0 minutes.
Servings: 2

Ingredients:

- 1 tablespoon unsweetened cocoa powder
- 1 tablespoon peanut butter
- 1 Avocado
- 1 teaspoon maca powder
- ½ cup unsweetened soy milk
- ¼ cup rolled oats
- 1 tablespoon flaxseeds
- 1 tablespoon maple syrup
- 1 cup water

Directions:

1. Add all the ingredients to a blender, then process until the mixture is smooth and creamy. Add water or soy milk if necessary.
2. Serve immediately.

Nutrition: Calories: 474 Fat: 16g Carbs: 27g Fiber: 18g Protein: 13g

137. Golden Milk

Preparation time: 5 minutes.
Cooking time: 0 minutes.
Servings: 2

Ingredients:

- ¼ teaspoon ground cinnamon
- ½ teaspoon ground turmeric
- ½ teaspoon grated fresh ginger
- 1 teaspoon maple syrup
- 1 cup unsweetened coconut milk
- Ground black pepper to taste
- 2 tablespoons water

Directions:

1. Combine all the ingredients in a saucepan. Stir to mix well.
2. Heat over medium heat for 5 minutes. Keep stirring during the heating.
3. Allow to cool for 5 minutes, then pour the mixture into a blender.
4. Pulse until creamy and smooth. Serve immediately.

Nutrition: Calories: 577 Fat: 57.3g Carbs: 19.7g Fiber: 6.1g Protein: 5.7g

CHAPTER 15:

Dinner

138. Pumpkin Frappe

Preparation time: 5 minutes
Cooking time: 0 minutes
Servings: 1
Ingredients:

- 1 sachet Essential Spiced Ginger
- 4 ounces strong brewed coffee
- 4 ounces unsweetened almond milk
- 1/8 teaspoon pumpkin pie spice
- ½ cup ice
- 1 tablespoon whipped topping

Directions:

1. In a blender, add the Spiced Ginger sachet, coffee, almond milk, pumpkin pie spice, and ice and pulse until smooth. Transfer the mixture into a glass and top with whipped topping. Serve immediately.

Nutrition: Calories: 138 Fat: 4.8g Carbohydrates: 16.4g Protein: 11.7g

139. Chocolate Frappe

Preparation time: 5 minutes
Cooking time: 0 minutes
Servings: 1
Ingredients:

- 1 sachet Essential Frosty Mint Chocolate Soft Serve Treat 4 ounces strong brewed coffee
- 4 ounces unsweetened almond milk
- 1½ tablespoons sugar-free chocolate syrup, divided.
- ¼ teaspoon peppermint extract
- ½ cup ice
- 1 tablespoon whipped topping

Directions:

1. In a blender, add the Chocolate sachet, coffee, almond milk, 1
2. tablespoon of chocolate syrup, peppermint extract, and ice and pulse until smooth.
3. Transfer the mixture into a glass and top with whipped topping.
4. Drizzle with remaining chocolate syrup and serve immediately.

Nutrition: Calories: 148 Fat: 4.8g Carbohydrates: 18g Protein: 11.7g

140. Peppermint Mocha Shake

Preparation time: 5 minutes
Cooking time: 0 minutes
Servings: 1
Ingredients:

- 1 sachet Essential Velvety Hot Chocolate
- 6 ounces freshly brewed coffee
- ¼ cup warm unsweetened almond milk
- ¼ teaspoon peppermint extract One tablespoon whipped topping
- Pinch of ground cinnamon

Directions:

1. In a serving mug, place the Hot Chocolate sachet, coffee, almond milk, and peppermint extract and stir until well blended.
2. Top the hot chocolate with whipped topping and sprinkle with cinnamon. Serve immediately.

Nutrition: Calories: 133 Fat: 1.1g Carbohydrates: 15.2g Protein: 14.6g

141. Max Power Smoothie

Preparation time: 5 minutes.
Cooking time: 0 minutes.
Servings: 2
Ingredients:

- 1 Avocado
- ¼ cup rolled oats, or 1 scoop plant protein powder 1 tablespoon flaxseed, or chia seeds
- 1 cup raspberries, or other berries
- 1 cup chopped mango (frozen or fresh)
- ½ cup non-dairy milk (optional)
- 1 cup water

Directions:

1. Purée everything in a blender until smooth, adding more water (or non-dairy milk) if needed.
2. Add none, some, or all the bonus boosters, as desired. Purée until blended.

Nutrition: Calories: 550 Fat: 9g Carbs: 116g Fiber: 29g Protein: 13g

142. Chai Chia Smoothie

Preparation time: 5 minutes.
Cooking time: 0 minutes.
Servings: 2
Ingredients:

- 1 Avocado
- ½ cup coconut milk
- 1 cup water
- 1 cup alfalfa sprouts (optional)
- 1 to 2 soft Medjool dates, pitted
- 1 tablespoon chia seeds, or ground flax or hemp hearts ¼ teaspoon ground cinnamon
- A pinch of ground cardamom
- 1 tablespoon grated fresh ginger, or ¼ teaspoon ground ginger

Directions:

1. Purée everything in a blender until smooth, adding more water (or coconut milk) if needed.

Nutrition: Calories: 477 Fat: 29g Carbs: 57g Fiber: 14g Protein: 8g

143. Trope-Kale Breeze

Preparation time: 5 minutes.
Cooking time: 0 minutes.
Servings: 2
Ingredients:

- 1 cup chopped pineapple (frozen or fresh)
- 1 cup chopped mango (frozen or fresh)
- ½ to 1 cup kale, chopped
- ½ avocado
- ½ cup coconut milk
- 1 cup water (or coconut water)
- 1 teaspoon matcha green tea powder (optional)

Directions:

1. Purée everything in a blender until smooth, add more water (or coconut milk) if needed.

Nutrition: Calories: 566 Fat: 36g Carbs: 66g Fiber: 12g Protein: 8g

144. Hydration Station

Preparation time: 5 minutes.
Cooking time: 0 minutes.
Servings: 2
Ingredients:

- 1 Avocado
- 1 orange, peeled and sectioned, or 1 cup pure orange juice 1 cup strawberries (frozen or fresh)
- 1 cup chopped cucumber
- ½ cup coconut water
- 1 cup water - ½ cup ice

Directions:

1. Purée everything in a blender until smooth, adding more water if needed.

2. Add bonus boosters, as desired, and purée until blended.

Nutrition: Calories: 320 Fat: 3g Carbs: 76g Fiber: 13g Protein: 6g

145. Mango Madness

Preparation time: 5 minutes.
Cooking time: 0 minutes.
Servings: 2
Ingredients:

- 1 Avocado
- 1 cup chopped mango (frozen or fresh)
- 1 cup chopped peach (frozen or fresh)
- 1 cup strawberries
- 1 carrot, peeled and chopped (optional)
- 1 cup water

Directions:

1. Purée everything in a blender until smooth, adding more water if needed.

Nutrition: Calories: 376 Fat: 2g Carbs: 95g Fiber: 14g Protein: 5g

146. Chocolate PB Smoothie

Preparation time: 5 minutes.
Cooking time: 0 minutes.
Servings: 2
Ingredients:

- 1 Avocado
- ¼ cup rolled oats, or 1 scoop plant protein powder 1 tablespoon flaxseed or chia seeds
- 1 tablespoon unsweetened cocoa powder
- 1 tablespoon peanut butter, or almond or sunflower seed butter 1 tablespoon maple syrup (optional)
- 1 cup alfalfa sprouts or spinach, chopped (optional) ½ cup non-dairy milk (optional)
- 1 cup water

Directions:

1. Purée everything in a blender until smooth, add more water (or non-dairy milk) if needed.

2. Add bonus boosters, as desired, and purée until blended.

Nutrition: Calories: 474 Fat: 16g Carbs: 79g Fiber: 18g Protein: 13g

147. Pink Panther Smoothie

Preparation time: 5 minutes.
Cooking time: 0 minutes.
Servings: 2
Ingredients:

- 1 cup strawberries
- 1 cup chopped melon (any kind)
- 1 cup cranberries or raspberries
- 1 tablespoon chia seeds

- ½ cup coconut milk or other non-dairy milk
- 1 cup water

Directions:

1. Purée everything in a blender until smooth, add more water (or coconut milk) if needed.
2. Add bonus boosters, as desired, and purée until blended.

Nutrition: Calories: 459 Fat: 30g Carbs: 52g Fiber: 19g Protein: 8g

148. Avocado Nut Smoothie

Preparation time: 5 minutes.

Cooking time: 0 minutes.

Servings: 2

Ingredients:

- 1 Avocado
- 1 tablespoon almond butter, or sunflower seed butter ¼ teaspoon ground cinnamon
- A pinch of ground nutmeg
- 1 to 2 tablespoons dates, or maple syrup
- 1 tablespoon ground flaxseed, or chia or hemp hearts ½ cup non-dairy milk (optional)
- 1 cup water

Directions:

1. Purée everything in a blender until smooth, add more water (or non-dairy milk) if needed.

Nutrition: Calories: 343 Fat: 14g Carbs: 55g Fiber: 8g Protein: 6g

~ 65 ~

CHAPTER 16:

After Dinner

149. Matcha Ice Cream

Preparation time: 5 minutes
Cooking time: 5 minutes
Servings: 2
Ingredients:

- ½ tsp. vanilla
- 2 tbsp. swerve
- 1 tsp. matcha powder
- 1 cup heavy whipping cream

Directions:

1. Add all ingredients into the glass jar.
2. Seal the jar with lid and shake for 4-5 minutes until mixture double.
3. Place in refrigerator for 3-4 hours.
4. Serve, chilled and enjoy.

Nutrition: Calories: 215 Fat: 22 g, Carbs: 3.8 g, Sugar: 0.2 g, Protein: 1.2 g, Cholesterol: 82 mg.

150. Moist Avocado Brownies

Preparation time: 10 minutes
Cooking time: 35 minutes
Servings: 2
Ingredients:

- 2 avocados, mashed
- 2 eggs
- 1 tsp. baking powder 2 tbsp. swerve
- 1/3 cup chocolate chips, melted
- 4 tbsp. coconut oil, melted
- 2/3 cup unsweetened cocoa powder

Directions:

1. Preheat the oven to 325 °F.
2. In a mixing bowl, mix together all dry ingredients.
3. In another bowl, mix together avocado and eggs until well combined.
4. Slowly add dry mixture to the wet along with melted chocolate and coconut oil. Mix well.
5. Pour batter in a greased baking pan and bake for 30-35 minutes.
6. Slice and serve.

Nutrition: Calories: 207, Fat: 18 g, Carbs: 11 g, Sugar: 3.6 g, Protein: 3.8 g, Cholesterol: 38 mg.

151. Mix Berry Sorbet

Preparation time: 10 minutes
Cooking time: 10 minutes
Servings: 2
Ingredients:

- ½ cup raspberries, frozen
- ½ cup blackberries, frozen
- 1 tsp. liquid stevia - 6 tbsp. water

Directions:

1. Add all ingredients into the blender and blend until smooth. Pour blended mixture into the container and place in refrigerator until hardened. Servings chilled and enjoy.

Nutrition: Calories: 63, Fat: 0.8 g, Carbs: 14 g, Sugar: 6 g, Protein: 1.7 g, Cholesterol: 0 mg.

152. Chia Almond Pudding

Preparation time: 5 minutes
Cooking time: 5 minutes
Servings: 2
Ingredients:

- 2 tbsp. almonds, toasted and crushed
- 1/3 cup chia seeds - ½ tsp. vanilla
- 4 tbsp. erythritol
- ¼ cup unsweetened cocoa powder
- 2 cups unsweetened almond milk

Directions:

1. Add almond milk, vanilla, sweetener, and cocoa powder into the blender and blend until well combined. Pour blended mixture into the bowl.
2. Add chia seeds and whisk for 1-2 minutes.
3. Pour pudding mixture into the serving bowls and place in the fridge for 1-2 hours.
4. Top with crushed almonds and serve.

Nutrition: Calories: 170, Fat: 12 g, Carbs: 12 g, Sugar: 1 g, Protein: 7 g, Cholesterol: 35 mg.

153. Chia Raspberry Pudding

Preparation time: 5 minutes
Cooking time: 5 minutes
Servings: 2

Ingredients:

- ¼ tsp. vanilla
- ¾ cup unsweetened almond milk
- 1 tbsp. erythritol
- 2 tbsp. proteins collagen peptides
- ¼ cup chia seeds
- ½ cup raspberries, mashed

Directions:

1. Add all ingredients into the bowl and stir until well combined.
2. Place in refrigerator for overnight.
3. Servings chilled and enjoy.

Nutrition: Calories: 102, Fat: 6 g, Carbs: 13 g, Sugar: 1.4 g, Protein: 4 g, Cholesterol: 0 mg.

154. Strawberry Frozen Yogurt Squares

Preparation time: 8 hours
Cooking time: 0 minute
Servings: 2

Ingredients:

- 1 cup barley, wheat cereal
- 3 cup fat-free strawberry yogurt
- 10 oz. frozen strawberries
- 1 cup fat-free milk
- 1 cup whipped topping

Directions:

1. Set a parchment paper on the baking tray.
2. Spread cereal evenly over the bottom of the tray.
3. Add milk, strawberries, and yogurt to the blender, and process into a smooth mixture.
4. Use yogurt mixture to top cereal, wrap with foil, and place to freeze until firm (about 8 hours).
5. Slightly thaw, cut into squares and serve.

Nutrition: Calories: 188, Net Carbs: 43.4 g, Fiber: 4 g, Fat: 3 g, Sugar: 7 g.

155. Lemon Mousse

Preparation time: 15 minutes
Cooking time: 4 hours to chill
Servings: 2

Ingredients:

- 1½ cups boiling water
- 1 (6-ounces) package Sugar:-free lemon-flavored gelatin
- 2 cups ice cubes
- 1½ cups whipped topping
- Fresh fruit, for servings (optional)

Directions:

1. In a large bowl, combine the boiling water and gelatin. Stir for at least 2 min, or until the gelatin is completely dissolved. Add the ice cubes, and stir until melted. Refrigerate until thickened, 5 to 10 min.
2. Fold in the whipped topping. Divide into four portions and refrigerate until firm, about 4 hours.
3. Garnish with fresh fruit before servings (if desired).

Nutrition: Calories: 85, Total Fat: 6 g, Protein: 1 g; Carbs: 6 g, Fiber: 0 g, Sugar: 3 g, Sodium: 45 mg.

156. Grilled Stone Fruit with Greek Yogurt

Preparation time: 5 minutes
Cooking time: 5 minutes
Servings: 2

Ingredients:

- Nonstick cooking time spray
- 3 large fresh peaches, halved and pitted
- 1 tsp. extra-virgin olive oil
- 6 ounces low-fat, honey-flavored Greek yogurt
- ¼ cup sliced almonds

Directions:

1. The ground cinnamon, for garnishing
2. Spray your grill (or a grill pan on the stovetop) with cooking time spray.
3. Heat the grill or grill pan to high heat, about 500 °F.
4. Brush each peach half with olive oil.
5. Place the cut fruit on the grill flesh-side down, and grill for two min.
6. Using tongs, turn the fruit over and cook for another 2 min.
7. Transfer to a serving dish. Serve the fruit with the Greek yogurt, and garnish with almonds and cinnamon.

Nutrition: Calories: 78, Total Fat: 3 g, Protein: 4 g, Carbs: 11 g, Fiber: 2 g, Sugar: 8 g, Sodium: 8 mg.

157. Mixed Berry Popsicles

Preparation time: 5 minutes
Cooking time: 5 minutes
Servings: 2

Ingredients:

- 1 cup fresh blackberries
- cup fresh blueberries
- 1 cup fresh raspberries
- 2 tbsp. fresh lemon juice
- 2 cups strawberries, sliced 2 tbsp. honey
  Directions:

Directions

1. Add all ingredients into the blender and blend until smooth.
2. Pour blended mixture into the Popsicle molds and place in the freezer for 4 hours or until set.
3. Servings and enjoy.

Nutrition: Calories: 44, Fat: 0.3 g, Carbs: 10.7 g, Sugar: 7.6 g, Protein: 0.7 g, Cholesterol: 0 mg.

158. Strawberry Yogurt

Preparation time: 5 minutes
Cooking time: 5 minutes
Servings: 2
Ingredients:

- 1 lb. frozen strawberries
- 1 cup non-fat yogurt
- 1 tsp. liquid stevia

Directions:

1. Add all ingredients into the blender and blend until smooth.
2. Pour blended mixture into the container.
3. Cover and place in the refrigerator for 2-3 hours.
4. Servings and enjoy.

Nutrition: Calories: 87, Fat: 0 g, Carbs: 19.8 g, Sugar: 12 g, Protein: 1.8 g, Cholesterol: 2 mg. 115.

159. Strawberry & Peach Crumble

Preparation time: 10 minutes
Cooking time: 6-7 hours on low
Servings: 2
Ingredients:

- 2 cups of sliced strawberries
- 2 cups of sliced peaches
- 1 tbsp. of grated lemon zest
- 1 cup of gluten-free oats
- 1 tbsp. of chia seeds, milled
- ½ tsp. of ground cinnamon

Directions:

1. Mix the strawberries, peaches and lemon zest, and place them in the slow cooker.
2. Mix the oats with the milled chia seeds and ground cinnamon, and top over the fruits.
3. Set the slow cooker to High for 2-3 hours or on Low for 6-7 hours.
4. The crumble is ready when the fruits are bubbling and the topping turns golden brown.

Nutrition: Calories: 138, Protein: 4 g, Carbs: 26 g, Fat: 3 g, Sugar: 8 g, Sodium: 3 mg, Potassium: 296 mg, Phosphorus: 142 mg, Calcium: 52 mg, Fiber: 6 g.

160. Poached Spiced Apples & Pears

Preparation time: 5 minutes
Cooking time: 7-8 hours on low
Servings: 2
Ingredients:

- 2 apples, peeled and halved
- 2 pears, peeled and halved
- 1/2 tbsp. of cloves
- 1 tsp. of allspice
- 1 cinnamon stick

Directions:

1. Turn the slow cooker to a low setting.
2. Peel and half the apples and pears.
3. Poke the cloves into the flesh of the fruits evenly.
4. Place into the slow cooker and cover with water.
5. Add the allspice and cinnamon stick. Mix.
6. Cover and cook for about 7-8 hours.
7. Remove the cinnamon stick before serving. The juices will have caramelized and formed a delicious sauce to serve with the fruits.
8. Add fat-free Greek yogurt if desired.

Nutrition: Calories: 84, Protein: 1 g, Carbs: 23 g, Fat: 0 g, Sugar: 15 g, Sodium: 2 mg, Potassium: 175 mg, Phosphorus: 18 mg, Calcium: 15 mg, Fiber: 4 g.

161. Almond Strawberry Chia Seed Pudding

Preparation time: 10 minutes + 4 hours to chill
Cooking time: 0 minute
Servings: 2
Ingredients:

- 2 cups almond milk
- 1 (16 ounces) package fresh strawberries, hulled
- ½ cup of chia seeds
- ¼ cup of honey
- 1 tsp. vanilla extract

Directions:

1. In a blender, purée the almond milk and strawberries until smooth; pour them into a bowl. In the strawberry puree, stir the chia seeds, butter, and vanilla extract.
2. Cover the bowl with a wrap of plastic and freeze it for 4 hours until set.

Nutrition: Calories: 209, Protein: 3.7 g, Carbs: 37.2 g, Fat: 6.3 g, Sodium: 84.9 mg.

162. Blueberry Muffins

Preparation time: 7 minutes
Cooking time: 18 minutes
Servings: 12
Ingredients:

- 1¾ cups whole flour

- 1/2 cup stevia
- 2½ tsp. baking powder
- ½ tsp. salt
- ¾ cup milk
- 1 egg, lightly beaten
- 1/2 cup butter, softened
- 1 cup blueberries, fresh or frozen

Directions:
1. Heat oven to 400 °F.
2. In a medium bowl, combine salt, baking powder, stevia and flour then set aside.
3. In a large bowl, beat butter and stevia until creamy; add egg and milk.
4. Add flour mixture to butter mixture and stir until the dry ingredients are moistened and a few lumps remain; fold in blueberries.
5. Spoon batter into twelve greased muffin cups; bake at 400 °F for 18 minutes, or until a toothpick can be inserted in the center and come out clean.

Nutrition: Calories: 162.8, Total Fat: 3.4 g, Total Carbs: 11.2 g, Protein: 7.5

163. Mashed Cauliflower

Preparation Time: 10 minutes
Cooking Time: 5 minutes
Servings: 2

Ingredients:
- 1 large head cauliflower
- ¼ cup water
- 1/3 cup low-fat buttermilk
- 1 tablespoon minced garlic 1 tablespoon extra-virgin olive oil

Directions:
1. Break the cauliflower into small florets. Place in a large microwave-safe bowl with the water. Cover and microwave for about 5 minutes, or until the cauliflower is soft. Drain the water from the bowl.
2. Using a food processor, puree the buttermilk, cauliflower, garlic, and olive oil on medium speed until the cauliflower is smooth and creamy. Serve immediately.
3. Ingredient tip: You can buy buttermilk in most supermarkets, but it's just as easy to make your own. Mix 1 teaspoon freshly squeezed lemon juice with 1/3 cup low-fat milk. Let the mixture sit for about 10 minutes, or until the milk begins to thicken. Cooking tip: For even more flavor, microwave the cauliflower with chicken or vegetable broth instead of water and add ½ cup shredded Parmigiano-Reggiano cheese when you puree the mixture.

4. You can add protein to this dish by blending in powdered egg whites or unflavored protein powder after the first puree (puree until smooth and creamy; then add the protein powder and puree to incorporate).

Nutrition: Per Serving (½ cup): Calories: 62; Total fat: 2g; Protein: 3g; Carbs: 8g; Fiber: 3g; Sugar: 3g; Sodium: 54mg

164. Pickle Roll-Ups

Preparation Time: 20 Minutes
Cooking Time: 20 Minutes
Servings: 2

Ingredients
- ¼ pound deli ham (nitrate-free), thinly sliced (about 8 slices) 8 ounces cheese, at room temperature
- 1 teaspoon dried dill
- 1 teaspoon onion powder
- 8 whole kosher dill pickle spears

Directions:
1. Get a large cutting board or clean counter space to assemble your roll-ups.
2. Lay the ham slices on the work surface and carefully spread on the cheese.
3. Season each lightly with the dill and onion powder.
4. Place an entire pickle on an end of the ham and carefully roll.
5. Slice each pickle roll-up into mini rounds about ½- to 1-inch wide.
6. Skew each with a toothpick for easier serving.

Nutrition: Per Serving (1 roll-up): Calories: 86; Total fat: 7g; Protein: 4g; Carbs: 4g; Fiber: 0 g; Sugar: 2g; Sodium: 540mg

165. Tomato, Basil, And Cucumber Salad

Preparation Time: 15 Minutes
Cooking Time: 30 Minutes
Servings: 2

Ingredients
- 1 large cucumber, seeded and sliced
- 4 medium tomatoes, quartered
- 1 medium red onion, thinly sliced
- ½ cup chopped fresh basil
- 3 tablespoons red wine vinegar
- 1 tablespoon extra-virgin olive oil
- ½ teaspoon Dijon mustard
- ½ teaspoon freshly ground black pepper

Directions:
1. In a medium bowl, mix together the cucumber, tomatoes, red onion, and basil.
2. In a small bowl, whisk together the vinegar, olive oil, mustard, and pepper.

3. Pour the dressing over the vegetables, and gently stir until well combined.

4. Cover and chill for at least 30 minutes prior to serving.

Nutrition: Per Serving (½ cup): Calories: 72; Total fat: 4g; Protein: 1g; Carbs: 8g; Fiber: 1g; Sugar: 4g; Sodium: 5mg

166. Raspberry Sorbet

Preparation time: 10 min
Cooking time: 0 min
Servings: 2
Ingredients:
- Honey (1 Tbsp.)
- Coconut water (.25 c.)
- Raspberries (12 oz.)

Directions:
1. We need to take all of those ingredients that we listed above and add them inside a prepared blender.
2. Blend until it is nice and smooth. Pour this into a container and add the lid to the top. Add to the freezer to set for a few hours before serving.

Nutrition: Calories 131, Fat 4, Carbs 8, Protein 6, Sodium 212

167. Avocado Hummus

Preparation time: 15 min
Cooking time: 0 min
Servings: 2
Ingredients:
- Edamame (1 c.)
- Chopped avocado (.5)
- Lemon juice (1 Tbsp.)
- Olive oil (2 Tbsp.)
- Minced garlic (.5 tsp.)
- Onion powder (.5 tsp.)
- Tahini (1 tsp.)

Directions:
1. Add all of these ingredients into a blender and blend to make smooth. Serve with some vegetables and enjoy it.

Nutrition: Calories 112, Fat 4, Carbs 18, Protein 7, Sodium 126

168. Avocado Detox Smoothie

Preparation time: 10 minutes
Cooking time: - 30 minutes
Servings: 2
Ingredients:
- ½ avocado, peeled and roughly chopped
- 1 Avocado, peeled and chopped
- Handful baby spinach, torn

- 1 tbsp powdered stevia
- 1 tsp turmeric, ground
- 1 tbsp flaxseed, ground
- 1 tbsp goji berries

Directions:
1. Peel the avocado and cut in half. Remove the pit and chop one half into small pieces. Wrap the other half in a plastic foil and refrigerate for later.
2. Peel the Avocado and cut into thin slices. Set aside.
3. Rinse the spinach thoroughly under cold running water using a colander.
4. Chop into small pieces and set aside.
5. Now, combine avocado, Avocado, spinach, turmeric, flaxseed, and goji berries in a blender. Process until well combined.
6. Transfer to a serving glass and add few ice cubes.
7. Serve immediately.

Nutrition information per serving: Calories: 221, Protein: 3.1g, Total Carbs: 28.6g, Dietary Fibers: 7.5g, Total Fat: 11.8g

169. Sweet Pumpkin Pudding

Preparation time: 15 minutes
Cooking time: 15 minutes
Servings: 2
Ingredients:
- 1 lb pumpkin, peeled and chopped into bite-sized pieces 2 tbsp honey
- 4 cups pumpkin juice, unsweetened
- 1 tsp cinnamon, ground
- 3 cloves, freshly ground

Directions:
1. Peel and prepare the pumpkin. Scrape out seeds and chop into bite-sized pieces. Set aside.
2. In a small bowl, combine pumpkin juice, honey, orange juice, cinnamon
3. Place the pumpkin chops in a large pot and pour the pumpkin juice mixture.
4. Stir well and then finally add cloves. Stir until well incorporated and heat up until almost boiling. Reduce the heat to low and cook for about 15 minutes, or until the mixture thickens.
5. Remove from the heat and transfer to the bowls immediately. Set aside to cool completely and then refrigerate for 15 minutes before serving, or simply chill overnight.

Nutrition information per serving: Calories: 232, Protein: 2.7g, Total Carbs: 56g, Dietary Fibers: 4.6g, Total Fat: 0.9g

CHAPTER 17:

From 6th To 8th Week Semi Solid Breakfast

170. Peanut Butter and Avocado Pancakes

Preparation Time: 10 minutes
Cooking Time: 20 minutes
Servings: 2
Ingredients:

- 1 cup white flour
- 1.25 tsp Baking Powder - 0.25 tsp Salt
- 1 tbsp Peanut Butter, chunky
- 1 cup non-fat Milk - 0.25 tps Vanilla Extract
- 1 small Avocado

Directions:

1. Combine flour, baking powder, salt and peanut butter in a large bowl. Add milk and vanilla. Stir until it's blended.
2. Chop the Avocado into small pieces. They are added when the pancakes are being cooked.
3. Oil the pan and keep it on medium heat. Spoon the batter into the pan.
4. Each pancake is approximately 2 tablespoons.
5. On every pancake sprinkle the Avocado pieces on. Cook until pancakes are golden brown on both sides and serve hot.

Nutrition: Serving size: 1 medium pancake Calories: 181.1 kcal Fat: 2.4 g Carbohydrates: 34.0 g Fiber: 1.8 g Protein: 6.5 g Sugar: 10 g

171. Pineapple Strawberry Blueberry Smoothie

Preparation Time: 5 minutes
Cooking Time: 0 minutes
Servings: 2
Ingredients:

- 0.5 cup Blueberries, fresh
- 1 cup, halves Strawberries, fresh
- 1 cup Lactaid Fat Free Milk
- 3 serving Truvia Natural Sweetener
- 1 cup Ice cubes

Directions:

1. Blend all ingredients together in blender or with an immersion blender. Enjoy!

Nutrition: Serving size: 1 cup Calories: 176.2kcal Fat: 0.6 g Carbohydrates: 42.9 g Fiber: 5.5 g Protein: 9.4 g Sugar: 20 g

172. Cinnamon Porridge with Blueberries and Greek Yogurt

Preparation Time: 10 minutes
Cooking Time: 15 minutes
Servings: 1
Ingredients:

- 1/3 cup Rolled oats
- 2/3 cup Water
- 1 dash Salt
- 172 tbsp Cinnamon
- 1 1/3 tbsp Greek Yogurt
- 2 tbsp Blueberries

Directions:

1. Place oats in a small saucepan and cover with water.
2. Add salt and cinnamon. Bring to the boil and then simmer gently for 10-15 minutes.
3. Put cooked porridge in a bowl.
4. Add yogurt and scatter blueberries. Serve and enjoy!

Nutrition: Serving size: 1 cup Calories: 131kcal Fat: 3 g Carbohydrates: 24 g Fiber: 4 g Protein: 5 g Sugar: 1.9g

173. Scrambled Eggs, Avocado, and Smoked Salmon on Toast

Preparation Time: 10 minutes
Cooking Time: 5 minutes
Servings: 1
Ingredients:

- 1 tbsp Reduced fat milk
- 1 1/3 large Egg
- 2/3 tbsp Butter
- 1/3 dash Salt
- 1/3 dash Pepper
- 2/3 fruit Avocados
- 2/3 tbsp Lemon juice
- 1 2/3 oz Chinook salmon

Directions:

1. Whisk milk and eggs in a large bowl. Melt butter in a large heavy
1. nonstick skillet over medium-low heat. Add egg mixture and season with salt and pepper.

2. Cook, occasionally scraping bottom of skillet with a heatproof spatula to form large, soft curds, until just barely set, 3-4 minutes.
3. Set aside.
4. Place a slice of toast onto each plate.
5. Put avocado into a bowl, mash with a fork, and season with lemon juice, salt, and pepper. Spread mashed avocado over each slice of toast. Spoon eggs over avocado.
6. Drape smoked salmon slices over eggs and season to taste with pepper. Enjoy!

Nutrition: Serving size: 1 toast Calories: 490 kcal Fat: 37 g Carbohydrates: 21 g Fiber: 10 g Protein: 23 g Sugar: 3 g

174.   **Protein Vegan Pancakes**

Preparation Time: 10 minutes
Cooking Time: 30 minutes
Servings: 2
Ingredients:

- 3/4 cup Bob's Red Mill Organic Spelt Flour
- 1 serving Protein Powder- Soy-Trader Darwin's- 2 Scoops 2 tsp Baking Powder
- 1/4 tsp Salt
- 1 cup Milk, Soy, Organic, Unsweetened, SILK
- 1 tbsp Flax Seed Meal (ground flax)
- 1 tsp Apple Cider Vinegar
- 1/2 tsp Vanilla Extract
  o   tbsp Coconut Oil
- 2 tbsp Turbinado Sugar
- 1/4 cup (8 fl oz) Water, tap

Directions:

1. Heat pan on medium heat.
2. Combine milk, water, flax seed and vinegar and whisk until foamy.
1. Let sit for 5 minutes.
2. Combine flour, protein powder, baking powder, salt and sugar. Add 2 tbsp of melted coconut oil to wet mixture. Make a well in center of dry ingredients and beat in wet ingredients until well combined.

3. Use the remaining oil on pan to cook the pancakes until golden brown.

Nutrition: Serving size: 1 pancake Calories: 168.5 kcal Fat: 7.6 g Carbohydrates: 16.5 g Fiber: 2.5 g Protein: 7.3 g Sugar: 12 g

175.   **Avocado Muffin (with Yogurt)**

Preparation Time: 10 minutes
Cooking Time: 15 minutes
Servings: 2
Ingredients:

- 1 cup all-purpose flour
- 1 tablespoon baking powder
- 1/2 teaspoon baking soda
- 1/4 teaspoon salt
- 1 cup mashed ripe Avocado
- 1/4 cup white sugar
- 1/4 cup nonfat plain yogurt
- 1 egg
- 1/2 teaspoon vanilla extract

Directions:

1. Preheat oven to 350 degrees F (175 degrees C). Grease muffin cups or line with paper muffin liners.
2. Mix together flour, baking powder, baking soda and salt.
3. In a separate bowl, beat together Avocado, sugar, egg and vanilla.
1. Stir in the yogur.
4. Stir Avocado mixture into flour until just combined. Scoop batter into prepared muffin cups.
5. Bake in preheated oven for 15 to 20 minutes, or until a toothpick inserted into center of a muffin comes out clean.
6. Let cool before serving

Nutrition: Serving size: 1 muffin Calories: 82kcal Fat: 0.2 g Carbohydrates: 18.6 g Fiber: 0.8 g Protein: 19 g Sugar: 10 g

176.   **Peanut Butter Avocado Breakfast Smoothie**

Preparation Time: 5 minutes
Cooking Time: 0 minutes
Servings: 1
Ingredients:

- 1 medium Avocado
- 2 Tbsp Peanut Butter
- 1 cup nonfat milk

Directions:

1. You blend ingredients together in blender with ice if you like.
2. It makes a very filling breakfast smoothie that keeps me full well until lunch.

3. Enjoy!

Nutrition: Serving size: 1 cup Calories: 374.3 kcal Fat: 12 g Carbohydrates: 53.5 g Fiber: 4.8 g Protein: 17.6 g Sugar: 12.3 g

177. Apple Strudel

Preparation Time: 70 minutes
Cooking Time: 35 minutes
Total time: 105 minutes
Servings: 2
Ingredients:

- 1 sheet puffed pastry
- 1 egg
- 1 tbsp water
- 2 tbsp granulated sugar
- 1 tbsp all-purpose flour
- 1/4 tsp ground cinnamon
- 2 large granny smith apples peeled, cored and sliced thinly.
- 2 tbsp raisins

Directions:

1. Thaw pastry at room temp for 40 minutes. Heat oven to 375.
1. Lightly grease baking sheet.
2. Stir the egg and water in small bowl. Mix sugar, flour and cinnamon in medium bowl. Add apples and raisins and toss to coat.
3. Unfold pastry sheet on lightly floured surface. Roll the sheet into a 16x12 inch rectangle. With the short side facing you, spoon apple mixture onto the bottom half of the pastry within 1 inch of edges.
4. Starting at the short side closest to you, roll up like a jelly roll.
5. Place seam side down on baking sheet. Tuck ends under to seal.
6. Brush with egg mixture.
4. Cut several 2-inch slits, 2 inches apart on top.
5. Bake 35 minutes or until golden. Cool baking sheet on wire rack for 30 minutes.
6. Slice and serve warm. Sprinkle with confectioners' sugar, if desired.

Nutrition: Serving size: 1 piece Calories: 178 kcal Fat: 8.9 g Carbohydrates: 21.3 g Fiber: 1.2 g Protein: 3.2 g Sugar: 9 g

178. Breakfast Quinoa Pumpkin Pudding

Preparation Time: 2 minutes
Cooking Time: 5minutes
Servings: 1
Ingredients:

- 0.25 cup quinoa
- 0.5 cup nonfat milk
- 0.5 oz raisins
- 0.25 cup canned pumpkin
- pumpkin pie spice to taste.
- Stevia - start small and add to taste.

Directions:

1. Add quinoa, raisins and milk to saucepan.
2. Heat to a boil and then simmer for 15 minutes.
3. Add pumpkin, spice, and sweetener.
4. Pour into bowl and add milk and butter - eat!

Nutrition: Serving size: 1 cup Calories: 375.6 kcal Fat: 8.2 g Carbohydrates: 62.8 g Fiber: 8.1 g Protein: 15.9 g Sugar: 15.6 g

179. Salmon Florentine

Preparation Time: 30 minutes
Cooking Time: 30 minutes
Total time: 60 minutes
Servings: 2

Ingredients

1 small onion diced/minced fine
1 lemon sliced and seeded
3 small, thin salmon fillets, fresh or thawed.
10-oz pkg freezing chopped spinach, thawed.
1 4-oz pkg, cheese free from fat.
Dill Weed, salt & pepper to taste.

Directions

1. Squeeze excess moisture from thawed spinach and combine with cream cheese and minced onion in a mixing bowl. Season with a pinch of salt and pepper to taste.
2. 1/2 of the spinach mixture should be patted into the bottom of a shallow baking dish big enough to hold the salmon fillets flat.
3. On top of the spinach layer, place salmon fillets. Lightly sprinkle dill over the salmon, then top with a few of lemon wedges. Cover the fish with the leftover spinach mixture and pat it down.
4.
5. Preheat oven to 350°F and bake for 30 minutes, or until fish flakes easily with a fork.
6. If the pan appears to be dry, add a splash of chicken broth (could use water too, just whatever is handy).Serve with cooked brown or wild rice.

Nutrition: Serving size: 1 plate Calories: 473.7 kcal Fat: 12.1 g Carbohydrates: 17.9 g
Fiber: 6.6 g Protein: 75.2 g Sugar: 8 g

180. Waffled Falafel

Preparation Time: 15 minutes
Cooking Time: 15 minutes
Total time: 30 minutes
Servings: 2
Ingredients:

- 2 (15 ounce) cans garbanzo beans (chickpeas), drained and rinsed.

- 1 small onion, chopped
- 2 large egg whites
- ¼ cup fresh chopped cilantro
- ¼ cup chopped fresh parsley
- 3 cloves roasted garlic, or more to taste.
- 1 ½ tablespoons all-purpose flour
- Cooking spray
- 2 tsp ground cumin
- 1 ¾ teaspoons salt
- 1 teaspoon ground coriander
- ¼ teaspoon ground black pepper
- ¼ teaspoon cayenne pepper
- 1 pinch ground cardamom

Directions:

1. Preheat a waffle iron as directed by the manufacturer. Cooking spray the interior of the waffle iron.
2. Garbanzo beans should be coarsely minced in a food processor.
3. Toss the garbanzo beans with the onion, egg whites, cilantro, parsley, garlic, flour, cumin, salt, coriander, black pepper, cayenne pepper, and cardamom. Pulse until the falafel batter resembles coarse meal, scraping down the sides of the basin as needed. Pour the batter into a mixing dish and whisk it together with a fork.
4. Fill each part of the preheated waffle iron with roughly 1/4 cup falafel batter. Cook for 5 minutes, or until uniformly browned.

Continue with the remaining batter.

Nutrition: Serving size: 1 medium waffle Calories: 210 kcal Fat: 2.1 g Carbohydrates: 38.7 g Fiber: 7.5 g Protein: 10 g Sugar: 1.4 g

181. Individual Baked Eggs

Preparation Time: 10 minutes
Cooking Time: 20 minutes
Servings: 1
Ingredients:

- 1 slice bacon
- 1 teaspoon melted butter
- 1 egg
- ¼ slice Cheddar cheese

Directions:

1. Preheat the oven to 350 degrees Fahrenheit (175 degrees C).
2. In a big, deep skillet, cook the bacon. Cook over medium-high heat, stirring occasionally, until uniformly browned but still pliable.
3. In a muffin cup, wrap a bacon piece around the inside. In the bottom of each muffin cup, place a teaspoon of butter (or bacon fat).
4. Pour in the egg.
5. Bake for 10 to 15 minutes in a preheated oven. Place 1/4 slice of cheese on top of the egg and heat until the cheese has melted and the egg is done..

Nutrition: Serving size: 1 cup Calories: 174kcal Fat: 14.3 g Carbohydrates: 0.6 g Protein: 10.7 g Sugar: 0.4 g

182. Western Omelet

Preparation Time: 15 minutes
Cooking Time: 5 minutes
Servings: 1
Ingredients:

- 2 teaspoons butter, divided
- ⅓ cup sliced fresh mushrooms (Optional)
- ¼ cup chopped green bell pepper
- 2 green onions sliced on the bias.
- ¼ cup cooked ham strips
- salt and ground black pepper to taste
- 2 eggs

Directions:

1. In a small skillet over medium heat, melt 1 teaspoon butter. Cook, stirring occasionally, until the mushrooms, bell pepper, and green onions are soft, about 5 minutes. Stir in the ham until it is fully cooked, about 1 minute. Salt & pepper to taste. Set aside the filling mixture in a small bowl to keep warm.
2. In a mixing dish, whisk together the eggs and season with salt and pepper.
3. In the same skillet, melt the butter over medium-high heat. 1 more to add
4. 1 tbsp. butter, heated till foaming Cook for 30 minutes after adding the eggs.
5. seconds. Lift the omelet's edges, allowing the uncooked egg to run under the cooked edges and into touch with the hot skillet.
6. To move the raw egg, shake and tilt the skillet. Repeat for another 2 minutes, or until the top is set but still wet and soft.
7. Fill one side of the omelet with the filling. Fold the remaining half of the omelet over the filling and place it on a plate.

Nutrition: Serving size: 1 omelet Calories: 320 kcal Fat: 24.5 g Carbohydrates: 5.5 g Fiber: 1.6 g Protein: 20.5 g Sugar: 2.8 g

183. Avocado Pudding and Yogurt Parfaits

Preparation Time: 20 minutes
Cooking Time: 0 minutes
Total time: 20 minutes
Servings: 2 parfaits
Ingredients:

- 2 Avocados, sliced

- 2 tsp lemon juice
- 2 cp heavy whipping cream
- 2 cups Greek yogurt
- 1 (2.5 ounce) instant vanilla pudding mix
- 2 cups coarsely crushed gingersnap cookies

Directions:

1. To keep avocado slices from browning, put them in a basin with lemon juice.
2. In a mixing bowl, whisk together heavy cream, Greek yogurt, and vanilla pudding mix until pudding is thick and creamy.
3. In the bottom of four 8-ounce clear drinking glasses, sprinkle 2 tablespoons smashed cookies. 2 to 3 tablespoons pudding mixture and 3 to 4 avocado slices on top of cookies Layers should be repeated twice more.

Nutrition: Serving size: 1 cup Calories: 230 kcal Fat: 16 g Carbohydrates: 20,25 g Fiber: 2.3 g Protein: 11.5 g Sugar: 46 g

184. Chia Seed Pudding

Preparation Time: 15 minutes
Cooking Time: 0 minutes
Servings: 2
Ingredients:

- 1 cup unsweetened vanilla-flavored almond milk 1 cup vanilla fat-free yogurt
- 2 tsp pure maple syrup
- 1 tsp pure vanilla extract
- ⅛ tsp salt
- ¼ cup chia seeds
- 1 pint strawberries, hulled and chopped
- 4 teaspoons pure maple syrup
- ¼ cup toasted almonds

Directions:

1. In a dish, whisk together almond milk, yogurt, 2 tablespoons maple syrup, vanilla, and salt until just combined; add chia seeds, swirl to integrate, and soak for 30 minutes.
2. To redistribute seeds that have collected throughout the chia seed mixture, stir it. Refrigerate the bowl for 8 hours to overnight, covered in plastic wrap.
3. In a mixing dish, drizzle 4 teaspoons maple syrup over strawberries and toss to coat. Stir in the almonds with the strawberries.
4. Divide the chia seed mixture among four bowls and top with a bit of the strawberry mixture in each.

Nutrition: Serving size: 1 cup Calories: 60 kcal Fat: 2 g Carbohydrates: 10 g Fiber: 1.5 g Protein: 1,8 g Sugar: 7,5 g

185. Low Carb Pancake Crepes

Preparation Time: 5 minutes
Cooking Time: 20 minutes
Total time: 25 minutes
Servings: 2
Ingredients:

- 3 ounces cream cheese, softened
- 2 eggs, beaten
- 1 teaspoon ground cinnamon
- 1 tablespoon sugar-free syrup
- 1 teaspoon butter

Directions:

1. Mash the cream cheese with the beaten eggs in a mixing basin, roughly 1 spoonful at a time at beginning, until the mixture is smooth and lump-free. Combine the cinnamon and sugar-free syrup in a mixing bowl.
2. In a nonstick skillet, melt the butter over medium heat. Reduce heat to medium-low and pour in several tablespoons of the batter once the butter has stopped foaming. Swirl to coat the skillet's bottom. Allow to cook until set on the first side, about 4 minutes; flip the crepe with a spatula and cook the other side until small, browned spots appear, 1 to 2 minutes more.

Nutrition: Calories: 240.7 kcal Fat: 21.8 g Carbohydrates: 2.4 g Fiber: 0.6 g Protein: 9.6 g Sugar: 0.5 g

186. Cheddar Biscuits

Preparation Time: 15 minutes
Cooking Time: 20 minutes
Servings: 2
Ingredients:

- 2 cups biscuit baking mix
- 1 cup shredded Cheddar cheese
- ⅔ cup milk
- ½ teaspoon garlic powder
- 2 tablespoons margarine, melted
- 2 teaspoons dried parsley
- 1 teaspoon garlic salt

Directions:

1. Preheat the oven to 400 degrees Fahrenheit (205 degrees C). Line a cookie sheet with parchment paper or grease it.
2. Combine baking mix, Cheddar cheese, and garlic powder in a large mixing bowl. Add the milk and mix well. Drop heaping tablespoonfuls of batter onto the prepared cookie sheet.
3. Bake for 10 minutes in a preheated oven. Brush the biscuits with melted margarine and season with garlic salt and parsley. 5 minutes in the oven

4. additional minutes, or until the bottom is lightly browned.

Nutrition: Serving size: 1 biscuit Calories: 214.4 kcal Fat: 12.3 g Carbohydrates: 19.9 g Fiber: 0.6 g Protein: 6.4 g Sugar: 1.7 g

187. Cloud Eggplant

Preparation Time: 10 minutes
Cooking Time: 30 minutes
Servings: 2
Ingredients:

- 3 large eggs, separated
- ¼ tsp cream of tartar
- 2 ounces cream cheese, very soft
- 1 tsp white sugar

Directions:

1. Preheat the oven to 350 degrees Fahrenheit (175 degrees C). Using parchment paper, line a baking sheet.
2. In a mixing bowl, whisk together the egg whites and cream of tartar until stiff peaks form.
3. In a second dish, combine egg yolks, cream cheese, and sugar using a wooden spoon, then beat with a hand-held eggbeater until smooth and no visible cream cheese remains.
4. Fold egg whites gently into cream cheese mixture, being careful not to deflate them.
5. Scoop the mixture onto the prepared baking sheet in 5 equal portions to a total of 6 "buns"
6. Bake for 30 minutes in a warm oven until cloud Eggplant is lightly browned.

Nutrition: Serving size: 1 cloud Eggplant Calories: 92.5 kcal Fat: 6.9 g Carbohydrates: 3.1 g Protein: 4.6 g Sugar: 2.8 g

188. Marinated Chicken Bruschetta

Preparation Time: 10 minutes
Cooking Time: 12 minutes
Additional: 40 minutes
Servings: 2
Ingredients:

- ¾ cup Wish-Bone® Italian Dressing, divided
- 6 (5 ounce) skinless, boneless chicken breast halves 2 medium beefsteak tomatoes, chopped
- ¼ cup diced red onion
- 1 tsp finely chopped fresh basil leaves* (Optional)

Directions:

1. In a large, shallow nonaluminum baking dish or plastic bag, pour 1/4 cup Wish-Bone® Italian Dressing over the chicken. Cover or tight bag and marinate in refrigerator for 30 minutes to 3 hours, turning occasionally.

2. In a medium mixing bowl, combine tomatoes, onion, basil, and 1/4 cup Dressing. Refrigerate for at least 30 minutes after covering.
3. Remove the chicken from the marinade and discard it. Grill or broil chicken until completely cooked, about 12 minutes, rotating once and brushing frequently with remaining 14 cup Dressing. Serve the tomato sauce over the chicken.

Nutrition: Serving size: 1 bruschetta Calories: 246.7 kcal Fat: 11.5 g Carbohydrates: 5.3 g Fiber: 0.6 g Protein: 29.9 g Sugar: 20 g

189. Keto Cupcakes

Preparation Time: 15 minutes
Cooking Time: 35 minutes
Additional: 2hours
Servings: 2
Ingredients:

- ⅔ cup coconut flour
- 2 teaspoons baking powder
- ½ cup butter, cut into small cubes.
- 2 ounces cream cheese, softened
- 1 cup coconut cream, chilled
- ¼ cup stevia powder
- 1 teaspoon vanilla extract
- 4 eggs

Directions:

1. Preheat the oven to 350°F (180°C) (175 degrees C). Paper liners should be used to line a cupcake pan.
2. In a large mixing basin, combine coconut flour and baking powder.
3. In a small microwave-safe bowl, combine the butter and cream cheese.
4. Microwave for 30 seconds, or until melted. Stir until everything is completely blended. Stir in the coconut cream, stevia, and vanilla essence.
5. Over the coconut flour mixture, pour the butter mixture. Stir everything together thoroughly. Incorporate the eggs. Evenly distribute the batter among the cupcake cups.
6. Bake for 35 minutes in a preheated oven, or until a toothpick inserted in the center comes out clean. Allow at least 2 hours for cooling before serving to avoid crumbling.

Nutrition: Serving size: 1 dozen Calories: 209.1 kcal Fat: 18.7 g Carbohydrates: 9.8 g Fiber: 3.5 g Protein: 4.3 g Sugar: 0.2 g

190. Broccoli and Cheddar Nuggets

Preparation Time: 15 minutes
Cooking Time: 25 minutes
Servings: 2

Ingredients:

- 1 tsp vegetable oil, or as needed.
- 1 (16 ounce) package frozen chopped broccoli, thawed.
- 1 cup Eggplant crumbs
- 1 ½ cups shredded Cheddar cheese
- 3 eggs
- ½ teaspoon dried basil
- ½ teaspoon dried oregano
- ¼ teaspoon garlic powder

Directions:

1. Preheat oven to 375 degrees Fahrenheit (190 degrees C). Using oil, grease a baking sheet.
2. Fill a pan with water to just under the bottom of a steamer insert. Bring a pot of water to a boil; add the broccoli, cover, and steam for 2 to 6 minutes, or until tender. Allow broccoli to cool at room temperature until it is safe to handle.
3. Broccoli should be placed in a large mixing dish. Toss the broccoli with the eggplant crumbs, Cheddar cheese, eggs, basil, oregano, and garlic powder. Form into nuggets or fun shapes and place on the baking sheet that has been prepped.
4. Bake for 15 minutes in a preheated oven, then flip and bake for another 10 to 15 minutes until heated through and firming up..

Nutrition: Calories: 372.2kcal Fat: 20.7 g Carbohydrates: 26.1 g Fiber: 4.8 g Protein: 22.1 g Sugar: 3.8 g

191. Baked Spaghetti Squash Casserole

Preparation Time: 20 minutes
Cooking Time: 55 minutes
Additional time: 5 minutes
Servings: 2

Ingredients:

- cooking spray
- 1 spaghetti squash
- 2 (14.5 ounce) cans chopped tomatoes
- 1 cup grated Parmesan cheese, divided
- ¼ cup chopped fresh oregano
- ¼ cup chopped fresh basil
- 2 cloves garlic, chopped
- ½ teaspoon salt

Directions:

1. Preheat the oven to 400 degrees Fahrenheit (200 degrees C). Using cooking spray, coat a 9x13-inch baking dish.
2. Using a knife, pierce the spaghetti squash in various places. Microwave on high for 10 to 15 minutes, rotating every 5 minutes until tender. Remove the dish from the microwave. Allow 5 to 10 minutes for cooling before handling.
3. Scoop out the seeds after cutting the squash in half. With a fork, scrape the insides of the squash into spaghetti strands. Place in a greased baking dish.
4. Mix together tomatoes, 3/4 cup Parmesan cheese, oregano, basil, garlic, and salt in a large mixing bowl. Top with the remaining 1/4 cup Parmesan cheese.
5. 45 to 60 minutes in a preheated oven until golden and bubbling.

Nutrition: Calories: 94.9 kcal Fat: 3.5 g Carbohydrates: 10.4 g Fiber: 0.9 g Protein: 5.4 g Sugar: 2.6 g

192. Spanish Tortilla

Preparation Time: 35 minutes
Cooking Time: 45 minutes
Additional time: 1 hour
Servings: 2

Ingredients:

- ½ cup olive oil
- 2 pounds baking Celeriac's peeled and split into 1/4-inch slices.
- salt and pepper to taste
- 2 tsp olive oil
- 2 onions, sliced into rings
- 5 eggs
- 1 roasted red pepper, drained and cut into strips.
- 3 ounces Spanish serrano ham, chopped
- 2 tsp chopped fresh Italian parsley

Directions:

1. In a large skillet, heat 1/2 cup olive oil over medium-low heat. Cook, stirring occasionally, until half of the cauliflower pieces are just cooked, 15 to 20 minutes. Remove the Celeriacs from the skillet and place them in a large mixing bowl, leaving the oil in the skillet. Cook until the remaining Celeriacs are cooked in the oil, then transfer to the bowl, leaving the oil in the skillet.
2. Season celeriac to taste with salt and pepper.
3. Meanwhile, in a pan over medium heat, heat 2 tablespoons olive oil. Stir in the onion rings and simmer, stirring occasionally, until they are tender and golden brown, about 15 minutes. Place the onions on a plate and set aside to cool while the celeriac cooks.

4. In a large mixing basin, whisk the eggs until smooth. In a large mixing bowl, combine the cooled onions, roasted peppers, and serrano ham. Fold in the cooked celeriac gently.

5. Heat the saved oil in a pan over low heat. Pour in the egg mixture and cook for 8 to 10 minutes, or until the sides have started to set and the bottom has turned golden brown. If necessary, loosen the tortilla with a spatula before carefully sliding it onto a big dish. Turn the skillet upside down and place it on the tortilla's uncooked side. Remove the plate and turn the skillet right side up. Return the skillet to the burner and cook for another 4 minutes, or until the tortilla has set in the center.

6. Allow it cool to room temperature before transferring the tortilla to a serving platter. To serve, cut into six wedges and top with parsley.

Nutrition: Calories: 476.6 kcal Fat: 32.3 g Carbohydrates: 35.8 g Fiber: 3.9 g Protein: 12.5 g Sugar: 5.3 g

193. Yummy Veggie Omelet

Preparation Time: 5 minutes
Cooking Time: 5 minutes
Servings: 2
Ingredients:

- 2 tablespoons butter
- 1 small onion, chopped
- 1 green bell pepper, chopped
- 4 eggs
- 2 tablespoons milk
- ¾ teaspoon salt
- ⅛ teaspoon freshly ground black pepper
- 2 ounces shredded Swiss cheese

Directions:

1. In a medium skillet, melt 1 tablespoon butter over medium heat.

2. Inside the skillet, place the onion and bell pepper. Cook, stirring occasionally, for 4 to 5 minutes, or until veggies are just soft.

3. While the vegetables are cooking, whisk together the eggs, milk, and 12 teaspoon salt and pepper in a mixing bowl.

4. Set aside the shredded cheese in a small bowl.

5. Remove the vegetables from the heat, place them in a separate bowl, and season with the remaining 1/4 teaspoon salt.

6. Over medium heat, melt the remaining 1 tablespoon butter (in the same skillet as the vegetables) Using the butter, coat the skillet. Add the egg mixture to the bubbling butter and cook for 2 minutes, or until the eggs begin to set on the bottom of the pan. Lift the omelet's edges gently with a spatula to allow the uncooked eggs to flow toward the edges and cook.

7. Cook for another 2 to 3 minutes, or until the omelet's middle appears to be dry.

8. Spread the cheese on top of the omelet, then ladle the veggie mixture into the center. Fold one edge of the omelet over the vegetables with a spatula. Allow the omelet to cook for another two minutes, or until the cheese has melted to your liking. Remove the omelet from the skillet and place it on a platter. Serve by slicing in half.

Nutrition: Calories: 386.4 kcal Fat: 29.8 g Carbohydrates: 9.1 g Fiber: 1.6 g Protein: 21.7 g Sugar: 4.8 g

CHAPTER 18:

Snacks

194. Beet Spinach Salad

Preparation time:15-20 minutes
Cooking time: 40 minutes
Servings: 2
Ingredients:

- 2 medium-sized beet, trimmed and sliced
- 1 cup fresh spinach, chopped
- 2 spring onions, finely chopped
- 1 small green apple, cored and chopped
- 3 tbsp olive oil
- 2 tbsp fresh lime juice
- 1 tbsp honey, raw
- 1 tsp apple cider vinegar
- 1 tsp salt

Directions:

1. Wash the beets and trim off the green parts. Set aside. Wash the spinach thoroughly and drain. Cut into small pieces and set aside.
2. Wash the apple and cut lengthwise in half. Remove the core and cut into bite-sized pieces and set aside.
3. Wash the onions and cut into small pieces. Set aside.
4. In a small bowl, combine olive oil, lime juice, honey, vinegar, and salt. Stir until well incorporated and set aside to allow flavors to meld. Place the beets in a deep pot. Pour enough water to cover and cook for about 40 minutes, or until tender. Remove the skin and slice. Set aside. In a large salad bowl, combine beets, spinach, spring onions, and apple. Stir well until combined and drizzle with previously prepared dressing. Give it a good final stir and serve immediately.

Nutrition information per serving: Calories: 215, Protein: 1.8g, Total Carbs: 23.8g, Dietary Fibers: 3.6g, Total Fat: 14.3g

195. Grilled Avocado in Curry Sauce

Preparation time: 15 minutes
Cooking time: 25-30 minutes
Servings: 2
Ingredients:

- 1 large avocado, chopped

- ¼ cup water
- 1 tbsp curry, ground
- 2 tbsp olive oil
- 1 tsp soy sauce
- 1 tsp fresh parsley, finely chopped
- ¼ tsp red pepper flakes
- ¼ tsp sea salt

Directions:

1. Peel the avocado and cut lengthwise in half. Remove the pit and cut the remaining avocado into small chunks. Set aside.
2. Heat up the olive oil in a large saucepan over a medium-high temperature.
3. In a small bowl, combine ground curry, soy sauce, parsley, red pepper and sea salt. Add water and cook for about 5 minutes, stirring occasionally.
4. Add chopped avocado, stir well and cook for 3 more minutes, or until all the liquid evaporates. Turn off the heat and cover. Let it stand for about 15-20 minutes before serving.

Nutrition information per serving: Calories: 338, Protein: 2.5g, Total Carbs: 10.8g, Dietary Fibers: 7.9g, Total Fat: 34.1g

196. Broccoli Cauliflower Puree

Preparation time: 10-15 minutes
Cooking time: 15-20 minutes
Servings: 2
Ingredients:

- 2 cups fresh broccoli chopped
- 2 cups fresh cauliflower, chopped
- ½ cup skim milk
- ½ tsp salt
- ½ tsp Italian seasoning
- ¼ tsp cumin, ground
- 1 tbsp fresh parsley, finely chopped
- 1 tbsp olive oil
- 1 tsp dry mint, ground

Directions:

1. Wash and roughly chop the cauliflower. Place it in a deep pot and add a pinch of salt. Cook for about 15-20 minutes. When done, drain and transfer it to a food processor. Set aside.

Gastric Sleeve Bariatric Cookbook

2. Wash the broccoli and chop into bite-sized pieces. Add it to the food processor along with milk, salt, Italian seasoning, cumin, parsley, and mint.
3. Gradually add olive oil and blend until nicely pureed.
4. Serve with some fresh carrots and celery.

Nutrition information per serving: Calories: 138, Protein: 6.1g, Total Carbs: 12.7g, Dietary Fibers: 4.6g, Total Fat: 7.5g

197. Peanut Butter Joy Cookies

Preparation time: 30 min
Cooking time: 45 min
Servings: 2
Ingredients:

- 250 ml quick oats
- 250 ml peanut butter, unsweetened
- 250 ml Splenda 1 tsp vanilla
- 1/2 tsp cinnamon, dried 1 egg

Directions:
1. Pre-heat oven to 350 degrees.
2. Place the peanut butter and Splenda in a mixing bowl. Using a sturdy spoon or hand beaters, beat the two together until smooth. Add in the egg, keep mixing, then add the vanilla.
3. Last, add in the oats and cinnamon. Continue to mix until everything is nice smooth dough.
4. Scoop the dough out a by dessert spoon and using your hands, roll into balls.
5. Place the balls on a cookie sheet and squish them gently down with a fork.
6. Place cookies in the oven for eight min until golden brown. Wait for them to cool before lifting off the pan.

Nutrition information per serving: Calories: 338, Protein: 2.5g, Total Carbs: 10.8g, Dietary Fibers: 7.9g, Total Fat: 34.1g

198. Chocolate Almond Ginger Mousse

Preparation time: 10 min
Cooking time: 30 min (4 hours cooling time)
Servings: 2
Ingredients:

- 325 ml milk, skim & cold
- 1 instant pudding package, fat-free and sugar-free 250 ml cool whip lite, thawed out
- 1/4 tsp ginger, dried
- 1 tbsp almonds, sliced

Directions:
1. Pour cold milk into a mixing bowl. Beating steadily with wire whisk, add the pudding mix and dried ginger. Keep whisking for two min. Fold in the cool whip topping.

2. Spoon into five pudding cups, refrigerate until needed. Garnish with sliced almonds just before servings.

Nutrition: Servings: 1g calories: 310kcal carbohydrates: 21g protein: 3.9g fat: 26.4g saturated fat: 9.5g polyunsaturated fat: 16.9g odium: 90mg fiber: 10.2g sugar: 7.1g

199. Bella's apple crisp

Preparation time: 20 min
Cooking time: 20 min
Servings: 2
Ingredients:

- Four apples, hard and crisp, cored and sliced 1/2 lemon
- 2 tbsp water
- 2 tbsp agave nectar or one tbsp honey
- Ingredients for toppings:
- 200 ml old-fashioned rolled oats
- 2 tbsp butter, cold
- 1/2 tsp cinnamon
- 125 ml chopped walnuts

Directions:
1. Heat oven to 350 degrees.
2. Place sliced apples in the bottom of an eight-inch pie plate or square cake pan.
3. Drizzle the water, lemon juice, and syrup over the apples.
4. In a mixing bowl, stir together the oats and cinnamon. Use a pastry cutter or two knives to cut in the butter mixture until it resembles coarse Eggplant crumbs.
5. Stir in the chopped nuts.
6. Sprinkle the mixture over the apples covering them completely.
7. Cover pan with tin foil and slide into the middle of the oven for twenty min.
8. Remove tin foil from pan and continue to bake for another ten to fifteen min until topping is golden brown.

Option: Servings: with a dab of fat-free, sugar-free ice cream.

Nutrition: Calories: 424kcal carbohydrates: 74.3g protein: 14.6g fat: 9.4g saturated fat: 2g polyunsaturated fat: 7.4g cholesterol: 94mg sodium: 572mg fiber: 11.3g sugar: 24.2g

200. Red energy wonders

Preparation time: 15 min
Cooking time: 15 min
Servings: 2
Ingredients:

- 75 ml almond butter
- 325 ml coconut, shredded and divided into a 225 ml portion and a 100 ml portion

~ 81 ~

- 125 ml oats, rolled 125 ml of strawberries 125 ml almonds 4 dates, Medrol, pit-less

Directions:

1. Place the 225 portions of coconut and all the rest of the ingredients in a food processor. On high speed, process until smooth and fully mixed.
2. Pour the remaining coconut onto a plate. With a spoon, scoop out one tablespoon of the mixture and form into a ball. Roll this ball around in the coconut, then place on a plate lined with parchment paper. Repeat until all of the mixtures are used.
3. Place the plate in the fridge for at least two hours before servings. Keep energy wonders in an airtight container in the fridge.

Nutrition: Calories: 191kcal carbohydrates: 17.9g protein: 6.3g fat: 12g saturated fat: 5.4g polyunsaturated fat: 6.6g cholesterol: 7mg sodium: 101mg fiber: 2.8g sugar: 8.6g

201. Chocolate Protein Pudding Pops

Preparation time: 5 min,
Cooking Time: 10 minutes
Servings: 2

Ingredients:

- 1 (3.9-ounce) package chocolate-flavored instant pudding 2 cups cold low-fat milk
- 2 scoops chocolate protein powder

Directions:

1. In a small bowl, whisk the pudding mix, milk, and protein powder for at least 2 min.
2. Spoon into ice pop molds or paper cups. Insert an ice pop stick in the center of each mold or cup.
3. F freeze for 4 hours, or until firm. Remove from the molds or cups before servings.
4. Post-op Servings: suggestions

Nutrition: Nutrition: calories: 215; total fat: 2g; protein: 12g; carbohydrates: 36g; fiber: 0g; sugar: 27g; sodium: 480mg.

202. Strawberry Frozen Yogurt

Preparation time: 5 min
Cooking Time: 4 hours
Servings: 2

Ingredients:

- 2 tablespoons honey
- 1 cup low-fat, plain Greek yogurt
- 4 cups frozen strawberries
- 2 teaspoons vanilla extract
- 1 teaspoon freshly squeezed lemon juice

Directions:

1. Combine the yogurt, strawberries, honey, vanilla, and lemon juice in a food processor. Pulse until the mixture is crumbly, then process until creamy. Fill a standard-size loaf pan halfway with batter. Cover and freeze for 2 hours, or until firm enough to scoop and serve. Post-op tips for servings Berry is a fantastic source of fiber and antioxidants, making it a terrific addition to your diet. Try this recipe using raspberries, blueberries, cranberries, or whatever berries are in season and available at the time.

Nutrition: Nutrition: calories: 135; total fat: 1g; protein: 6g; carbohydrates: 25g; fiber: 3g; sugar: 17g; sodium: 39mg.

203. Mozzarella Balls Recipe

Preparation Time: 10 minutes
Cooking Time: 5 minutes
Servings: 2

Ingredients

- 1 package string cheese
- 2 cups of Panko Eggplant Crumbs
- 2 tsp Italian seasoning
- 1 tsp parsley
- 1 cup of milk
- 1 cup of flour
- Marinara Sauce (homemade or store bought)
- Oil for frying

Direction:

1. Split 1-inch pieces of string cheese
2. In a bowl By pouring milk and setting aside, prepare the coating form. Put 1
3. cup of flour in a plastic bag and add 2 cups of panko, mixed with seasonings, into another bag.
4. Place the cheese, one handful at a time, in the milk.
5. Toss it in your bag of flour and shake well.
6. Put the cheese back in your bowl of milk, then coat it full.
7. Toss and shake in the panko bag until uniformly covered.
8. Place bites of mozzarella on a plate or in a bag and freeze for a minimum of 2 hours.
9. Heat oil on medium heat. Fry until golden brown in hot oil. Be sure to take out them of the oil until they get too hot, or from the Egg planting, cheese will ooze.
10. With marinara sauce, serve soft. ENJOY!

Nutrition: Amount Per Serving Fat 1g; Cholesterol 3mg; Sodium 124mg; Potassium 92mg; Carbohydrates 24g; Fiber 1g; Sugar 2g; Protein 4g; Vitamin A 55IU; Calcium 71mg; Iron 1.6mg

204. Chocolate Protein Balls

Preparation time: 40 mins
Cooking time: 0 mins
Servings: 1

Ingredients

- 1 cup of rolled oats
- ½ cup of natural peanut butter
- ⅓ cup of honey
- ¼ cup of chopped dark chocolate
- 2 tbsp flax seeds
- 2 tbsp chia seeds
- 1 tbsp chocolate-flavored protein powder, or as need

Directions

1. In a bowl, whisk together the oats, peanut butter, honey, chocolate, flax seeds, chia seeds and protein powder until mixed evenly. Cover the plastic wrap with a bowl and refrigerate for 30 minutes.
2. Scoop the balls into a chilled mixture. Keep it cold before you serve.

Nutrition: 188 calories; protein 5.8g 12% DV; carbohydrates 21.5g 7% DV; fat 9.9g 15% DV; cholesterol 0.2mg; sodium 67.5mg 3% DV.

205. Instant Frozen Berry Yogurt

Preparation time: 2 mins
Cooking time: 0 minutes
Serving: 2

Ingredients

- 250g frozen mixed berry
- 250g Greek yogurt
- 1 tbsp honey

Direction:

1. In a food processor, mix the berries, yogurt, and honey or agave syrup for 20 seconds, until the ice cream texture is smooth.
2. Scoop and serve in bowls.

Nutrition: per serving low in kcal 70; fat 0g; carbs 10g; sugars 10g; fiber 2g; protein 7g; low in salt 0.1g

206. Chocolate Avocado Pudding

Preparation time: 40 mins
Cooking time: 0 mins
Servings: 2

Ingredients

- 2 large avocados - peeled, pitted, and cubed ½ cup of unsweetened cocoa powder
- ½ cup of brown sugar
- ⅓ cup of coconut milk
- 2 tsp vanilla extract
- 1 pinch ground cinnamon

Directions

1. In a blender, mix the avocado, cocoa powder, brown sugar, coconut milk, vanilla extract, and cinnamon until soft.
2. Refrigerate the pudding for about 30 minutes until it is chilled

Nutrition: 400 calories; protein 5.4g 11% DV; carbohydrates 45.9g 15% DV; fat 26.3g 41% DV; sodium 22.6mg 1% DV.

207. Choco Frosty

Preparation Time: 5 minutes
Cooking Time: 5 minutes
Servings: 2

Ingredients:

- 1 tbsp. vanilla
- 8 drops liquid stevia
- 2 tbsp. unsweetened cocoa powder
- tbsp. almond butter
- 1 cup heavy cream

Directions:

1. Add all ingredients into the mixing bowl and beat with immersion blender until soft peaks form.
2. Place in refrigerator for 30 minutes.
3. Add frosty mixture into the piping bag and pipe in serving glasses.
4. Serve and enjoy.

Nutrition Calories 240   Fat 25 g Carbohydrates 4 g Sugar 3 g Protein 3 g Cholesterol 43 mg

208. Cheesecake Fat Bombs

Preparation Time: 10 minutes
Cooking Time: 10 minutes
Servings: 2

Ingredients:

- 8 oz. cream cheese
- ½ tsp. vanilla - 2 tbsp. erythritol
- 4 oz. coconut oil
- 4 oz. heavy cream

Directions:

1. Add all ingredients into the mixing bowl and beat using immersion blender until creamy.
2. Pour batter into the mini cupcake liner and place in refrigerator until set.
3. Serve and enjoy.

Nutrition Calories 90 Fat 9.8 g Carbohydrates 1.4 g Sugar 0.1 g Protein 0.8 g Cholesterol 17 mg

209. Green Ice Cream

Preparation Time: 5 minutes
Cooking Time: 5 minutes
Servings: 2

Ingredients:

- ½ tsp. vanilla

- 2 tbsp. swerve
- 1 tbsp. matcha powder
- 1 cup heavy whipping cream

Directions:
1. Add all ingredients into the glass jar.
2. Seal jar with lid and shake for 4-5 minutes until mixture double.
3. Place in refrigerator for 3-4 hours.
4. Servings chilled and enjoy.

Nutrition Calories 215 Fat 22 g Carbohydrates 3.8 g Sugar 0.2 g Protein 1.2 g Cholesterol 82 mg

210. Smoked Tofu Quesadillas

Preparation Time: 6 minutes
Cooking Time: 5 minutes
Servings: 2
Ingredients:

- 1 lb. extra firm sliced tofu
- 12 tortillas
- 2 tbsps. coconut oil
- 6 slices cheddar cheese
- 2 tbsps. sundried tomatoes
- 1 tbsp. cilantro
- 5 tbsps. sour cream

Directions:
1. Lay one tortilla flat and fill with tofu, tomato, cheese and top with oil. Repeat for as many as you need.
2. Bake for 5 minutes and remove from flame.
3. Top with sour cream.

Nutrition Net carbs 13 g Fiber 3 g Fat 6 g Sugar 3 g Calories 136

211. Zucchini Pizza Boats

Preparation Time: 5 minutes
Cooking Time: 30 minutes
Servings: 2
Ingredients:

- 2 medium Zucchini
- ½ cup Tomato Sauce
- ½ cup shredded Mozzarella cheese
- 2 tbsps. Parmesan cheese

Directions:
1. Set oven to 350 degrees F.
2. Slice zucchini in half lengthwise and spoon out the core and seeds to form boats.
3. Place zucchini halves skin side down in a small baking dish.
4. Add remaining ingredients inside the hollow center then set to bake until golden brown and fork tender (about 30 minutes).
5. Serve and enjoy.

Nutrition Net carbs 23.6 g Fiber 4 g Fats 7.9 g Sugar 1 g Calories 214

212. Pear-Cranberry Pie with Oatmeal Streusel

Preparation Time: 10 minutes
Cooking Time: 1 hour
Servings: 2
Ingredients:
Streusel:

- ¾ cup oats
- 1/3 cup stevia
- ½ tsp. cinnamon
- ¼ tsp. nutmeg
- 1 tbsp. cubed butter

Filling:

- 3 cup cubed pears
- 2 cup cranberries
- ½ cup stevia

Directions:
1. Set oven to 350 degrees F.
2. Combine all streusel ingredients in a food processor and process into a coarse crumb.
3. Next, combine all filling ingredients in a large bowl and toss to combine.
4. Transfer filling into pie crust, then top with streusel mix.
5. Set to bake until golden brown (about an hour). Cool and serve.

Nutrition Net carbs 47 g Fiber 4 g Fats 9 g Sugar 1 g Calories 280

213. Caramel Custard

Preparation Time: 15 Minutes
Cooking Time: 7 Minutes
Servings: 2
Ingredients:

- 4 cups milk - 6 eggs
- 4 tablespoons sugar
- 3/4 cup sugar
- 1 teaspoon vanilla extract
- 1 pinch sea salt
- 1/4 teaspoon ground cinnamon
- Round stainless-steel pan
- 2 tablespoons water

Directions:
1. Beat the milk, eggs, sugar, cinnamon, vanilla extract and salt in the bowl until they become smooth.
2. Transfer the mixture to the steel pan.
3. Set a cup of water into Instant Pot and place the trivet inside.
4. Cover the bowl with tin foil, poke some holes in it then place it over the trivet.
5. Secure the lid and cook on Manual for 7 minutes at high pressure.

1. When it beeps; do a quick release and remove the lid.
6. Boil the sugar with 2 tablespoons of water in the skillet and let it caramelize, Pour this mixture on top of custard then serve when cool.

Nutrition: Calories: 361 Fat: 11.5g Protein: 16.2g Carbs: 50.2g Net Carbs: 50.1g Fiber: 0.1g

214. Chocolate Cheesecake

Preparation Time: 10 Minutes
Cooking Time: 18 Minutes
Servings: 2
Ingredients:
- 3/4 tablespoon cocoa powder
- 1/4 cup Swerve sugar Sweetener
- 1 egg
- 8 ounces (227 g) cream cheese softened
- 1 tablespoon powdered peanut butter
- 1/2 teaspoon pure vanilla extract

Directions:
1. Blend the eggs and cream cheese in a blender to form a smooth mixture.
2. Add the brown sugar, peanut butter and vanilla extract to the egg mixture and blend.
3. Transfer the mixture to a greased ramekin.
4. Pour water into Instant Pot and place the trivet inside.
5. Arrange the ramekin over the trivet.
6. Secure the lid and cook on Manual function for 18 minutes at high pressure.
7. When it beeps; do a quick release and remove the lid.
8. Let the ramekin cool and refrigerate the cake for 8 hours. Serve.

Nutrition: Calories: 224 Fat: 21.1g Protein: 6.6g Carbs: 17.7g Net Carbs: 17.2g Fiber: 0.5g

215. Crème Brûlée

Preparation Time: 10 Minutes
Cooking Time: 14 Minutes
Servings: 2
Ingredients:
- 1/4 cup superfine sugar
- 5 egg yolks
- 2 cups heavy cream
- 1 tablespoon vanilla extract
- 1/2 cup sugar

Directions
1. Beat the egg yolks, cream, vanilla extract and sugar in a large bowl.
2. Divide the mixture into 4 ramekins.
3. Set a cup of water into Instant Pot and place the trivet inside.
4. Arrange the ramekins over the trivet.
5. Secure the lid and cook on Manual function for 13 minutes at high pressure.
6. When it beeps; do a quick release and remove the lid.
7. Let the ramekin cool and refrigerate for 4 hours. Sprinkle superfine sugar on top and serve.

Nutrition Calories: 378 Fat: 27.7g Protein: 4.5g Carbs: 27.6g Net Carbs: 27.6g Fiber: 0g

216. Maple-Mashed Sweet celeriac

Preparation time: 5 minutes
Cooking time: 10 minutes
Servings: 2
Ingredients:
- 1 pound sweet celeriac
- 1 cup carrots, thinly sliced
- Ingredients from the Kitchen Store:
- 2 tbsp. maple syrup
- ¼ tsp. nutmeg
- ¼ tsp. fresh ground pepper
- 4 cup water

Directions:
1. Wash and clean sweet celeriac.
2. Peel and cut into small chunks.
3. In a large bowl, pour water and bring to boil.
4. Put carrots and sweet celeriac into it.
5. Reduce heat and continue cooking for about 10 minutes until the carrots and sweet celeriac become soft.
6. Drain the vegetables using a colander and put them into a bowl.
7. Mas the vegetables until it becomes smooth.
8. Sprinkle ground pepper and nutmeg into it and stir.
9. Drizzle maple syrup over it, and stir.

Nutrition: Calories: 212, Fat: 4 g, Carbs: 18 g, Protein: 6 g, Sodium: 176 mg.

217. Garlic-Parmesan Cheesy Chips

Preparation time: 2 minutes + 20 minutes to cool
Cooking time: 7 minutes
Servings: 2
Ingredients:
- ¼ cup shredded Parmesan cheese
- ¼ cup shredded sharp Cheddar cheese
- ¼ tsp. garlic powder
- Dash salt

Directions:

1. Preheat the oven to 400 °F. Line a large baking sheet with parchment paper.
2. In a medium mixing bowl, combine the Parmesan cheese, Cheddar cheese, garlic powder, and salt. Mix well.
3. Place 2 tsp. of the cheese mixture about an inch or two apart on the baking sheet, making about 12 chips.
4. Bake for 5 to 7 minutes, or until the chips are golden brown around the edges.
5. Remove from the oven and let sit for 15 to 20 minutes, or until the chips start to crisp. Enjoy.

Nutrition: Per Serving (6 Chips): Calories: 98, Protein: 8 g, Fat: 7 g, Carbs: 1 g, Fiber: 0 g, Sugar: 0 g, Sodium: 333 mg.

218. Cheesy Baked Radish Chips

Preparation time: 5 minutes
Cooking time: 35 minutes
Servings: 2
Ingredients:

- 1 cup thinly sliced radishes (2 bunches radishes)
- 1 tbsp. extra-virgin olive oil
- 3 tbsp. nutritional yeast flakes
- ¼ tsp. salt
- Dash freshly ground black pepper (optional) Directions:

Directions

1. Preheat the oven to 375 °F. Line a baking sheet with parchment paper.
2. Place the radishes into a small bowl and toss in the oil.
3. In a small cup, mix the nutritional yeast, salt, and pepper (if using).
4. Place the oil-coated radish slices onto the prepared baking sheet in a single layer and sprinkle the nutritional yeast mixture lightly onto each slice.
5. Bake for about 15 minutes, then flip the chips and bake for another 15 minutes. Remove crispy chips, then continue to bake any remaining chips for a few minutes more at a time, until crispy and golden brown.
6. Serve and enjoy alone or with your favorite low-carb dip.

Nutrition: Per Serving (½ Cup Chips): Calories: 99, Protein: 5 g, Fat: 7 g, Carbs: 4 g, Fiber: 2 g, Sugar: 0 g, Sodium: 313 mg.

219. Savory Cheese Biscuits

Preparation time: 5 minutes
Cooking time: 15 minutes
Servings: 2
Ingredients:

- 1 cup almond flour

- ¼ cup shredded Parmesan cheese
- ¼ cup shredded Cheddar cheese
- 2 tsp. baking powder
- 2 tsp. garlic powder
- ½ tsp. salt - 2 large eggs

Directions:

1. Preheat the oven to 350 °F. Line a large baking sheet with parchment paper and set it aside.
2. In a large bowl, add the almond flour, Parmesan cheese, Cheddar cheese, baking powder, garlic powder, and salt. Mix well. Add the eggs and combine.
3. Scoop a heaping tbsp. of the mixture onto the baking sheet. Using a spatula, flatten the batter slightly into about 2-inches circles.
1. Repeat, placing biscuits about an inch apart. This should yield 8 small biscuits.
4. Bake for 15 minutes, or until the top of the biscuit is slightly golden brown. Serve warm.

Nutrition: Per Serving (2 Biscuits): Calories: 275, Protein: 15 g, Fat: 23 g, Carbs: 8 g, Fiber: 3 g, Sugar: 1 g; Sodium: 447 mg.

220. Italian Herb Muffins

Preparation time: 5 minutes
Cooking time: 12 minutes
Servings: 2
Ingredients:

- Nonstick cooking spray
- 8 tbsp. almond flour
- ¼ cup shredded Parmesan cheese
- 1 large egg
- 1 tsp. garlic powder
- 1 tsp. Italian seasoning
- 1 tsp. baking powder
- ¼ tsp. salt

Directions:

1. Preheat the oven to 350 °F. Line a muffin pan with 4 cupcake liners and spray the liners with nonstick cooking spray.
2. In a large mixing bowl, combine the almond flour, Parmesan cheese, egg, garlic powder, Italian seasoning, baking powder, and salt. Mix well until fully incorporated.
3. Scoop heaping tbsp. of the mixture into the lined cups until all the batter is used.
4. Bake for 12 minutes or until golden brown on the tops. Enjoy warm.

Nutrition: (1 Muffin): Calories: 128, Protein: 7 g, Fat: 10 g, Carbs: 5 g, Fiber: 2 g, Sugar: 1 g, Sodium: 217 mg.

221. Cheesy Cauliflower Tots

Preparation time: 5 minutes
Cooking time: 15 minutes
Servings: 2

Ingredients:

- 1 cup cauliflower rice
- ½ cup almond flour
- ½ cup shredded mozzarella cheese
- 1 large egg
- ¼ tsp. salt

Directions:

1. Preheat the oven to 400 °F. Line a large baking sheet with parchment paper and set it aside.
2. In a large mixing bowl, combine the cauliflower rice, almond flour, mozzarella cheese, egg, and salt. Mix well until fully incorporated.
3. Scoop heaping tbsp. of the mixture onto the baking sheet about an inch apart until all the batter is used. This recipe should make about 16 tots.
4. Bake for 13 to 15 minutes, until crispy and golden brown. Serve and enjoy.

Nutrition: Per Serving (4 Tots): Calories: 152, Protein: 9 g, Fat: 11 g, Carbs: 6 g, Fiber: 2 g, Sugar: 1 g, Sodium: 253 mg.

222. Mozzarella Mushroom Caps

Preparation time: 5 minutes
Cooking time: 20 minutes
Servings: 2

Ingredients:

- 12 white mushroom caps
- 4 ounces fresh mozzarella pearls
- 2 tbsp. almond flour
- 1 tbsp. whipped butter
- ½ tsp. garlic powder
- Dash salt

Directions:

1. Preheat the oven to 350 °F. Line a baking sheet with parchment paper.
2. Wash the mushrooms and carefully remove the cap from each one.
1. Place the mushrooms onto the lined baking sheet.
2. Place about three mozzarella pearls (about 1 tbsp.) in each mushroom cap.
3. In a small bowl, mix the almond flour, whipped butter, garlic powder, and salt. Sprinkle the mixture on top of each mushroom cap.
4. Bake for about 20 minutes or until the cheese has melted. Enjoy warm.

Nutrition: Per Serving (3 Mushroom Caps): Calories: 117, Protein: 8 g, Fat: 9 g, Carbs: 4 g, Fiber: 1 g, Sugar: 0.25 g, Sodium: 141 mg.

223. Subtly Sweet Coconut Milk "Flan"

Preparation time: 5 minutes + 1 hour to chill
Cooking time: 5 minutes
Servings: 2

Ingredients:

- ½ cup light unsweetened coconut milk
- 2 tsp. vanilla extract 1 tsp. stevia or no-calorie sweetener
- 1 tbsp. (1 packet) plain gelatin powder
Directions:

Directions

1. In a small saucepan, heat the coconut milk for 1 to 2 minutes, then sprinkle in the vanilla extract and stevia and stir to dissolve.
2. Sprinkle in the gelatin while stirring constantly to dissolve the gelatin completely. Remove from the heat.
3. Transfer the mixture to a blender and blend for about 30 seconds or so, until frothy. Pour into a small jar or mug.
4. Allow the dessert to set in the refrigerator for about an hour to firm.
5. Serve and enjoy.

Nutrition: Per Serving (6 Tbsp.): Calories: 130, Protein: 6 g, Fat: 7 g, Carbs: 5 g, Fiber: 0 g, Sugar: 3 g, Sodium: 51 mg.

224. Chia Chocolate Pudding

Preparation time: 5 minutes + 2-8 hours to chill
Cooking time: 0 minute
Servings: 2

Ingredients:

- ½ cup unsweetened almond milk
- ½ cup non-fat plain Greek yogurt
- 2 tbsp. chia seeds
- 1 tbsp. vanilla whey Protein:
- 1 tsp. unsweetened cocoa powder
- ½ tsp. stevia or no-calorie sweetener Directions:

Directions

1. In a canning jar, combine the almond milk, yogurt, chia seeds, whey protein cocoa powder, and stevia.
2. Seal with lid and let sit in the refrigerator overnight.
3. Enjoy straight from the jar, or in a separate bowl if you are consuming a smaller serving.

Nutrition: Per Serving (1¼ Cup): Calories: 257, Protein: 25 g, Fat: 12 g, Carbs: 21 g Fiber: 11 g; Sugar: 5 g, Sodium: 122 mg.

225. Simply Vanilla Frozen Greek Yogurt

Preparation time: 5 minutes + 8 hours to freeze
Cooking time: 0 minute
Servings: 2
Ingredients:

- 4 cups non-fat plain Greek yogurt
- 4 tbsp. vanilla whey protein powder
- 4 tbsp. vanilla extract
- 4 tsp. stevia or no-calorie sweetener Directions:

Directions

1. In a large bowl or loaf pan, combine the yogurt, protein powder, vanilla extract, and stevia.
2. Cover and freeze overnight or for at least 8 hours.
3. About an hour before serving, set in the refrigerator to thaw slightly. Serve and enjoy.

Nutrition: Per Serving (1 Cup): Calories: 183, Protein: 28 g, Fat: 1 g, Carbs: 12 g, Fiber: 1 g, Sugar: 8 g, Sodium: 96 mg.

226. Garlic Eggplant

Preparation Time: 5 minutes
Cooking Time: 5 minutes
Servings: 2
Ingredients:

- ½ cup butter, melted
- Pinch salt
- 1 tablespoon fresh parsley, chopped
- 4 cloves garlic, roasted and minced
- 1 loaf French Eggplant, sliced in half lengthwise

Directions:

1. Mix the butter, salt, parsley and garlic in a bowl.
2. Spread mixture on top of French Eggplant.
3. Air fry at 400 degrees F for 3 minutes.
4. Let cool for 2 minutes before serving.

Nutrition: Calories 312, Fat 6, Carbs 18, Protein 9, Sodium 385

227. Mozzarella Bites

Preparation Time: 5 minutes
Cooking Time: 5 minutes
Servings: 2
Ingredients:

- 8 mozzarella sticks
- 2 tablespoons butter
- ¼ Eggplant crumbs

Directions:

1. Dip the mozzarella sticks in butter.
2. Dredge with Eggplant crumbs.
3. Arrange in the air fryer basket.

4. Cook at 320 degrees F for 5 minutes, stirring once.

Nutrition: Calories 312, Fat 6, Carbs 18, Protein 9, Sodium 385

228. Ranch Pretzels

Preparation Time: 5 minutes
Cooking Time: 5 minutes
Servings: 2
Ingredients:

- 10 oz. pretzels
- 2 tablespoons olive oil
- 1 packet dry ranch seasoning mix

Directions:

1. Coat the pretzels with olive oil.
2. Sprinkle all sides with ranch seasoning.
3. Arrange the pretzels in the air fryer basket.
4. Cook at 320 degrees F for 3 minutes.
5. Turn and cook for another 2 minutes.

Nutrition: Calories 312, Fat 6, Carbs 18, Protein 9, Sodium 385

229. Maple Barbecue Cashews

Preparation Time: 5 minutes
Cooking Time: 5 minutes
Servings: 2
Ingredients:

- 2 tablespoons olive oil
- 2 teaspoons maple barbecue rub
- 1 cup raw cashews

Directions:

1. Blend olive oil and maple barbecue rub.
2. Coat cashews with this mixture.
3. Add to the air fryer basket.
4. Air fry at 370 degrees F for 5 minutes, stirring once.

Nutrition: Calories 312, Fat 6, Carbs 18, Protein 9, Sodium 385

230. Smoky Chickpeas

Preparation Time: 5 minutes
Cooking Time: 18 minutes
Servings: 2
Ingredients:

- 15 oz. chickpeas, rinsed and drained
- 1 tablespoon sunflower oil
- Salt to taste
- 2 tablespoons lemon juice
- ½ teaspoon ground cumin
- ¾ teaspoon smoked paprika
- ½ teaspoon granulated garlic

Directions:

1. Preheat your air fryer to 390 degrees F.
2. Cook chickpeas for 15 minutes, shaking the basket once.

3. In a bowl, mix the oil, salt, lemon juice and spices.
4. Toss the chickpeas in the spice mixture.
5. Air fry at 360 degrees F for 3 minutes.

Nutrition: Calories 312, Fat 6, Carbs 18, Protein 9, Sodium 385

231. Cauliflower Chips

Preparation Time: 5 minutes
Cooking Time: 15 minutes
Servings: 2
Ingredients:

- Cooking spray
- 1 Cauliflower, sliced thinly
- Salt to taste

Directions:

1. Spray your air fryer basket with oil.
2. Spray the Cauliflower slices with oil.
3. Sprinkle Cauliflower with salt.
4. Air fry at 450 degrees F for 15 minutes, stirring once or twice.

Nutrition: Calories 312, Fat 6, Carbs 18, Protein 9, Sodium 385

232. Roasted Macadamia

Preparation Time: 5 minutes
Cooking Time: 10 minutes
Servings: 2
Ingredients:

- 1 lb. macadamia nuts
- Salt to taste

Directions:

1. Spread the macadamia nuts in the air fryer basket.
2. Cook at 250 degrees F for 10 minutes, shaking the basket halfway through.
3. Sprinkle with salt.

Nutrition: Calories 312, Fat 6, Carbs 18, Protein 9, Sodium 385

233. Apricot Brie Snack

Preparation Time: 10 minutes
Cooking Time: 5 minutes
Servings: 2
Ingredients:

- 1 package crescent dough sheets
- 4 oz. brie cheese, sliced
- ½ cup apricot preserves

Directions:

1. Spread the crescent dough sheet on your kitchen table.
2. Press the sheet onto muffin cups.
3. Top with the cheese and apricot preserves.
4. Air fry at 340 degrees F for 5 minutes.

Nutrition: Calories 312, Fat 6, Carbs 18, Protein 9, Sodium 385

Ingredients:

- 1 cup almond flour
- ¼ cup shredded Parmesan cheese
- ¼ cup shredded Cheddar cheese
- 2 teaspoons baking powder
- 2 teaspoons garlic powder
- ½ teaspoon salt
- 2 large eggs

Directions:

1. Preheat the oven to 350°F. Line a large baking sheet with parchment paper and set aside.
2. In a large bowl, add the almond flour, Parmesan cheese, Cheddar cheese, baking powder, garlic powder, and salt. Mix well. Add the eggs and combine.
3. Scoop a heaping tablespoon of the mixture onto the baking sheet. Using a spatula, flatten the batter slightly into about 2-inch circles. Repeat, placing biscuits about an inch apart. This should yield 8 small biscuits.
4. Bake for 15 minutes, or until the top of biscuits is slightly golden brown.
5. Serve warm.

Nutrition: (2 BISCUITS): Calories: 275; Protein: 15g; Fat: 23g; Carbohydrates: 8g; Fiber: 3g; Sugar: 1g; Sodium: 447mg

234. Almond-Crusted Mozzarella Sticks

Preparation Time: 10 minutes
Cooking Time: 6 minutes
Servings: 2
Ingredients:

- 8 tablespoons almond flour
- ½ teaspoon Italian seasoning
- ¼ teaspoon salt
- 2 large eggs
- 6 (1-ounce) light mozzarella sticks
- 1 tablespoon extra-virgin olive oil

Directions:

1. On a separate small plate, mix the almond flour, Italian seasoning, and salt. Beat the eggs in a small bowl and place between the two plates.
2. Cut the mozzarella sticks in half. Lightly coat each mozzarella, then dip and coat in the egg, and then coat well in the almond flour mixture. Coat each mozzarella piece well with the batter to enclose the cheese in the mixture so it doesn't spread onto the baking sheet while baking.
3. Place each coated mozzarella piece on a large plate. Repeat until all the mozzarella pieces are coated.

4. Cover the plate with plastic wrap and place the mozzarella sticks in the freezer for about 2 hours.
5. Preheat the oven to 400°F. Line a baking sheet with parchment paper.
6. Place the mozzarella pieces about 1-inch apart on the baking sheet. Using a basting brush, coat each side of each mozzarella piece lightly with the oil.
7. Bake for 4 to 6 minutes, until the cheese starts to bubble, and the crust starts to turn slightly golden. Watch closely to make sure the cheese does not start to spread. Enjoy warm.

Nutrition (2 mozzarella sticks): Calories: 182; Protein: 11g; Fat: 15g; Carbohydrates: 4g; Fiber: 1g; Sugar: 1g; Sodium: 311mg

CHAPTER 19:

Lunch

235. Summer Quinoa Bowls

Preparation time: 5 minutes
Cooking time: 20 minutes
Servings: 2

Ingredients:

- 1 sliced peach
- 1/3 cup quinoa
- 1 cup low-fat milk
- ½ tsp. vanilla extract
- 2 tsp. natural stevia
- 12 raspberries
- 14 blueberries - 2 tsp. honey

Directions:

1. Add natural stevia, 2/3 cup milk, and quinoa to a saucepan, and stir to combine.
2. Over medium-high heat, bring to a boil then cover and reduce heat to a low simmer for a further 20 minutes (you should be able to fluff quinoa with a fork).
3. Grease and preheat grill to medium. Grill peach slices for about a minute per side. Set aside.
4. Heat remaining milk in the microwave and set aside.
5. Split cooked quinoa evenly between 2 serving bowls and top evenly with remaining ingredients. Enjoy!

Nutrition: Calories: 180, Net Carbs: 36 g, Fiber: 4 g, Fat: 4 g, Sugar: 3 g.

236. Perfect Granola

Preparation time: 10 minutes
Cooking time: 30 minutes
Servings: 1

Ingredients:

- ¼ cup canola oil
- 4 tbsp. honey - 1½ tsp. vanilla
- 6 cup old fashioned rolled oats
- 1 cup almond
- ½ cup shredded unsweetened coconut
- 2 cup bran flakes
- ¾ cup chopped walnuts
- 1 cup raisins - Cooking spray

Directions:

1. Prepare oven to preheat at 325 °F.

2. In a saucepan, cook oil and vanilla gently over low flame, occasionally stirring for roughly 5 mins.
3. Place all ingredients except raisins into a large bowl and combine.
4. Stir in honey and oil mixture slowly, ensuring all grains are properly coated.
5. Set a parchment paper on the baking tray or use cooking spray to grease lightly. Spread cereal evenly in the tray and bake for 25
6. mins, occasionally stirring to keep the mixture from burning, or until very lightly browned.
7. When ready, remove cereal and put it aside to cool.
8. Add raisins and mix well.

Nutrition: Calories: 458, Net Carbs: 62 g, Fiber: 2 g, Fat: 21 g, Sugar: 3 g.

237. Sweet Millet Congee

Preparation time: 5 minutes
Cooking time: 1 hour 10 minutes
Servings: 2

Ingredients:

- 1 cup millet
- 5 cup of water
- 1 cup diced sweet Cauliflower
- 1 tsp. cinnamon
- 1 tbsp. stevia
- 1 cup diced apple
- ¼ cup honey

Directions:

1. In a deep pot, add stevia, sweet Cauliflower, cinnamon, water, and millet, then stir to combine. Bring to boil over high heat, then decrease to a simmer on low for an hour or until the water is fully absorbed and millet is cooked. Stir in remaining ingredients and serve.

Nutrition: Calories: 136, Fat: 1 g, Carbs: 28.5 g, Protein: 3.1 g.

238. Vanilla Egg Custard

Preparation time: 5 minutes
Cooking time: 30 minutes
Servings: 2

Ingredients:

- 4 large eggs

- 2 tsp. vanilla extract
- 2/3 cup Splenda
- 12 oz. can evaporate milk
- 2 cup milks ½ cup nutmeg, grated

Directions:
1. Preheat the oven at 325 °F.
2. Place six ramekins in a baking tray and set them aside.
3. Add vanilla, Splenda, eggs, evaporated milk, and milk in a blender and blend until smooth.
4. Pour mixture into the ramekins then pour enough water in a baking tray and bake in preheated oven for 30 minutes.
5. Serve chilled and enjoy.

Nutrition: Calories: 255, Fat: 8.4 g, Carbs: 29.5 g, Sugar: 29.5 g, Protein: 9.4g, Cholesterol: 144 mg.

---

239. Mushroom Frittata

Preparation time: 10 minutes
Cooking time: 30 minutes
Servings: 2
Ingredients:

- 6 eggs, lightly beaten
- 2 oz. butter
- 2 oz. green onion, chopped
- 3 oz. fresh spinach
- 5 oz. mushrooms, sliced
- 4 oz. feta cheese, crumbled
- Pepper - Salt

Directions:
1. Preheat the oven to 350 °F/ 0 °C.
2. Whisk eggs, cheese, pepper, and salt in a bowl.
3. Melt butter in a pan over medium heat.
4. Add mushrooms and green onion to the pan and sauté for 5-10
5. minutes. Add spinach and sauté for 2 minutes.
6. Pour egg mixture into the pan.
7. Bake in preheated oven for 20 minutes.
8. Serve and enjoy.

Nutrition: Calories: 226, Fat: 10.2 g, Carbs: 11.2 g, Sugar: 4.7 g, Protein: 24.2 g, Cholesterol: 164 mg.
64.

---

240. Avocado Shrimp Salad

Preparation time: 10 minutes
Cooking time: 15 minutes
Servings: 2
Ingredients:

- 1 ripe avocado
- 1 tbsp. Tabasco
- 1 tsp. ranch dressing
- ½ cup yogurt
- 1 lb. shrimp, cooked
- 1 grapefruit, cut into sections

Directions:
1. Combine together Tabasco, ranch dressing, and yogurt. Place shrimp, avocado, and grapefruit in a large bowl.
2. Pour dressing over shrimp and avocado mixture. Serve and enjoy.

Nutrition: Calories: 226, Fat: 10.2 g, Carbs: 11.2 g, Sugar: 4.7 g, Protein: 24.2 g, Cholesterol: 164

---

241. Farmer's Egg Casserole with Broccoli, Mushroom, and Onions

Preparation time: 10 minutes
Cooking time: 40 minutes
Servings: 2
Ingredients:

- Nonstick cooking spray
- 2 tsp. extra-virgin olive oil
- 1 onion, diced
- ½ cup chopped mushrooms
- 2 cups roughly chopped broccoli florets
- 12 eggs
- 2 tbsp. low-fat milk
- ½ tsp. dried oregano
- ½ tsp. dried basil
- ¼ tsp. dried thyme
- 1 cup chopped or shredded cooked poultry breast, such as leftover
- turkey or chicken, canned chicken breast, or turkey lunch meat (nitrate-free)
- 1 cup shredded Swiss cheese
- ¼ cup shredded Parmigiano-Reggiano cheese

Post-Op:

- 1 (3-by-4-inches) piece

Directions:
1. Preheat the oven to 350 °F. Spray a 9-by-13-inches baking dish with the cooking spray.
2. In a large skillet over medium heat, add the olive oil. When the oil is hot, add the onion and sauté for 1 to 2 minutes, or until tender.
3. Add the mushrooms and cook for an additional 2 to 3 minutes, or until tender.
4. In a steamer or microwave-safe bowl, place the broccoli florets and 2 tbsp. of water.

5. Cover and microwave/steam for about 4 minutes or just until tender. Drain off any liquid and set it aside.

6. In a large bowl, whisk together the eggs, milk, oregano, basil, and thyme.

7. Add the cooked vegetables, poultry, and Swiss cheese to the egg mixture and stir to combine.

8. Pour the mixture into the baking dish and sprinkle the Parmigiano-Reggiano cheese over the top. Bake for 35 to 40 minutes, or until lightly browned. Let the casserole rest for 5 minutes before serving.

9. Store leftovers in the refrigerator for up to 1 week. Reheat before eating.

Nutrition: Calories: 147, Total Fat: 10 g, Protein: 12 g, Carbs: 2 g, Fiber: 1g;Sugar: 0 g, Sodium: 1 mg.

242. Apple and Goat Cheese Sandwich

Preparation time: 1 minute
Cooking time: 5 minutes
Servings: 1
Ingredients:

- 2 slices 100-percent whole-wheat Eggplant, toasted
- 1 ounce goat cheese, at room temperature
- 1 tbsp. natural peanut butter
- ½ medium apple, cored and thinly sliced, divided
- ¼ tsp. cinnamon

Directions:

1. Spread a bit of toast with goat cheddar and the other with nutty spread. Make a sandwich with a large portion of the apple cuts sprinkled with cinnamon. Present with residual apple cuts.

Nutrition: Calories: 408, Fat: 17 g, Carbs: 49 g, Sugar: 15 g, Protein: 17 g.

243. Mushroom And Wild Rice Soup

Preparation time: 10 min
Cooking time: 4 hours
Servings: 2
Ingredients:

- Onion, white, chopped (1/2 piece)
- White wine (1/2 cup) or chicken broth, fat free, low sodium (1/2 cup) Thyme, dried (1/4 teaspoon)
- Carrots, chopped (1/4 cup)
- Milk, half and half, fat free (1 cup)
- Wild rice, cooked (1 cup)
- Olive oil, extra virgin (1 tablespoon)
- Celery, chopped (1/4 cup)
- White mushrooms, fresh, sliced (1 ½ cups)
- Chicken broth, fat free, low sodium (2 ½ cups) Flour (2 tablespoons)

- Black pepper, freshly ground (1/2 teaspoon)

Directions:

1. Heat a stock pot on medium, then add the olive oil. Stir in the chopped onion as well as carrots and celery. Cook for two to three min or until tender and fragrant.

2. Pour in the chicken broth and white wine. Add the mushrooms as well, then stir to combine. Cover and allow the mixture to get heated through.

3. Meanwhile, place the flour in a large bowl. Add the milk, pepper, and thyme; stir to combine. Add the cooked rice and toss until well-combined.

4. Transfer the rice mixture into the vegetable pot. Stir well before cooking time on medium until bubbly and thickened.

5. Servings: immediately.

Nutrition: Calories: 270kcal carbohydrates: 18.5g protein: 34.8g fat: 7.1g saturated fat: 0.7g cholesterol: 75mgsodium: 994mg fiber: 1g

244. Cheesy grits

Preparation time: 10 min
Cooking time: 10 min
Servings: 2
Ingredients:

- 1 cup grits, uncooked
- 3 eggs, lightly beaten
- 1 cup cheddar cheese, shredded
- ¼ cup half-and-half

Directions

1. Preparation time the grits according to the package directions Meanwhile, in a small bowl, combine the beaten eggs with the cheese.

2. When the grits are almost done, stir 3 tablespoons of the hot grits into the egg mixture.

3. Add the egg mixture to the cooking time grits; whisk the egg mixture into the grits until the grits are smooth.

4. Add half-and-half; continue whisking until the grits are of desired consistency.

Nutrition Calories 304.5 Total fat 9.6g Total carbohydrate 36.4g Protein 16.9g

245. Oat Meal Mush With Polish Sausage

Preparation time: 10 min
Cooking time: 10 min
Servings: 2
Ingredients:

- 1 (16-ounce) package refrigerated oat meal mush ½ (16-ounce) package skinless polish sausage ½ tablespoon butter

- Stevia to taste

Directions

1. Set aside both the mush and the sausage slices, which should be cut into 1-inch slices.
2. Melt butter in a large pan over medium heat; add mush, layering pieces side by side. Cook for 10 minutes on one side until softened and gently browned, then flip to cook the other side.
3. Add sausage to skillet after turning mush over to brown the other side; place around rims of skillet and between mush pieces to keep warm (you may also use a separate skillet to heat sausage).

Servings: with maple syrup drizzled on top.

Nutrition: calories 110.4 /total fat 1.1g /total carbohydrate 23.4 g /protein 2.5g

246. Mexican scrambled eggs

Preparation time: 10 min
Cooking time: 5 min
Servings: 2

Ingredients:

- Eggs (6, lightly beaten)
- Tomato (1, diced)
- Cheese (3 oz., shredded)
- Butter (1 tbsp., for frying)

Directions

1. Set a large skillet with butter over medium heat and allow to melt.
2. Add tomatoes and green onions then cook, while stirring, until fragrant (about 3 min).
3. Add eggs, and continue to cook, while stirring, until almost set (about 2 min) Add cheese, and season to taste continue cooking time until the cheese melts (about another minute).
4. Servings: and enjoy.

Nutrition Calories 239 Total fat 3.7g Total carbohydrate

247. Spinach Omelet

Preparation time: 10 min
Cooking time: 10 min
Servings: 2

Ingredients:

- 2 tbsp olive oil
- 1 cup spinach, chopped
- 1 cup swiss chard, chopped
- 3 eggs
- 1 tsp garlic powder
- ½ tsp sea salt
- ¼ tsp red pepper flakes

Directions

1. Grease the pressure cooker's bottom with 2 tablespoons of olive oil.

2. Press beans/lentils button and add greens. Stir-fry for 5 min. Remove from the cooker and set aside.
3. Whisk together eggs, garlic powder, salt, and red pepper flakes. Pour the mixture into the stainless-steel insert.
4. Spread the eggs evenly with a wooden spatula and cook for about 2-3 min.
5. Using a spatula, ease around the edges and slide to a Servings: plate. Add greens and fold it over in half.

Nutrition Calories 227 Total fat 3g Total carbohydrate 2.3 g Protein 20g

248. Slow Cooker Apple Oatmeal

Preparation time: 1 hour
Cooking time: 7 hour
Servings: 2

Ingredients:

- 4 cups oatmeal
- 2 cups apple juice
- 4½ cups water
- 2 teaspoons cinnamon
- ¼ cup stevia
- 2 apples, peeled and chopped

Directions

1. In a slow cooker, add oatmeal, apple juice, water, cinnamon, and stevia. Mix well.
2. Add apples evenly across top; push down into oatmeal.
3. Cover; cook on low for 8 hours, or overnight.

Nutrition Calories 290 Total fat 7.7g Total carbohydrate 24.3 g Protein 8.1g

249. Cheesy Radish

Preparation time: 20 min
Cooking time: 40 min
Servings: 2

Ingredients

- 16 oz. Monterey jack cheese, shredded
- 2 cups radish
- ½ cup heavy cream
- 1 teaspoon lemon juice
- Salt and white pepper, to taste

Directions

1. Preheat the oven to 3000f and lightly grease a baking sheet.
2. Heat heavy cream in a small saucepan and season with salt and white pepper.
3. Stir in Monterey jack cheese and lemon juice.
4. Place the radish on the baking sheet and top with the cheese mixture.

5. Bake for about 45 min and remove from the oven to serve hot.

Nutrition calories 387 Total fat 32g Saturated fat 20.1g 1 Cholesterol 97mg Sodium 509mg Total carbohydrate 2.6g Dietary fiber 0.7g Total sugars 1.3g Protein 22.8g

250. Parmesan Garlic Oven Roasted Mushrooms

Preparation time: 10 min
Cooking time: 20 min
Servings: 2

Ingredients

- 3 tablespoons butter
- 12 oz. Baby Bella mushrooms
- ¼ cup pork rinds, finely ground
- Pink Himalayan salt and black pepper, to taste ¼ cup parmesan cheese, grated

Directions

1. Preheat the oven to 4000f and lightly grease a baking sheet.
2. Heat butter in a large skillet over medium high heat and add mushrooms.
3. Sauté for about 3 min and dish out.
4. Mix together pork rinds, parmesan cheese, salt and black pepper in a bowl.
5. Put the mushrooms in this mixture and mix to coat well.
6. Place on the baking sheet and transfer to the oven.
7. Bake for about 15 min and dish out to immediately serve

Nutrition Calories 94 Total fat 7.7g Saturated fat 4.7g Cholesterol 22mg Sodium 228mg Total carbohydrate 3g Dietary fiber 0.9g Total sugars 1g Protein 4.5

251. Garlicky Green Beans Stir Fry

Preparation time: 25 min
Cooking time: 15 min
Servings: 2

Ingredients

- 2 tablespoons peanut oil
- 1-pound fresh green beans
- 2 tablespoons garlic, chopped
- Salt and red chili pepper, to taste
- ½ yellow onion, slivered

Directions

1. Heat peanut oil in a wok over high heat and add garlic and onions.
2. Sauté for about 4 min add beans, salt and red chili pepper.
3. Sauté for about 3 min and add a little water.
4. Cover with lid and cook on low heat for about 5 min.

5. Dish out into a bowl and serve hot.

Nutrition Calories 107 Total fat 6.9g Saturated fat 1.2g Cholesterol 0mg Sodium 8mg Total carbohydrate 10.9g Dietary fiber 4.3g Total sugars 2.3g Protein 2.5g

252. Collard Greens With Burst Cherry Tomatoes

Preparation time: 25 min
Cooking time: 25 min
Servings: 2

Ingredients

- 1-pound collard greens
- 3 strips bacon, cooked and crisped
- ¼ cup cherry tomatoes
- Salt and black pepper, to taste
- 2 tablespoons chicken broth

Directions

1. Put the collard greens, cherry tomatoes and chicken broth in a pot and stir gently.
2. Cook for about 8 min and season with salt and black pepper.
3. Cook for about 2 min and stir in the bacon.
4. Cook for about 3 min and dish out into a bowl to serve hot.

Nutrition Calories 110 Total fat 7.6g Saturated fat 2.3g Cholesterol 0mg Total carbohydrate 6.7g Dietary fiber 3.9g Total sugars 0.3g Protein 5.7g

253. Southwestern Scrambled Eggs

Preparation time 15 min
Cooking time: 15 min
Servings: 2

Ingredients

- Olive oil (one tsp)
- Cilantro (.25 cup, fresh and finely chopped) Red onion (.25 cup, chopped)
- Eggs (3 large, with omega 3)
- Non-fat milk (.25 cup, no added vitamin a & d) Salt (.5 teaspoon) - Black pepper (.25, ground)
- Muir glen medium salsa (.5 cup)

Directions

1. Mince the garlic. Heat up healthy oil in skillet.
2. Add garlic, onion and cilantro.
3. Sauté five min or until veggies are soft.
4. In a bowl, beat the eggs. Add milk, salt and pepper. Mix together.
5. Pour egg mixture into skillet and let cook for two min, stirring and lifting up the eggs.
6. Put eggs onto plate and top with salsa.

Nutrition: Protein: 10.62 grams Calories: 169.8

254. Swiss steak

Preparation time: 20 min
Cooking time: 1 hour 15 min
Servings: 1
Ingredients:

- Round or flank steak (2 pounds, 1.5 inches thick) Cooked tomatoes (#1 tall can)
- Onion (one, sliced) - Celery (one stalk, diced)
- Flour (as needed to coat steak)
- Salt (as needed to season coating)
- Healthy oil (as needed to brown the steak

Directions:

1. Cut up the onion and the celery and set aside.
2. Put flour and salt into a bowl and mix together.
3. Coat the steak in the flour and salt mixture.
4. Heat up oil in heavy skillet.
5. Brown the steak on both sides in the hot oil.
6. Add the cooked tomatoes and the sliced fresh vegetables to the pan.
7. Cover and cook over low heat (or bake in oven set at 300 degrees Fahrenheit) for 2-2.5 hours.

Nutrition: Protein: 46 kcal Fat: 72 kcal Carbohydrates: 14 kcal

255. Braised Pork Chops With Sweetened Apple Ring

Preparation time: 10 min
Cooking time: 50 min
Servings: 2
Ingredients:

- Pork chops (one to three, as desired)
- Flour (as needed)
- Salt (as needed)
- Apple (1 fresh, tart, cut into one .75-inch thick slice for each chop) Healthy oil (as needed)
- Sugar-free brown sugar (to taste)
- Water (as needed)

Directions:

1. Put enough flour, seasoned to taste with salt, to coat the pork chops.
2. Heat up healthy oil in an oiled heavy skillet.
3. Coat pork chops and place them into the hot skillet. Brown both sides of all chops.
4. Place one apple ring on top of each chop. Sprinkle brown sugar on top of the apple rings.
5. Add a bit of water to the bottom of the pan. Cover and cook (braise) over low heat for 35-40 min or until tender.

Nutrition: Protein: 107 kcal Fat: 160 kcal Carbohydrates: 0 kcal

256. Chicken Salad

Preparation time: 10 min
Cooking time: 20 min
Servings: 2
Ingredients:

- Chicken (2 cups, cooked, chopped, cold)
- Eggs (2-3 eggs, hard-boiled, chopped, cold; one could be reserve for presentation)
- Celery (1 cup, fresh)
- Lemon juice (one tbsp)
- Seasonings (pepper and salt)
- Low-fat mayonnaise (.5 cup)
- Tomato (one, fresh, optional)
- Lettuce (optional)
- Olives (optional)
- Sweet pickles (optional)
- Parsley (optional)

Directions:

1. Bake, cool and chop the chicken.
2. Boil, cool and chop the eggs that will be mixed with the chicken.
3. Chop the celery.
4. Put the chicken, celery, lemon juice, salt and pepper in a bowl. Mix.
5. Add and mix in the mayonnaise.
6. Add and mix in the chopped eggs.
7. Optional presentation:
8. Cover bottom of plate with lettuce leaves.
9. Cut the tomato downward from the top, but not through the bottom, between two and four times so as to make a tomato flower cup for the salad.
10. Put the tomato flower on top of the lettuce and fill with the chicken.
11. Top the chicken with fresh parsley.
12. Slice the remaining boiled egg into slices.
13. Line the edge of the flower with the egg slices, olives, sweet pickles, etc., as desired.

Nutrition: Protein: 39 kcal Fat: 17 kcal Carbohydrates: 9 kcal

257. Cabbage Salad

Preparation time: 10 min
Cooking time: 15 min
Servings: 2
Ingredients:

- Cabbage (2.5 cups, shredded)
- Salt (one tsp)
- Low-fat mayonnaise (as needed to coat)

Directions:

1. Mix all ingredients together.

Nutrition: Protein: 3 kcal Fat: 55 kcal Carbohydrates: 50 kcal

258. Cauliflower salad

Preparation time: 20 mi
Cooking time: 2 hour
Servings: 2

Ingredients:

- celeriac (3 cups, cubed, boiled, cold)
- Onion (one tbsp, finely chopped)
- Salt (dash)
- Black pepper (dash)
- Pimiento (to taste, optional)
- Parsley (to taste, optional)
- French dressing (.25 cup)
- Low-fat mayonnaise (.75 cup)

Directions:

1. Boil the eggs. Let cool. Chill.
2. Peel, cube, boil the celeriac until soft but not falling apart. Cool.
3. Chop the onions.
4. Put the cooled celeriac and the onions together in a bowl.
5. Season with salt and pepper. Mix gently.
6. Add the French dressing. Mix gently. Chill 1-2 hours.
7. Add the mayonnaise, pimiento and parsley. Mix gently.
8. Dice and add the chilled eggs. Mix gently.
9. Add extra seasonings to taste.
10. Dish up into individual bowls. For more variety, place on individual plates surrounded with salad greens, cucumber sticks, slices of boiled eggs, and/or tomato sections.

Nutrition: Protein: 11 kcal Fat: 74 kcal Carbohydrates: 45 kcal

259. Hummus

Preparation time: 2 hours
Cooking time: 30 minutes
Servings: 2

Ingredients:

- 1 can chickpeas, drained and rinsed
- 1 tbsp peanut butter
- 1/2 lemon, juice only
- 1 tsp lemon rind, minced
- 1 tsp salt
- 1/4 tsp red pepper flakes, crushed
- 1 tbsp olive oil
- 1 clove garlic
- Option, substitute pesto for peanut butter

Directions:

1. Place everything in the food processor. Start to puree while slowly drizzling in two tablespoons of water. Puree until exceptionally creamy.

2. Place in a bowl and keep cool in the fridge until ready to enjoy with any chopped, sliced, or whole vegetable of your choice. These could include sweet bell peppers, cherry tomatoes, radishes, fennel, jicama, and snap peas.

Nutrition: Protein: 19 kcal Fat: 77 kcal Carbohydrates: 80 kcal

260. Cheese Chips

Preparation time: 20 min
Cooking time: 30 min
Servings: 2

Ingredients:

- 10 tbsp parmesan cheese shredded
- Garlic powder
- 2 tbsp fresh basil finely chopped

Directions:

1. Heat the oven to 350 degrees. Line a baking sheet with parchment paper.
2. Scoop one tablespoon of cheese and drop in a plop on the baking sheet.
3. With your fingers, gently spread the cheese into a thin circle and add a pinch of garlic powder and a pinch of basil.
4. Repeat until all of the cheese is gone.
5. Place sheet in oven until circle edges are golden brown. Give them a minute to cool.

Nutrition: Protein: 26 kcal Fat: 239 kcal Carbohydrates: 231 kcal

261. Basil Parmesan Tomatoes

Preparation time: 30 min
Cooking time: 20 min
Servings: 2

Ingredients

- ½ teaspoon dried oregano
- 4 roam tomatoes
- Spices: onion powder, garlic powder, sea salt and black pepper ½ cup parmesan cheese, shredded
- 12 small fresh basil leaves

Directions

1. Preheat the oven to 4250f and grease a baking sheet lightly.
2. Mix together dried oregano, onion powder, garlic powder, sea salt and black pepper in a small bowl.
3. Arrange the tomato slices on a baking sheet and sprinkle with the seasoning blend.
4. Top with parmesan cheese and basil leaves and transfer to the oven. Bake for about 20 min and remove from the oven to servings.

Nutrition Calories 49 Total fat 2.2g Saturated fat 1.4g Cholesterol 7mg Sodium 91mg Total carbohydrate 4.3g Dietary fiber 1.2g Total sugars 2.4g Protein 3.9g

262. Caprese Salad Bites

Preparation time: 10 min
Cooking time: 15 min
Servings: 2
Ingredients:

- For the bites
- 24 cherry tomatoes
- 12 mozzarella balls
- 12 fresh basil leaves
- For the balsamic glaze
- ½ cup balsamic vinegar
- 2 tablespoons extra-virgin olive oil
- 1 garlic clove, minced
- 1 teaspoon Italian seasoning

Directions:

1. To prepare the bites
2. Using 12 toothpicks or short skewers, gather each with 1 cherry tomato, 1 mozzarella ball, 1 basil leaf, and another tomato. Place on a Servings: platter or in a large glass storage container that can be sealed.
3. To make the glaze
4. In a small pan, bring the balsamic to a simmer. Simmer for 15 min, or until syrupy. Set aside to cool and thicken.
5. In a small bowl, whisk olive oil, garlic, Italian seasoning, and cooled vinegar.
6. Sprinkle the olive oil and balsamic glaze over the skewers. Servings: immediately or keep in the refrigerator for a tasty snack.
7. Ingredient tip: if you don't have mozzarella balls, you can use string cheese
8. cut each piece into sixths.

Nutrition: calories: 39; total fat: 3g; protein: 1g; carbohydrates: 3g; fiber: 0g; sugar: 0g; sodium: 11mg.

263. Easy Chicken Parmesan

Preparation time: 20 min
Cooking time: 35 min
Servings: 2
Ingredient

- 2 pounds of chicken cutlets (pounded thin)
- 1 jar spaghetti sauce (low sodium)
- 8 oz part-skim mozzarella cheese (shredded) ¾ cup parmesan cheese (grated)
- 2 eggs
- ¾ cup of flour
- 1 ¾ cups Italian Eggplant crumbs
- ½ cup vegetable oil
- Salt and pepper, to taste

Directions

1. Preheat oven to 375 f.
2. In a medium bowl, beat together eggs and 2 tablespoons of water.

3. Set up 3 shallow dishes: 1 with flour + salt + pepper ; 1 with Eggplant crumbs ; 1 with the eggs.
4. Dip chicken in flour. Shake off excess. Dip chicken in eggs. Drain excess.
5. Dip in Eggplant crumbs. Coat chicken thoroughly.
6. In a big skillet, heat vegetable oil over medium-high heat. Add Egg planted chicken and cook until golden, about 2 min per side.
7. In a 13" baking pan, pour half of spaghetti sauce. Add one layer of chicken.
8. Cover with half of mozzarella and parmesan. Layer with leftover chicken, sauce, and cheeses.
9. Bake for about 20 min, or until cheese is bubbling. Servings: warm.

Nutrition: Calories :177.8 Saturated fat 1.6 g Total fat : 12.7 g Polyunsaturated fat 4.1 g

264. Kale, Butternut Squash, And Sausage Pasta

Preparation time: 35 minutes
Cooking time: 25 minutes
Servings: 2
Ingredients:

- 6 links Italian sausage (spicy or sweet)
- 4 cups kale (roughly chopped)
- 1 cup butternut squash (diced)
- 3 cloves garlic (grated)
- ¼ cup parsley (minced)
- 1 pound whole wheat pasta (orecchiette) ½ cup parmigiano-reggiano (grated)
- ¼ cup olive oil (divided)
- Salt and pepper, to taste

Directions

1. Preheat oven to 400 f.
2. Line a baking sheet with foil. Coat butternut squash with olive oil, salt, and pepper. Arrange onto a single layer on the baking sheet. Roast until golden brown, about 25-30 min. Toss once, halfway through.
3. Prepare orecchiette pasta according to package directions using a timer. 1 cup of the liquid from the cooked pasta should be set aside. Set aside the cooked pasta.
4. Heat 1 tablespoon olive oil in a deep pan over medium-high heat. Remove the sausage from the casings and place it in the pan. Brown the meat first.
5. When the sausage is halfway cooked, add the grated garlic. Cook for another 7-9 minutes, or until the chicken is completely done. Deglaze the pan using the liquid from the cooked pasta.

6. 6. In a sausage pan, combine the kale, 2 tablespoons olive oil, salt, and pepper. Wait 2-3 minutes for the kale to turn brilliant green.
7. Chuck in a cooked pasta, roasted butternut squash, parsley, and Parmigiano-Reggiano.
8. Servings, topped with Parmigiano-Reggiano and parsley as preferred.

Nutrition: Calories : 177.8 Calories: 384kcal carbohydrates: 53.2g protein: 24g fat: 12.2g saturated fat: 3.9g

cholesterol: 54mg sodium: 820mg fiber: 7.9g

265. Lemon Juice Salmon With Quinoa

Preparation time: 10 min
Cooking time: 15 min
Servings: 2
Ingredients

- 2 8-ounce boneless salmon fillets
- 14 cherry tomatoes (halved)
- 10 white button mushrooms (thinly sliced)
- 8-10 asparagus spears
- 1 lemon
- 2 tablespoon dill (roughly chopped)
- 2 cloves garlic (minced)
- 2 teaspoons olive oil
- 2 teaspoons capers (optional)

Directions
1. Preheat the oven to 350 degrees Fahrenheit.
2. Layer minced garlic on a big sheet of parchment paper. Arrange the asparagus on top of the garlic. On top of the asparagus, place a salmon fillet.
3. Surround the fish with mushrooms and cherry tomatoes.
4. Drizzle with olive oil and lemon juice. Add salt, pepper, dill, and capers to taste.
5. Fold the paper up above the ingredients, being careful to keep the layers in place. Fold the edges numerous times to create a tight seal.
6. Preheat oven to 200°F and bake for 20-25 minutes, or until salmon is flaky.
7. Rice, pasta, or quinoa can be served as a side dish.

Nutrition: Calories: 302kcal carbohydrates: 2.2g protein: 30.4g fat: 18.9g saturated fat: 3g cholesterol: 88mg sodium: 634mg

266. Greek Chop-Chop Salad

Preparation time: 15 minutes
Cooking time: 20 minutes
Servings: 2
Ingredients

- 1 medium of English cucumber, chopped (2 cups) 1 cup halved cherry tomatoes

- 1 red bell pepper, seeded and diced
- ½ red onion, diced
- ½ cup pitted kalamata olives, roughly chopped 1 cup smashed feta cheese
- ½ cup balsamic dressing

Directions:
1. In a big bowl, chuck the cucumber, tomatoes, bell pepper, onion, olives, and cheese with the dressing, and serve.

Ingredient tip: looking for a protein boost? Add diced chicken breast or chickpeas.

Nutrition: calories: 173; total fat: 13g; protein: 4g; carbohydrates: 10g; fiber: 1g; sugar: 4g; sodium: 883mg.

CHAPTER 20:

Snacks

267. Pears with Coconut Butter

Preparation Time: 10 Minutes
Cooking Time: 15 Minutes
Servings: 2
Ingredients:

- 2 large pears, peeled and cut into wedges
- 2 tablespoons coconut oil
- 3 tablespoons coconut butter, melted
- 1 teaspoon cinnamon
- 1 cup water

Directions

1. Pour the water into the Instant Pot.
2. Place the pears inside the steamer basket and lower the basket into the pot.
3. Close the lid and cook for 2 minutes.
4. Quickly let the pressure and open the lid.
5. Transfer the bowl to a plate and discard the water from the pan.
6. Melt the coconut butter in the Instant Pot on Sauté and add the pears inside.
7. Sprinkle with cinnamon and cook until they become browned.
8. Serve drizzled with the melted coconut butter.
9. Enjoy!

Nutrition: Calories: 241 Fat: 17.1g Protein: 1.0g Carbs: 22.0g Net Carbs: 16.0g Fiber: 6.0g

268. Green Beans with Lemon

Preparation Time: 10 Minutes
Cooking Time: 10 Minutes
Servings: 2
Ingredients:

- 4 ounces (113 g) trimmed green beans
- 1 teaspoon fresh lemon juice
- 1/2 teaspoon extra-virgin olive oil
- Pinch of sea salt

Directions:

1. Steam the green beans in your instant pot for about 5 minutes for until crisp-tender.
2. Drizzle with fresh lemon juice, olive oil and sprinkle with sea salt.
3. Enjoy!

Nutrition Calories: 30 Fat: 1.2g Protein: 1.0g Carbs: 4.0g Net Carbs: 2.0g Fiber: 2.0g

269. Peppermint Cheesecake

Preparation Time: 10 Minutes
Cooking Time: 34 Minutes
Servings: 2

Ingredients:

- 1 cups organic cream cheese, softened, 1/4 cup sour cream 1 large organic eggs
- 1/2 cup swerve or erythritol sweetener
- 1/2 tablespoon coconut, Pinch of salt
- 1 teaspoons pure vanilla extract,
- 1/2 teaspoons pure peppermint extract

Chocolate Ganache:

- 3 ounces (85 g) unsweetened chocolate chips, melted 1/3 cup organic heavy cream, Pinch of salt

Crust:

- 1/2 cup almond flour
- 1 tablespoons swerve or Erythritol sweetener
- 1 tablespoons ghee or goat butter, melted

Directions

1. Combine ingredients for crust. Press down in a spring form pan; choose pan suitable for Instant Pot. Place in freezer for 10 minutes.
2. In a large bowl or blender, combine filling ingredients. Stir well.
3. Pour cheesecake filling in spring form pan. Cover with aluminum foil.
4. Add 1 cup of water, and trivet to Instant Pot. Place spring form pan on top.
5. Close, seal the lid. Press Manual button. Cook on High 35 minutes.
6. When done, naturally release pressure 15 minutes, then quick release remaining pressure. Remove the lid.
7. Remove pan from pot. Cool on counter 30 minutes, then refrigerate 4 hours.
8. In a bowl, combine chocolate ganache ingredients. Microwave 30 seconds. Stir. Repeat until smooth.
9. Transfer cheesecake to platter. Drizzle over ganache. Serve.

Nutrition: Calories: 454 Fat: 33.2g Protein: 8.8g Carbs: 30.1g Net Carbs: 29.2g Fiber: 0.9g

270. Strawberry Sorbet

Preparation Time: 10 Minutes
Cooking Time: 0 Minutes
Servings: 1
Ingredients:

- 3 cups Almond Breeze Almond Coconut Milk Blend Unsweetened 2 cup, unthawed Strawberries, frozen, unsweetened cup, sliced Avocado, frozen
- 1/8 piece of Fresh Lime with skin
- 6 tsp. Organic cane sugar,

Directions:

1. Place all ingredients into your Vitamin in the order listed. Set the blender on to Variable 1, then quickly increase the speed to Variable 10.
2. Set to high then blend for about 30-60 seconds. Set the tamper to press the ingredients into the blades.
3. Stop the machine as soon as the mounds form. Serve.

Nutrition: Calories: 47 Fat: 1.1 g Carbs: 9.1 g Protein: 0.6 g

271. Pumpkin Balls

Preparation Time: 15 Minutes
Cooking Time: 0 Minutes
Servings: 1
Ingredients:

- 1 cup almond butter
- 5 drops liquid stevia.
- 2 tbsp. coconut flour
- 2 tbsp. pumpkin puree
- 1 tsp. pumpkin pie spice

Directions:

1. Mix pumpkin puree in a large bowl and almond butter until well combined. Add liquid stevia, pumpkin pie spice, and coconut flour and mix well.
2. Make small balls from the mixture and place onto a baking tray in the freezer for 1 hour.
3. Serve and enjoy.

Nutrition: Calories: 95.1 Fat: 5.2 g Carbs: 10.8 g Protein: 2.3 g

272. Smooth Peanut Butter Cream

Preparation Time: 10 Minutes
Cooking Time: 0 Minutes
Servings: 2
Ingredients:

- 1/4 cup peanut butter
- 4 overripe Avocados, chopped.
- 1/3 cup cocoa powder
- 1/4 tsp. vanilla extract
- 1/8 tsp. salt

Directions:

1. In the blender, add all the listed ingredients and blend until smooth.
2. Serve immediately and enjoy.

Nutrition: Calories: 101 Fat: 5 g Carbs: 14 g Protein: 3 g

273. Vanilla Avocado Popsicles

Preparation Time: 20 Minutes
Cooking Time: 0 Minutes
Servings: 2
Ingredients:

- 2 avocadoes
- 1 tsp. vanilla
- 1 cup almond milk
- 1 tsp. liquid stevia
- 1/2 cup unsweetened cocoa powder

Directions:

1. In the blender, add all the listed ingredients and blend smoothly.
2. Pour blended mixture into the Popsicle molds and place in the freezer until set. Serve and enjoy.

Nutrition: Calories: 130 Fat: 12 g Carbs: 7 g Protein: 3 g

274. Cocoa Chocolate Chips Cookies

Preparation Time: 20 Minutes
Cooking Time: 11 Minutes
Servings: 2
Ingredients:

- 12 tablespoons butter, melted
- 1/2 cup light brown sugar
- 1 cup granulated sugar
- 1 large egg
- 1 large egg yolk
- teaspoon vanilla extract
- 1 3/4 cups all-purpose flour
- 1/4 cup unsweetened cocoa powder
- 1/2 teaspoon salt
- 1/2 teaspoon baking soda
- 1 1/2 cups semisweet chocolate chips

Directions:

1. Merge melted butter with brown sugar and granulated sugar until smooth. Cool slightly and beat in egg and egg yolk. Beat in vanilla.

2. Merge the flour, cocoa, salt, and baking soda. Slowly beat into the butter and sugar mixture until well blended. Fold in chocolate chips.
3. Chill the dough for at least 1 hour, or until firm.
4. Heat oven to 350°.
5. With a cookie scoop or tablespoon, scoop mounds of dough onto a silicone-lined or greased baking sheet, leaving about 1 1/2 to 2
1. inches between cookies. Bake for 12 to 15 minutes, until set.
6. Cool on baking sheet on a rack, then remove cookies to rack to cool completely.
7. Makes 2 to 3 dozen cookies.

Nutrition: Calories: 490.3 Fat: 21.7 g Carbs: 58.7 g Protein: 3.0 g

275. Amazing Rice Pudding

Preparation Time: 10 Minutes
Cooking Time: 45 Minutes
Servings: 2

Ingredients:
- 3 cups cooked white rice
- cups skim milk
- tbsp. light margarine
- 1/2 cup sugar
- 1/2 cup raisins
- Tsp. vanilla extract
- 1/2 tsp. nutmeg
- Tsp. cinnamon

Directions:
1. Cook the rice.
2. Let the rice cool for a few minutes. In a medium sized pot, merge the rice, milk, margarine, sugar, raisins, and vanilla.
3. Cook until the liquid is mostly absorbed. Stir frequently to keep the rice from sticking to the bottom of the pot.
4. Attach the cinnamon and nutmeg, stirring well.
5. Cook another 5 minutes.
6. Serve

Nutrition: Calories: 137.8 Fat: 1.0 g Carbs: 28.1 g Protein: 3.2 g

276. Mini Molten Lava Cakes

Preparation Time: 15 Minutes
Cooking Time: 20 Minutes
Servings: 2

Ingredients:
- Butter, unsalted, 170 grams
- Semisweet chocolate, 1 cup chips (6 oz. package) Egg, fresh, 3 larges
- Cocoa, dry powder, unsweetened, 3 tbsp.
- Granulated Sugar, 0.5 cup
- Flour, white, 0.33 cup

Directions:
1. Pre-heat oven to 350.
2. Melt chocolate and butter in bowl over boiling water.
3. Sift flour and cocoa in separate bowl.
4. Mix sugar and eggs in another bowl until it turns a lighter color.
5. Mix chocolate mixture to egg and sugar mixture. Blend in flour and cocoa.
6. Put into ramekins or muffin pan (grease muffin pan).
7. Bake until top starts to split a little.
8. Inside will be deliciously gooey!

Nutrition: Calories: 78.7 Fat: 5.7 g Carbs: 6.9 g Protein: 1.0 g

277. Raspberry Compote

Preparation Time: 10 Minutes
Cooking Time: 20 Minutes
Servings: 2

Ingredients:
- 2 cups raspberries, fresh or frozen (thawed)
- 3 tbsp. honey
- juice of 1/2 an orange (preferably a blood orange) Pinch salt
- 2 tbsp. cold water

Directions:
1. Set raspberries, honey, orange juice and salt in a small saucepan.
2. Place to a low simmer over medium heat and cook, stirring occasionally, until the berries are mostly broken down, 3 to 5 minutes.
3. Whisk together the cold water until smooth and stir into the cooking mixture.
4. Cook until mixture thickens.
5. Set to at least room temperature before serving. Store in fridge.

Nutrition: Calories: 33.5 Fat: 0.1 g Carbs: 8.5 g Protein: 0.3 g

278. Chocolate Popsicle

Preparation Time: 20 Minutes
Cooking Time: 10 Minutes
Servings: 2

Ingredients:
- 4 oz. unsweetened chocolate, chopped.
- 6 drops liquid stevia
- 1 1/2 cups heavy cream

Directions:
1. Add heavy cream into the microwave-safe bowl and microwave until it just begins the boiling. Add chocolate into the heavy cream and set aside for 5 minutes.

2. Add liquid stevia into the heavy cream mixture and stir until chocolate is melted. Pour mixture into the Popsicle molds and place in freezer for 4 hours or until set. Serve and enjoy.

Nutrition: Calories: 198 Fat: 21 g Carbs: 6 g Protein: 3 g

279. Raspberry Ice Cream

Preparation Time: 10 Minutes
Cooking Time: 0 Minutes
Servings: 2
Ingredients:

- 1 cup frozen raspberries
- 1/2 cup heavy cream
- 1/8 tsp. stevia powder

Directions:

1. Blend all the listed fixings in a blender until smooth. Serve immediately and enjoy.

Nutrition: Calories: 144 Fat: 11 g Carbs: 10 g Protein: 2 g

280. Wrapped Pears with Vanilla Bean Sauce

Preparation Time: 35 Minutes
Cooking Time: 2 hours 5 Minutes
Servings: 2
Ingredients:

- 3 cups water - 3/4 cup sugar
- 1/2 vanilla bean,
- 4 Bartlett or Bosc pear cored and peeled.
- 1/2 cup heavy cream
- 1/2 of a 17.3-ounce package Pepperidge Farm Puff Pastry Sheets (1 sheet), thawed
- 1cup fresh raspberries

Directions:

1. Warmth the water, sugar and vanilla bean in a 2-quart saucepan over low heat until the sugar is dissolved, stirring occasionally.
2. Attach the pears to the saucepan and cook for 10 minutes or until the pears are tender, turning occasionally. Detach the pears from the saucepan. Secure and refrigerate for 1 hour or until the pears are cold.
3. Stir the cream into the saucepan. Cook until the mixture is reduced to about 3/4 cup, stirring often. Detach the vanilla bean and scrape the seeds into the saucepan. Remove the saucepan from the heat. Heat the oven to 400F.
4. Set the pastry sheet on a lightly floured surface. Divide the pastry sheet crosswise into 8 (3/4-inch wide) strips. Garnish the strips with water and sprinkle with additional sugar.
5. Set the ends of 2 pastry strips together. Set the wrapped pears onto a baking sheet. Loosely cover the wrapped pears with aluminum foil.

6. Bake. Spoon the vanilla sauce onto 4 plates. Top each with 1 pear and garnish with the raspberries.

Nutrition: Calories: 571 Fat: 21 g Carbs: 96.1 g Protein: 4.5 g

281. Chocolate Almond Butter Brownie

Preparation Time: 10 Minutes
Cooking Time: 16 Minutes
Servings: 2
Ingredients:

- 1 cup Avocados, overripe
- 1/2 cup almond butter, melted.
- 1 scoop protein powder
- 2 tbsp unsweetened cocoa powder

Directions:

1. Warm air fryer to 325 F. Grease air fryer baking pan and set aside.
2. Blend all fixings in a blender until smooth.
3. Pour batter into the prepared pan and place in the air fryer basket and cook for 16 minutes. Serve and enjoy.

Nutrition: Calories: 82 Fat: 2 g Carbs: 11 g Protein: 7 g

282. Peanut Butter Fudge

Preparation Time: 10 Minutes
Cooking Time: 10 Minutes
Servings: 2
Ingredients:

- 1/4 cup almonds toasted and chopped.
- 12 oz. smooth peanut butter
- 15 drops liquid stevia
- 3 tbsp. coconut oil
- 4 tbsp. coconut cream
- Pinch of salt

Directions:

1. Line baking tray with parchment paper. Dissolve coconut oil in a pan over low heat. Add peanut butter, coconut cream, stevia, and salt in a saucepan. Stir well.
2. Pour fudge mixture into the prepared baking tray and sprinkle chopped almonds on top. Place the tray in the refrigerator for 1
1. hour or until set. Slice and serve.

Nutrition: Calories: 131 Fat: 12 g Carbs: 4 g

283. Avocado Chocolate Cake

Preparation Time: 15 Minutes
Cooking Time: 35 Minutes
Servings: 1
Ingredients:

- 2 very ripe medium Avocados
- 1/4 cups all-purpose flour

- 3/4 cup sugar
- 1/4 cup unsweetened cocoa powder
- 1/3 cup canola oil
- 1/3 cup water
- 1teaspoon baking soda
- 1teaspoon white vinegar
- 1/4 teaspoon salt
- 1/3 cup semisweet chocolate chips

Directions:
1. Warmth oven to 350
2. Press Avocados or blend with electric beater.
3. Blend in wet ingredients and brown sugar.
4. Sift dry ingredients together then add to wet.
5. Blend well. Sprinkle chocolate chips over batter.
6. Bake until toothpick inserted in the center comes out clean. Cool completely, about 45 minutes.

Nutrition: Calories: 142.5 Fat: 5.8 g Carbs: 24.9 g Protein: 1.7 g

284. Chia Pudding

Preparation Time: 20 Minutes
Cooking Time: 0 Minutes
Servings: 2

Ingredients:
- 4 tbsp. chia seeds
- 1 cup unsweetened coconut milk
- 1/2 cup raspberries

Directions:
1. Add raspberry and coconut milk into a blender and blend until smooth. Pour mixture into the glass jar. Add chia seeds in a jar and stir well.
2. Seal the jar with a lid and shake well and place in the refrigerator for 3 hours.
3. Serve chilled and enjoy.

Nutrition: Calories: 360 Fat: 33 g Carbs: 13 g Protein: 6 g

285. Lean Green Smoothie

Preparation Time: 10 Minutes
Cooking Time: 0 Minutes
Servings: 1

Ingredients:
- cup frozen tropical fruit mix (papaya, pineapple, guava) 1/2 cup chilled green tea, unsweetened
- 1/2 cup plain low-fat yogurt
- 1tbsp.. green powder
- 2tbsp flax seed (or chia seeds)
- 1tbsp vanilla protein powder (whey or soy)
- a pinch of fresh mint (optional)
- sweeten to taste with stevia or agave nectar (nutrition count includes 2 tsp. agave)

Directions:
1. Combine in a blender until smooth, about 30 seconds. Makes about 14 ounces.
2. It can substitute either cultured soy or more tea and ice, to make this vegan or less calories.

Nutrition: Calories: 403 Fat: 8.9 g Carbs: 48.9 g Protein: 34.8 g

286. Light Ice Cream Sandwich Cake

Preparation Time: 10 minutes
Cooking Time: 2 hours
Servings: 1

Ingredients:
- Low fat,. Hy-Vee brand could be a good one.
- Light, fat free hot fudge topping
- Light Cool Whip 12 oz. tub

Directions:
1. Set your whipped topping. Set a 9x13 pan with the ice cream sandwiches, you will have to cut them to cover the whole bottom of the pan.
2. Warmth the fudge and spread over the ice cream sandwiches.
3. Secure the whole thing with Cool Whip and refreeze.

Nutrition: Calories: 173.8 Fat: 3.8 g Carbs: 37.9 g Protein: 3.2 g

287. Carrot Gelatin Salad

Preparation Time: 15 minutes
Cooking Time: 5 hours
Servings: 2

Ingredients:
- (6 ounce) package lemon flavored gelatin mix
- (20 ounce) can crushed pineapple, drained with juice 4 large carrots, shredded.

Directions:
1. In a large bowl, set the lemon gelatin according to package directions using reserved pineapple juice in place of some of the water. Refrigerate until thickened, about 1 hour.
2. When the gelatin has thickened, set in pineapple and shredded carrot. Cover and refrigerate until set, at least 4 hours.

Nutrition: Calories: 54.8 Fat: 0.1 g Carbs: 12.8 g Protein: 0.6 g

288. Vegan Chocolate Almond Milk Ice Cream Fudgsicle Style

Preparation Time: 10 minutes
Cooking Time: 0 minutes
Servings: 2

Ingredients:
- 2 cups unsweetened almond milk
- 1/2 cup Cocoa, dry powder, unsweetened
- 1/2tsp Vanilla Extract

- 300 grams avocados - 1 cup coconut sugar

Directions:

1. Set everything into a blender and puree.
2. Freeze it in a plastic bag, squishing it together as it freezes..

Nutrition: Calories: 183.5 Fat: 8.0 g Carbs: 31.0 g Protein: 2.2 g

289. Avocado Pudding

Preparation Time: 20 Minutes
Cooking Time: 0 Minutes
Servings: 2

Ingredients:

- 2 ripe avocados pitted and cut into pieces.
- 1 tbsp. fresh lime juice
- 14 oz. coconut milk
- 2 tsp. liquid stevia
- 2 tsp. vanilla

Directions:

1. Inside the blender, Add all ingredients and blend until smooth.
2. Serve immediately and enjoy.

Nutrition: Calories: 317 Fat: 30 g Carbs: 9 g Protein: 3 g

290. Strawberry Granita

Preparation Time: 10 minutes
Cooking Time: 3 hours
Servings: 2

Ingredients:

- 3 cups sliced fresh strawberries.
- 1/2 cup sugar
- 1/2 cup warm water
- 2 TBS fresh lemon juice = 1 oz.

Directions:

1. In a blender dissolve the sugar with the water. Once dissolved add in the strawberries and the lemon juice.
2. Puree until smooth. Pour into an 8 X 8 dish. Freeze for 3 hours.
3. Stir completely.
4. Freeze for another 5 hours or overnight. Let sit on counter around 10 minutes. Grate with the tines of a fork and serve in 1 cup dishes.

Nutrition: Calories: 68.0 Fat: 0.2 g Carbs: 17.2 g Protein: 0.4 g

291. Peanut Butter Coconut Popsicle

Preparation Time: 15 Minutes
Cooking Time: 0 Minutes
Servings: 2

Ingredients:

- 1/2 cup peanut butter
- 1 tsp. liquid stevia
- 2 cans unsweetened coconut milk

Directions:

1. In the blender, add all the listed ingredients and blend until smooth. Pour mixture into the Popsicle molds and place in the freezer for 4 hours or until set. Serve!

Nutrition: Calories: 155 Fat: 15 g Carbs: 4 g Protein: 3 g

292. Brownie Bites

Preparation Time: 20 minutes
Cooking Time: 0 minutes
Servings: 1

Ingredients:

- 1/4 cup unsweetened chocolate chips
- 1/4 cup unsweetened cocoa powder
- 1 cup pecans, chopped.
- 1/2 cup almond butter
- 1/2 tsp. vanilla
- 1/4 cup monk fruit sweetener
- 1/8 tsp. pink salt

Directions:

1. Add pecans, sweetener, vanilla, almond butter, cocoa powder, and salt into the food processor and process until well combined.
2. Transfer brownie mixture into the large bowl.
3. Add chocolate chips and fold well. Make small round shape balls from brownie mixture and place onto a baking tray. Place in the freezer for 20 minutes. Serve and enjoy.

Nutrition: Calories: 108 Fat: 9 g Carbs: 4 g Protein: 2 g

293. Peanut Butter Brownie Ice Cream Sandwiches

Preparation Time: 20 Minutes
Cooking Time: 20 Minutes
Servings: 1
Ingredients:
Brownies

- 1/2 cup Coconut oil or butter
- 1/2 cup Crazy Richard's Creamy Peanut Butter
- 2 cups semi-sweet chocolate chips
- 4 eggs
- 2/3 cup granulated sugar
- 1/2 cup unsweetened cocoa powder
- 1/2tsp pure vanilla extract
- 1/2 tsp. sea salt

Filling:

- 3 cups ice cream
- 1/4 to 1/2 cup creamy peanut butter
- Optional drizzle:
- 1/2 cup chocolate chips
- TBS Peanut butter

Directions:

1. Warmth oven to 350 degrees F

2. Set and grease two 8x8" square baking pans 3. In a mixing bowl, dissolve together butter, peanut butter and chocolate chips. Stir until smooth.

3. Attach the eggs and stir until smooth.

4. Attach sugar, sea salt, vanilla, and cocoa powder and mix until the batter is smooth.

5. Set mixture evenly between the two prepared 8x8" baking pans.

6. Bake until the edges and top of the brownie looks set and feels firm to the touch.

7. Detach the brownies from the oven and let them cool in the baking pans.

8. While the brownies are cooling, detach 3 cups of ice cream from the freezer and let it sit at room temperature to soften.

9. Once the brownies are completely cool, detach ONE batch of brownies from its baking pan.

10. Set the pan of brownies with peanut butter in the freezer to harden for at least 15 minutes.

11. Detach the brownies from the freezer and spread softened ice cream over the peanut butter layer.

12. Set the baking pan in the freezer to harden for at least 5 hours or overnight.

13. Detach the brownie ice cream sandwiches from the freezer and place on a cutting board.

14. Divide the sandwiches into 9 pieces, and then cut each of those 9 pieces in half, with a large, sharp knife.

15. If desired, set topping by melting chocolate chips and peanut butter together, then drizzle as desired on the cut ice cream sandwiches.

Nutrition: Calories: 257 Fat: 18.5 g Carbs: 21.4 g Protein: 6.8 g

294. **Vegan Porridge**

Preparation time: 5 minutes
Cooking time: 15 minutes
Servings: 1
Ingredients:

- 2 tbsp. coconut flour
- 3 tbsp. flaxseed meal
- 2 tbsp. Protein: powder
- 1½ cup unsweetened almond milk
- Powdered erythritol to taste

Directions:

1. Mix the golden flaxseed, coconut flour, and protein powder in a bowl.

2. Add to a saucepan, along with almond milk, and cook over medium heat. When the mixture starts to thicken, stir in a preferred portion of sweetener. Serve with your favorite toppings.

Nutrition: Calories: 112, Fat: 5.7, Carbs: 11 g, Protein: 3.7 g.

295. **Cheesy Tomato Omelet**

Preparation time: 2 minutes
Cooking time: 15 minutes
Servings: 1
Ingredients:

- ½ tsp. butter - 1 large egg
- 1 tbsp. milk or water
- Salt Black pepper
- Garlic powder 1 slice cheddar cheese
- 1 tbsp. chopped tomato

Directions:

1. In a 6-inches nonstick skillet, melt butter over medium heat; turn the skillet to coat evenly.

2. In a small bowl, whisk egg and milk or water; pour into skillet.

1. Sprinkle garlic powder, pepper, and salt over the top of the egg.

2. When edges of egg mixture begin to cook, lift edges with a spatula and tip the skillet so uncooked egg flows underneath to cook.

3. Repeat step 3 until the top is almost dry. Place cheese slice on top, then the tomatoes over half of the omelet. When the cheese begins to melt, fold in half and serve.

Nutrition: Calories: 272.4, Fat: 19.1 g, Carbs: 6.4 g, Protein: 18.4 g.

296. **Colorful Scrambled Eggs**

Preparation time: 10 minutes
Cooking time: 10 minutes
Servings: 2
Ingredients:

- 4 eggs
- ⅛ tsp. salt
- ⅛ tsp. pepper
- 2 tbsp. olive oil
- 2 tbsp. chopped red bell pepper
- 1 chopped garlic clove
- 1½ tsp. chopped chives

Directions:

1. Set aside a bowl containing eggs, pepper, and salt.

2. Heat the oil in a large skillet and add the red bell pepper and garlic. Cook for 5 minutes over medium heat, stirring regularly.

3. Cook and whisk the egg mixture and chives in a pan over low heat until the eggs are done.

Nutrition: Calories: 199, Fat: 15.21 g, Carbs: 1.96 g, Protein: 13.01 g.

297. Chunky Mediterranean Tomato Soup

Preparation time: 10 minutes
Cooking time: 15 minutes
Servings: 2
Ingredients:

- 400 g grilled vegetable mix, frozen
- 2 tbsp. garlic, chopped
- Fresh basil leaves
- 400 g can chopped tomato
- 1 reduced-salt vegetable stock cube
- 50 g ricotta

Directions:

Heat the pan to medium, add the vegetable mixture and garlic, and simmer until the veggies begin to soften, about 5 minutes.

Blend the basil, tomatoes, stock cube, and two cans of water until smooth.

Nutrition: Calories: 212, Fat: 7 g, Carbs: 24 g, Protein: 11 g.

298. Grilled Cheese and Tomato Sandwich

Preparation time: 5 minutes
Cooking time: 15 minutes
Servings: 2
Ingredients:

- 8 slices of soft Eggplant
- 4 tbsp. Softened butter
- 4 slices cheddar cheese
- 4 slices sliced tomato

Directions:

1. 12 tablespoons butter on one side of each eggplant slice
2. Place 4 slices of Eggplant side by side in a big skillet or griddle; the butter side should face down. Each piece should be topped with a tomato slice and a slice of cheese; the unbuttered side should be topped with another Eggplant slice.
3. Cook until one side is lightly browned over low heat, then turn and cook until the second side is lightly browned and the cheese is melted. Serve immediately.

Nutrition: Calories: 475.9, Fat: 26.8 g, Carbs: 41 g, Protein: 20.9 g.

299. Fried Deli Turkey Mushroom Sandwich

Preparation time: 5 minutes
Cooking time: 15 minutes
Servings: 1
Ingredients:

- 1 slice of deli turkey
- 1 grilled Portobello mushroom
- Ketchup
- Mustard

Directions:

1. Cut deli turkey from the center of the slice to the outside edge so that it will lay flat in the skillet.
2. Place a frypan on average heat; place deli turkey in the pan and cook until it begins to brown; turn over and cook another side until lightly browned.
3. Place fried deli turkey into grilled mushroom; top up with ketchup, and mustard if desired.

Nutrition: Calories: 259, Fat: 5.2 g, Carbs: 11 g, Protein: 8.2 g.

300. Ham and Swiss Sandwich

Preparation time: 30 minutes
Cooking time: 0 minute
Servings: 2
Ingredients:

- 1/2 cup mayonnaise
- 1 tsp. parsley flakes
- ½ tsp. prepared mustard
- ¼ tsp. onion powder
- 5 oz. ground smoked ham
- ½ cup shredded Swiss cheese
- 2 Portobello mushrooms
- 2 tomato slices

Directions:

1. Combine mayonnaise, parsley, mustard, and onion powder in a medium mixing basin and toss until thoroughly combined.
2. Mix in the ham and cheese until everything is well mixed. Chill before serving.
3. Fill Portobello mushrooms with ham and cheese mixture; top with a tomato slice, if preferred.

Nutrition: Calories: 390, Fat: 11 g, Carbs: 36 g, Protein: 24 g.

301. Egg Salad Sandwich

Preparation time: 1 hour
Cooking time: 0 minute
Servings: 2
Ingredients:

- ½ cup mayonnaise
- 2 tbsp. pickle relish
- 1 tsp. prepared mustard
- ¼ tsp. salt
- ¼ tsp. black pepper
- 4 chopped hard-cooked eggs
- 1 sliced
- 2 Portobello mushrooms

Directions:

1. Combine mayonnaise, relish, mustard, salt, and pepper in a medium mixing bowl.
2. Mix in the diced eggs gradually. Chill before serving.
3. Fill Portobello mushrooms with cold egg salad and tomato slices, if preferred.

Nutrition: Calories: 259, Fat: 9.5 g, Carbs: 10 g, Protein: 12.8 g.

302. Easy Baked Tomatoes

Preparation time: 10 minutes
Cooking time: 50 minutes
Servings: 2
Ingredients:

- ¼ cup pine nuts
- Greek seasoning as needed
- ¼ cup low-fat parmesan
- Olive oil spray as needed
- 5-6 whole tomatoes

Directions:

1. Preheat your oven to 350 °F.
2. Slice tomatoes in half lengthwise and transfer to a pan with the cut side up.
3. Spray tops of tomato with olive oil spray.
4. Season with pine nuts, cheese, and Greek seasoning.
5. Bake for 50 minutes and serve, enjoy!

Nutrition: Calories: 74, Total Fat: 5 g, Saturated Fat: 1 g, Protein: 3 g, Carbs: 6 g, Fiber: 1 g.

303. Black Bean Chipotle Hummus

Preparation time: 10 min
Cooking time: 0 min
Servings: 2
Ingredients:

- 1 (15 ounces) can, black beans, drained and rinsed
- 1 lime, juiced
- 1 chipotle pepper in adobo sauce
- 1 tsp. adobo sauce
- 1 tsp. garlic, minced
- 2 tsp. ground cumin
- 2 tbsp. extra-virgin olive oil
- ¼ cup fresh cilantro, chopped

Directions:

1. Take your food processor and add black beans, lime juice, chipotle pepper, adobo sauce, garlic, cumin, olive oil, cilantro, and blend on high for 2-3 minutes until smooth.

Nutrition: Calories: 143, Fat: 2 g, Carbs: 18 g, Protein: 5 g, Sodium: 125 mg.

304. Finely Crispy Wok Veggies

Preparation time: 10 minutes
Cooking time: 20 minutes
Servings: 2
Ingredients:

- 1 medium red bell pepper, cut into strips
- 1 medium green bell pepper, cut into strips
- ½ cup button mushrooms, canned
- 1 cup cauliflower, chopped into bite-sized pieces - 1 medium carrot, peeled and cut into strips
- 1 tsp. oyster sauce
- 1 tbsp. olive oil - 1 tsp. salt

Directions:

1. Wash bell peppers and cut them in half.
2. Remove seeds and cut them into strips.
3. Take a large wok pan and heat up olive oil over medium heat, add carrots and cauliflower and cook for 8-10 minutes.
4. Add red and green pepper strips, button mushrooms, oyster sauce, cook for 5-7 minutes.

Nutrition: Calories: 234, Fat: 1 g, Carbs: 21 g, Protein: 12 g, Sodium: 322 mg.

305. Chickpea and Mango Wraps

Preparation time: 15 minutes
Cook time: 0 minutes
Servings: Makes 3 wraps
Ingredients:

- 3 tablespoons tahini
- 1 tablespoon curry powder
- ¼ teaspoon sea salt (optional)
- Zest and juice of 1 lime
- 3 to 4 tablespoons water
- 1½ cups cooked chickpeas
- 1 cup diced mango
- ½ cup fresh cilantro, chopped
- 1 red bell pepper, deseeded and diced
- 3 large whole-wheat wraps
- 1½ cups shredded lettuce

Directions:

1. In a large bowl, stir together the tahini, curry powder, lime zest, lime juice and sea salt (if desired) until smooth and creamy. Whisk in 3 to 4 tablespoons water to help thin the mixture.
2. Add the cooked chickpeas, mango, cilantro and bell pepper to the bowl. Toss until well coated.
3. On a clean work surface, lay the wraps. Divide the chickpea and mango mixture among the wraps. Spread the shredded lettuce on top and roll up tightly. Serve immediately.

Nutrition: Calories: 436 fat: 17.9g carbs: 8.9g protein: 15.2g fiber: 12.1g

306. Tofu and Pineapple in Lettuce

Preparation time: 2 hours 20 minutes
Cooking time: 15 minutes
Servings: 2

Ingredients:

- ¼ cup low-sodium soy sauce
- 1 garlic clove, minced
- 2 tablespoons sesame oil (optional)
- 1 tablespoons coconut sugar (optional)
- 1 (14-ounce / 397-g) package extra firm tofu, drained, cut into ½-inch cubes 1 small white onion, diced
- ½ pineapple, peeled, cored, cut into cubes
- Salt and ground black pepper, to taste (optional) 4 large lettuce leaves
- 1 tablespoon roasted sesame seeds

Directions

1. Combine the soy sauce, garlic, sesame oil (if desired), and coconut sugar in a bowl. Stir to mix well.
2. Add the tofu cubes to the bowl of soy sauce mixture, then press to coat well. Wrap the bowl in plastic and refrigerate to marinate for at least 2 hours.
3. Pour the marinated tofu and marinade in a skillet and heat over medium heat. Add the onion and pineapple cubes to the skillet and stir to mix well.
4. Sprinkle with salt (if desired) and pepper and sauté for 15 minutes or until the onions are lightly browned and the pineapple cubes are tender.
5. Divide the lettuce leaves among 4 plates, then top the leaves with the tofu and pineapple mixture. Sprinkle with sesame seeds and serve immediately.

Nutrition: Calories: 259 fat: 15.4g carbs: 20.5g protein: 12.1g fiber: 3.2g

307. Quinoa and Black Bean Lettuce Wraps

Preparation time: 30 minutes
Cooking time: 15 minutes
Servings: 2

Ingredients:

- 2 tablespoons avocado oil (optional)
- ¼ cup deseeded and chopped bell pepper
- ½ onion, chopped
- 2 tablespoons minced garlic
- 1 teaspoon salt (optional)
- 1 teaspoon pepper (optional)
- ½ cup cooked quinoa
- 1 cup cooked black beans

- ½ cup almond flour
- ½ teaspoon paprika
- ½ teaspoon red pepper flakes
- 6 large lettuce leaves

Directions:

1. Heat 1 tablespoon of the avocado oil (if desired) in a skillet over medium-high heat.
2. Add the bell peppers, onions, garlic, salt (if desired), and pepper.
1. Sauté for 5 minutes or until the bell peppers are tender.
2. Turn off the heat and allow to cool for 10 minutes, then pour the vegetables in a food processor. Add the quinoa, beans, flour.
3. Sprinkle with paprika and red pepper flakes. Pulse until thick and well combined.
4. Line a baking pan with parchment paper, then shape the mixture into 6 patties with your hands and place on the baking pan.
5. Put the pan in the freezer for 5 minutes to make the patties firm.
6. Heat the remaining avocado oil (if desired) in the skillet over high heat.
7. Add the patties and cook for 6 minutes or until well browned on both sides. Flip the patties halfway through.
8. Arrange the patties in the lettuce leaves and serve immediately.

Nutrition: Calories: 200 fat: 10.6g carbs: 40.5g protein: 9.5g fiber: 8.2g

308. Rice and Bean Lettuce Burgers

Preparation time: 1 hour 25 minutes
Cooking time: 45 minutes
Servings: 2

Ingredients:

- 1 cup uncooked medium-grain brown rice
- 2 cups water - ½ cup grated carrots
- ¾ cup chopped red onion
- ½ cup raw sunflower seeds
- ¾ cup cooked pinto beans
- 5 cloves garlic, peeled - 2 tablespoons oat flour
- 2 teaspoons arrowroot powder
- 2 tablespoons nutritional yeast
- ¼ cup chopped fresh basil
- 4 Teaspoons ground cumin
- 4 Teaspoons low-sodium soy sauce
- 2 tablespoons low -sodium tomato paste
- Salt and ground black pepper, to taste (optional) 1 to 2 tablespoons water
- 8 large lettuce leaves, for serving

Directions

1. Pour the rice and water in a pot. Bring to a boil over medium heat.

1. Reduce the heat to low and simmer for 15 more minutes or until the rice is tender. Transfer the rice in a large bowl. Allow the rice to cool and fluff with a fork.
2. Put the carrots, onions, sunflower seeds, beans, and garlic in a food processor and pulse until well combined and chunky. Pour the mixture over the rice.
3. Add the remaining ingredients, except for the lettuce, to the bowl of rice, then toss to combine well. Shape the mixture into 8 patties and arrange them on a parchment-lined baking pan. Refrigerate for an hour until firm.
4. Preheat the oven to 350°F (180°C).
5. Place the baking pan in the oven and bake for 30 minutes or until well browned on both sides. Flip the patties halfway through.
6. Unfold the lettuce leaves on 8 plates, then top each leaf with a patty.
7. Wrap and serve.

Nutrition: Calories: 197 fat: 5.9g carbs: 30.5g protein: 7.4g fiber: 4.7g

309. Bulgur and Pinto Bean Lettuce Wraps

Preparation time: 30 minutes

Cooking time: 10 minutes

Servings: 2

Ingredients:

- 1½ cups plus 2 tablespoons water, divided
- Salt and ground black pepper, to taste (optional) ⅔ cup bulgur, rinsed
- ¾ cup walnuts
- ½ cup fresh basil leaves
- 2 garlic cloves, minced
- 1 large beet (about 9 ounces / 255 g), peeled and shredded 1 (15-ounce / 425-g) can pinto beans, rinsed
- 1 (4-ounce / 113-g) jar carrot
- 1 tablespoon Dijon mustard
- 1½ cups panko Eggplant crumbs
- 6 tablespoons avocado oil (optional)
- 8 large lettuce leaves

Directions

1. Pour 1½ cups of water in a pot and sprinkle with salt (if desired) to taste. Bring to a boil, then turn off the heat. Pour the bulgur in the boiling water. Cover the lid and let sit for 15 minutes or until the bulgur is soft. Drain the bulgur and spread it on a baking pan to cool.
2. Meanwhile, combine the walnuts, basil, garlic, and beet in a food processor.

3. Pulse to mix well. Then add the beans, carrot, 2 tablespoons of water, Dijon mustard, salt (if desired) and pepper.
1. Pulse to combine well.
2. Pour the mixture in a large bowl and fold in the cooked bulgur and panko. Shape the mixture into 8 patties.
3. Heat the avocado oil (if desired) in the skillet over medium-high heat.
4. Arrange the patties in a skillet and cook for 8 minutes or until well browned on both sides. Flip the patties halfway through. Work in batches to avoid overcrowding.
5. Unfold the lettuce leaves on 8 plates, then top the leaves with the patties and wrap to serve.

Nutrition: Calories: 317 fat: 17.2g carbs: 33.9g protein: 8.9g fiber: 6.5g

CHAPTER 21:

Dinner

310. Tuna Salad

Preparation time: 25 min
Cooking time 20 min
Servings: 2
Ingredients:

- 2 cans of tuna
- 1/8 teaspoon mustard
- 1 tablespoon parsley
- Salt and pepper to taste
- 1 minced garlic clove
- 1 small onion
- ½ celery stick
- 1 tablespoon lemon juice

Directions

1. Pour tuna in sieve and drain
2. Use a spoon to mash it
3. Pour in bowl and put all ingredients except mayonnaise and Dijon Mix very well
4. Mayonnaise and Dijon mix again and Servings:

Nutrition Calories: 404 kale; protein 49g; carbohydrate: 12.5g; fat 17.5;

311. Beef Stew

Preparation time:8 hours min
Cooking time: 1 hour
Serving: 2
Ingredients:

- 3 ounces of red celeriac
- 1 carrot
- 1 small red onion, cut into wedges
- ¼ pound of beef
- 3 ounces of condensed cream of mushroom soup
- 1 cup beef broth
- 1/3 teaspoon of thyme
- 1/3 teaspoon of curry
- 2 ounces of package frozen cut green beans
- 1 stock cube
- ¼ teaspoon salt

Directions

1. Quarter the celeriac
2. Cut onion into cubes
3. Dice carrots

4. In a soup pot, pour in celeriac's, carrots, onion, beef, mushroom soup, broth, thyme, and curry.
5. Stir and add stock cube and salt
6. Cook on medium heat for 7 hours
7. Add green beans
8. Cook for 15 min
9. Service hot

Nutrition: Calories: 660kcal carbohydrates: 50g protein: 80g fat: 15g saturated fat: 7g cholesterol: 191mg sodium: 1639mg potassium: 1075mg fiber: 2g sugar: 6g vitamin a: 348iu vitamin c: 8mg calcium: 273mg iron: 3mg

312. Meatloaf

Preparation time: 1 ½ hours
Cooking time: 1 hour
Servings: 2
Ingredients:

- 2 pounds lean ground beef
- ¾ cup dry whole-wheat Eggplant crumbs
- 2 stalks celery
- 1 onion
- 1 green bell pepper
- 1 tablespoon canola oil
- 4 tablespoons ketchup
- 3 tablespoons Worcestershire sauce
- 1 tablespoon whole-grain mustard
- 1 tablespoon paprika
- 1 teaspoon crushed garlic
- Salt to taste
- Pepper to taste
- 1 egg

Directions

1. Chop onions
2. Chop celery
3. Chop pepper
4. Beat egg lightly
5. Preheat oven to 375 degrees f
6. Spray baking tray with low fat baking spray Put in onions, pepper, celery in food processor and make smooth Put oil in skillet on medium heat
7. Pour in vegetables into pt. and stir fry until they are soft Take out and let cool
8. Add Worcestershire, mustard, garlic, paprika, salt, pepper and half of the ketchup.

9. Mix Eggplant an egg crumbs
10. Pour in mix
11. Put in ground beef
12. With your hands mix the mixture
13. Spread out the mixture on baking pan
14. Pour left over ketchup
15. Bake for 45 min at 165 degrees f

Nutrition: Calories: 660kcal carbohydrates: 50g protein: 80g fat: 15g saturated fat: 7g cholesterol: 191mg

sodium: 1639mg potassium: 1075mg fiber: 2g sugar: 6g vitamin a: 348iu vitamin c: 8mg calcium: 273mg iron: 3mg

313. Tuna Burger

Preparation time: 30 min
Cooking time: 30 min
Servings: 2
Ingredients:

- 6 ounces light tuna
- 2 slices tomato
- ¼ of cup whole wheat Eggplant crumbs 1/3 cup of low-fat mayonnaise
- 3 tablespoons of roasted red peppers
- ½ stalk of chopped celery
- 3 tablespoons finely chopped onion
- 2 teaspoons extra-virgin olive oil
- 2 whole-wheat hamburger buns or English muffins, toasted 2 lettuce leaves
- ½ stock cube

Directions

1. In a large bowl, put in drained tuna
2. Pour half of mayonnaise, pepper, and celery Sprinkle stock cube and mix well
3. The form is to hold together
4. Form two patties
5. Put in the other half of the mayonnaise and peppers Heat oil
6. Place molded patties and fry for two min on each side Spread the mayonnaise and peppers on the top side of each bun.
7. Arrange the patty, onions, lettuce and tomato in the bun

Nutrition: Calories: 338kcal carbohydrates: 29.4g protein: 24.8g fat: 15.6g saturated fat: 1.5g polyunsaturated fat: 14.1g trans-fat: 0g cholesterol: 42mg sodium: 933mg fiber: 4.2g sugar: 3.3g iron: 3mg

314. Low Fat Blackberry Yoghurt

Preparation time: 15 min
Cooking time: 30 min
Servings: 2
Ingredients:

- 2 cups low fat yogurt
- 1 cup blackberries

Directions

1. Dice blackberries and freeze
2. Pour in yoghurt in food processor
3. Put in frozen blackberries process for 5-15 seconds Freeze
4. Servings: cold

Nutrition: Calories: 231kcal carbohydrates: 32.5g protein: 17.9g fat: 3.5g saturated fat: 0.6g cholesterol: 2mg sodium: 74mg fiber: 7.9g

315. Strawberry smoothie

Preparation time: 15 min
Cooking time: 15 min
Servings: 2
Ingredients:

- 1 1/3 cup strawberries
- 1 cup crushed ice
- 1/2 cup of non-fat and plain yogurt
- 1 teaspoon lemon juice
- 1 tablespoon stevia sugar

Directions

1. Slice strawberries and freeze
2. Take out and set aside
3. Place yogurt in blender
4. Put in strawberries

Nutrition: Calories: 231kcal carbohydrates: 32.5g protein: 17.9g fat: 3.5g saturated fat: 0.6g cholesterol: 2mg

sodium: 74mg fiber: 7.9g

316. Autumn Coleslaw

Preparation time: 5 min
Cooking time:15 min
Servings: 2
Ingredients

- Flat leaf parsley, chopped, 3 tbs
- Mixed nuts, 2 ounces (chop them if they are large) Black pepper
- Salt
- Wholegrain mustard, ½ tsp
- Extra light mayonnaise, 4 tbs
- Fat-free Greek yogurt, 4 tbs
- Lemon, 1 juiced
- Small apples, cored and sliced thin, 2
- A red onion that has been chopped
- Celery, 2 stalks (that have been chopped)
- Red cabbage, shredded, 4 ounces White cabbage, shredded, 4 ounces

Directions:

1. Put the onion, celery, red cabbage, and white cabbage into a large bowl.
2. Add the apples to a bowl and toss them with the lemon juice. Toss to coat well. Add to the cabbage mixture. Toss to combine.

3. Add the mustard, mayonnaise, yogurt, pepper, and salt to a different bowl and mix well to combine everything.
4. Pour dressing over the cabbage and apples. Add parsley and nuts. Toss well to combine all ingredients together.
5. Cover and refrigerate until you are ready to use them. You can even store them for up to four days.

Nutrition: Calories: 112 Fat: 5.5 g Protein: 4.9 g Carb: 10.7 g

317. Roasted Salmon

Preparation time: 10 min
Cooking time:14 min
Servings: 2

Ingredients

- Lemon, 1 - Black pepper - Salt
- Low-fat cooking time spray
- Thin asparagus spears, 3 or 4
- Cherry tomatoes, 6 cut in half
- Red onion, half of one that has been sliced Small salmon fillet
- Spinach leaves, one handful Dill for garnish

Directions:

1. Preheat your oven to 400 degrees.
2. On a cookie sheet, place a large piece of parchment paper or aluminum foil.
3. Place down the handful of spinach leaves. On top of the spinach, place the salmon skin side up. On top of the salmon, place the asparagus, tomatoes, and onion.
4. Give everything a good spray with the cooking time spray. Sprinkle with pepper and salt.
5. Slice the lemon in half and slice one of the halves into slices. Squeeze one half of the lemon over the salmon. Place the slices of lemon on top of the salmon.
6. Slide this into the oven for 10 to 14 min. It will depend on how thick your salmon is as to the cooking time . If you like your vegetables softer, cook them for ten min before adding the salmon. Then cook for another ten to 14 min.
7. When cooked through, place on a plate and garnish with fresh dill.

Nutrition: Calories: 310 Fat: 15.9 g Protein: 30.3 g Carb: 11.3 g

318. Steak and Cauliflower skewers

Preparation time: 15 min
Cooking time:30 min
Servings: 2

Ingredients

Dressing:
- Water, 4 tbs
- Sugar-free syrup or maple syrup, 1 tbs
- Lemon juice, 2 tbs
- Tahini, 4 tbs
- Skewers:
- Black pepper
- Salt
- Low-fat cooking time spray
- Cherry tomatoes, 4
- A red onion that has been peeled and cut into wedges Mushrooms
- Multi-colored peppers, 3
- Steak, 1.5 pounds that have been cut into cubes New celeriac, 8 ounces

Directions:

1. Pour some water into a pot and add salt. Place on a burner and bring to a boil.
2. Wash the celeriac. Cut each one into quarters or halves depending on their size. Put into the pot of boiling water and cook for eight min until tender.
3. Remove from heat and drain.
4. Put the tomatoes, onions, mushrooms, peppers, and steak into a bowl and spray generously with cooking time spray. Sprinkle with pepper and salt. Mix well to combine.
5. Take the ingredients and alternate them onto four different skewers.
6. Cook them either on an inside or outside grill for ten min. Turn them frequently to ensure even cooking time.
7. While skewers are cooking time, make the dressing. Place all ingredients for the dressing into a bowl and whisk until incorporated and smooth.
8. When skewers are cooked through, take off grill and place onto Servings: plates. Drizzle with some of the dressing. Place remaining dressing into a small bowl for dipping.

Nutrition: Calories: 425 Fat: 16.8 g Protein: 44.5 g Carb: 24.7 g

319. Easy Pork Stir-Fry

Preparation time: 25 min
Cooking time:10 min
Servings: 2

Ingredients

- Straight to wok ribbon rice noodles, 5 ounces Garlic paste, 1 tsp
- Ginger paste, 1 tsp
- Low-fat cooking time spray
- Frozen stir-fry vegetable medley, 7 ounces
- Hoisin sauce, 2 tbs
- Pork, 8 ounces diced

Directions:

1. Put the pork in a bowl and pour in the hoisin sauce. Mix well to coat and let marinate for 20 min.
2. Take the peppers out of the vegetable medley and slice them thinly. Chop any of the remaining vegetables into smaller pieces if needed. Spray a wok with nonstick spray generously. Put on the burner and heat up.
3. Add garlic and ginger paste and half of the peppers. Cook for one minute.
4. Place the pork in with the marinade and let it cook for four min. Take out of the wok with a slotted spoon and place it to the side.
5. Respray the wok if needed and add in the vegetables and cook for an additional two min.
6. Add the noodles to the wok along with one to two tablespoons of water.
7. Cover and let cook for another two min until it reaches the desired doneness.
8. Place the pork back into the wok and toss well to combine. Divide evenly into bowls and top with preserving peppers if you want.

Nutrition: Calories: 315 Fat: 4.3 g Protein: 30.5 g Carb: 36.1 g

320. Sugar-Free Strawberry Limeade

Preparation time: 0 min
Cooking time:3 min
Servings: 1
Ingredients

- Ice cubes, 6 - Strawberry extract, ½ tsp
- Cold water, 1 ½ cups
- Juice of half a lime

Directions:

1. Mix together the strawberry extract, lime juice, and water. Add the ice cubes to a cup and pour in the strawberry mixture. If you want, you can sweeten with a calorie-free sweetener.

Nutrition: Calories: 12 Fat: 0 g Protein: .1 g Carb: 2.1 g

321. Rooibos Mint Tea

Preparation time: 3 min
Cooking time:30 min
Servings: 2
Ingredients

- Boiling water, 1 gallon
- Sweetener, 1-2 tbsp (don't sweeten if you have just had your surgery) Fresh mint, 2 tbs
- Sliced lemon
- Rooibos tea, 6 bags

Directions:

1. Place the water on high heat. After it has started boiling, turn the heat off and add in the tea bags.

2. Pour into a pitcher and mix in everything else. Place the pitcher in the sunlight and allow the tea to steep for at least 30 min.
3. Servings: over ice.

Nutrition: Calories: 4 Fat: 0 g Protein: .2 g Carb: 1.4 g

322. Curried Root Soup

Preparation time: 10 min
Cooking time:50 min
Servings: 2
Ingredients

- A squeeze of lemon juice
- Vegetable stock, 5 cups
- Curry powder, 1 tsp
- Crushed garlic, 2 cloves
- Pepper
- Salt
- Chopped carrots, 1 lb.
- Chopped rutabaga, 1 lb.
- Sliced leeks, 2
- Chopped onion
- Cooking time spray

Directions:

1. Give a large skillet a generous spritz of cooking time spray and allow it to heat up. Add in the carrots, rutabaga, leeks, and onions along with a sprinkling of pepper and salt. Allow this to fry up for around 30 min, stirring occasionally. Add some water or a little more cooking time spray if the pan starts to look dry. The vegetables need to soften up, but they should not take on a deep color.
2. Add in the curry powder and garlic, allowing this to cook for one to two min.
3. Mix in the stock and allow everything to come to a boil. Lower the heat down and let it simmer for 15 min.
4. Once cooked, add batches to a blender and puree until smooth. You can also use an immersion blender if you have one.
5. Place back in the pan and add in a squeeze of lemon juice. Check the seasonings and adjust if needed. Servings: with some yogurt, mint leaves, or mango chutney if you would like.

Nutrition: Calories: 125 Fat: 2.5 g Protein: 4.5 g Carb: 22.3 g

323. DZ's Grilled Chicken Wings

Preparation time: 15 minutes
Cooking time: 20 minutes
Servings: 1
Ingredients:

- 11/2 pounds frozen chicken wings
- Freshly ground black pepper
- 1 teaspoon garlic powder

- 1 cup buffalo wing sauce
- 1 teaspoon extra-virgin olive oil

Directions:

1. Preheat the grill to 350F.
2. Season the wings with the black pepper and garlic powder.
3. Grill the wings for 15 minutes per side. They will be browned and crispy when finished.
4. Toss the grilled wings in the buffalo wing sauce and olive oil.
5. Serve immediately.

Nutrition: Calories: 82 Total fat: 6g Protein: 7g Carbs: 1g Fiber: 0g Sugar: 0g Sodium: 400mg

324. Ranch-Seasoned Crispy Chicken Tenders

Preparation time: 15 minutes
Cooking time: 15 minutes
Servings: 2

Ingredients:

- Nonstick cooking spray
- 6 chicken tenderloin pieces (about 11/4 pounds) 2 tablespoons whole-wheat pastry flour
- 1 egg, lightly beaten
- 1/2 cup whole-wheat Eggplant crumbs
- 2 tablespoons grated Parmigiano-Reggiano cheese 2 teaspoons dried parsley
- 3/4 teaspoon dried dill
- 1/4 teaspoon garlic powder
- 1/4 teaspoon onion powder
- 1/4 teaspoon dried basil
- 1/8 teaspoon freshly ground black pepper

Directions:

1. Preheat the oven to 425F. Spray a baking sheet with the cooking spray.
2. Prepare three small dishes for coating the chicken. Place the flour in one, the egg in the second, and in the last dish mix together the Eggplant crumbs, Parmigiano-Reggiano cheese, parsley, dill, garlic powder, onion powder, basil, and black pepper.
3. Working one at a time, dip each tenderloin into the flour. Shake off any excess, then dip the chicken into the egg. Finally, place the tenderloin in the Eggplant crumbs and press to coat in the mixture.
1. Place on the baking sheet.
4. Bake for like 20 minutes, or until crispy, brown and cooked through. Serve immediately.

Nutrition Calories: 162 Total fat: 2g Protein: 25g Carbs: 8g Fiber: 1g Sugar: 1g Sodium: 239mg

325. Chicken "Nachos" with Sweet Bell Peppers

Preparation time: 15 minutes
Cooking time: 25 minutes
Servings: 1

Ingredients:

- Nonstick cooking spray
- 1 (1-pound) package mini bell peppers, stemmed, seeded, and halved
- 2 teaspoons extra-virgin olive oil
- 1/2 onion,
- 2 cups cooked shredded chicken breast
- 1 large tomato,
- 1 teaspoon garlic powder
- 1 teaspoon ground cumin
- 1/2 teaspoon smoked paprika
- 1 cup shredded Colby Jack cheese
- 1/4 cup sliced black olives
- 3 scallions, finely sliced
- 1 jalapeño pepper, seeded, thinly sliced (optional) 2 mini bell pepper halves

Directions:

1. Preheat the oven to 400F. Set a baking sheet with aluminum foil and coat the foil with the cooking spray.
2. Set the bell pepper halves on the baking sheet cut-side up.
3. Warmth the olive oil in a large skillet over medium heat. Add the onion and sauté for 1 to 2 minutes, or until tender. Attach the chicken, tomato, garlic powder, cumin, and paprika and cook for like 5 minutes, or until the tomato has softened and the chicken is heated through.
4. Set 1 heaping tablespoon of the chicken mixture into each mini bell pepper half. Set each with the cheese, black olives, scallions, and jalapeño (if using). Bake until cheese has melted and browned.
1. Enjoy immediately.

Nutrition: Calories: 189 Total fat: 3g Protein: 29g; Carbs: 9g Fiber: 2g Sugar: 2g Sodium: 143mg

326. Baked "Fried Chicken" Thighs

Preparation time: 15 minutes
Cooking time: 35 minutes
Servings: 2

Ingredients:

- Nonstick cooking spray
- 1 teaspoon smoked paprika
- 1/2 teaspoon garlic powder
- 1/2 teaspoon freshly ground black pepper
- 1/2 teaspoon cayenne pepper
- 1/2 teaspoon dried oregano

- 4 (5-ounce) boneless, skinless chicken thighs
- 2 large eggs
- 1 tablespoon water
- 1 teaspoon Dijon mustard
- 21/2 cups bran flakes

Post-Op Serve.

- 1/2 chicken thigh (2 to 4 ounces)
- 1 chicken thigh (4 to 6 ounces)

Directions:

1. Preheat the oven to 400F. Set a large rimmed baking sheet with aluminum foil, and place it in the oven below a clean oven rack.
1. Spray the clean rack with the cooking spray.
2. In a large zip-top bag, combine the paprika, garlic powder, black pepper, cayenne pepper, and oregano. Add the chicken thighs to the bag, seal the bag, and shake to coat the thighs with the seasonings. Set aside.
3. In a small bowl, lightly whisk together the eggs, water, and mustard.
4. Crush the bran flakes in another large plastic bag.
5. To Eggplant the chicken, dredge the seasoned chicken thighs in the egg mixture, and then put them in the bag of crushed cereal. Shake to coat well.
6. Place the chicken thighs on the clean oven rack, making sure the baking sheet is directly under the chicken to catch any drippings.
7. Bake for 35 minutes, or until the thighs are crispy and reach an internal temperature of 165F, and serve.

Nutrition: Calories: 272 Total fat: 8g Protein: 35g Carbs: 15g Fiber: 3g Sugar: 3g Sodium: 279mg

327. Egg Roll in a Bowl

Preparation time: 15 minutes
Cooking time: 20 minutes
Servings: 2

Ingredients:

- 2 teaspoons sesame oil, divided
- 1 teaspoon minced garlic
- 1 onion, finely diced
- 1 pound extra-lean ground chicken or turkey
- 11/2 tablespoons low-sodium soy sauce or Bragg Liquid Aminos 1/2 cup low-sodium beef broth
- 2 teaspoons ground ginger
- 1/2 teaspoon freshly ground black pepper
- 4 cups green cabbage, chopped or shredded into 1-inch ribbons 11/2 cups shredded carrots

- 1 cup fresh bean sprouts or 1 (14-ounce) can, drained and rinsed 2 scallions, finely chopped, for garnish

Post-Op Serve.

- 3/4 cup

Directions:

2. Preheat a large skillet to medium-high. 1 teaspoon sesame oil and the garlic are added. 1 minute of stirring Cook for 1 to 2 minutes, or until the onion is soft. Add the ground chicken to the mix. Cook for 7 to 9 minutes, breaking up the meat into smaller pieces as it browns.
3. In a small bowl, combine the remaining 1 teaspoon sesame oil, soy sauce, broth, ginger, and black pepper while the beef is browning.
4. Stir the sauce into the skillet once the chicken is done. Combine the cabbage, carrots, and bean sprouts in a large mixing bowl. To blend, stir everything together. Cover the skillet and cook for 5 to 7 minutes, or until the cabbage is soft.
5. Serve in a bowl and top with scallions and more soy sauce, if desired.

Nutrition: Calories: 133 Total fat: 3g Protein: 19g Carbs: 7g Fiber 2g Sugars: 4g Sodium: 356mg

328. Chicken Cordon Bleu

Preparation time: 15 minutes
Cooking time: 30 minutes
Servings: 2

Ingredients:

- Nonstick cooking spray
- 6 boneless, skinless chicken breasts, thinly sliced 6 slices lean deli ham
- 6 slices reduced-fat Swiss cheese (3 ounces total), halved 2 large eggs
- 1 tablespoon water
- 1/4 cup whole-wheat Eggplant crumbs
- 2 tablespoons grated Parmigiano-Reggiano cheese Post-Op Serve.
- 1 chicken breast

Directions:

1. Preheat the oven to 450 degrees Fahrenheit. Using the cooking spray, coat a baking sheet.
2. Preheat the oven to 350°F and pound the chicken breasts to a thickness of 1/4 inch.
3. On each chicken breast, layer 1 ham slice and 1 cheese slice (2 halves). Roll the chicken with care. Place it on the baking sheet seam-side down.
4. Lightly whisk the eggs in a small bowl. Combine the Eggplant crumbs and Parmigiano-Reggiano cheese in a second small bowl.
5. Lightly coat each chicken roll with the egg wash with a pastry brush, then top with the eggplant-crumb mixture.

6. Bake for 30 minutes, or until the chicken is well cooked and the top is gently browned.

Nutrition: Calories: 174 Total fat: 7g Protein: 24g Carbs: 3g Fiber: 0g Sugar: 0g Sodium: 321mg

329. Zoodles with Turkey Meatballs

Preparation time: 15 minutes
Cooking time: 15 minutes
Servings: 2
Ingredients:

- Nonstick cooking spray - 1 large egg
- 1/2 cup whole-wheat Eggplant crumbs
- 1/3 cup chopped onion
- 1/2 teaspoon freshly ground black pepper
- 1 pound extra-lean ground turkey
- 1 pound zucchini (about 3 medium zucchini)
- 1 teaspoon extra-virgin olive oil
- 2 cups Marinara Sauce with Italian Herbs, or a low-sugar jarred marinara sauce

Post-Op Serve.

- 1 meatball with 2 ounces sauce
- 2 meatballs with 2 to 4 ounces sauce and 1/4 cup zoodles

Directions:

1. Preheat the oven to 400 degrees Fahrenheit. Using the cooking spray, coat the bottom of a shallow baking pan.
2. Combine the egg, eggplant crumbs, onion, and pepper in a large mixing basin.
3. Mix in the ground turkey thoroughly with clean hands until the mixture is equally distributed.
4. Place the meat mixture in the baking pan and roll it into 2-inch balls.
5. Bake for 15 minutes, uncovered.
6. Remove the zucchini's ends and discard them. Slice the zucchini into long, thin strips using a mandolin, spiralizer, or the side of a box grater.
7. Heat the olive oil in a medium skillet over medium heat. Sauté the zucchini strips for about 5 minutes, or until they are soft.
8. Serve in a serving bowl.
9. Serve the meatballs with zoodles and marinara sauce on top.

Nutrition: Calories: 191 Total fat: 5g Protein: 22g Carbs: 15g Fiber: 3g Sugar: 4g Sodium: 205mg

330. Slow Cooker Barbecue Shredded Chicken

Preparation time: 15 minutes
Cooking time: 2 hours 15 minutes
Servings: 2
Ingredients:

- 4 (4-ounce) boneless, skinless chicken breasts 1 cup catsup (free of high-fructose corn syrup) 1/2 cup water

- 1 tablespoon freshly squeezed lemon juice
- 1 tablespoon dried onions
- 1/2 teaspoon dried mustard
- 1/4 teaspoon red pepper flakes
- 3 tablespoons Worcestershire sauce
- 1 tablespoon white vinegar

Post-Op Serve.

- 1/4 cup (2 ounces)
- 1/2 cup (4 ounces)
- 1/2 cup (4 ounces)

Directions:

1. Set the chicken breasts in a slow cooker.
2. In a small bowl, whisk together the catsup, water, lemon juice, dried onions, dried mustard, red pepper flakes, Worcestershire sauce, and white vinegar. Pour the mixture over the chicken.
3. Seal the slow cooker and turn on low to cook for 6 to 8 hours.
4. Bring the chicken to a plate and shred it with a fork. Return it to the slow cooker, and cook on low for 30 minutes more before serving, allowing the chicken to absorb some of the liquid.

Nutrition: Calories: 188 Total fat: 3g Protein: 22g Carbs: 16g Fiber: 0g Sugar: 10g Sodium: 750mg

331. Whole Herbed Roasted Chicken

Preparation time: 7 hours 10 minutes
Cooking time: 20 minutes
Servings: 2
Ingredients:

- 1 teaspoon garlic powder
- 1 teaspoon smoked paprika
- 1 teaspoon onion powder
- 1 teaspoon dried thyme
- 1/2 teaspoon freshly ground black pepper
- 1/2 teaspoon dried sage
- 1 (4-pound) whole chicken
- 2 sprigs fresh rosemary
- 2 lemon wedges
- Post-Op Serve.
- 1/4 cup (2 ounces)
- 1/2 cup (4 ounces)
- 1/2 to 3/4 cup

Directions

1. In a small bowl, merge together the garlic powder, paprika, onion powder, thyme, black pepper, and sage.
2. Detach any giblets from the chicken cavity. Clean the outside and inner cavity of the chicken under cold water and use a paper towel to pat dry. Place the chicken in the slow cooker.

3. Massage the chicken with the herb mixture, getting as much as possible under the skin.
4. Set the inside of the chicken with the rosemary and lemon wedges.
5. Secure the slow cooker and turn on low to cook for 7 hours, or until the temperature of the innermost part of a thigh and thickest part of the breast has reached 165°F.

Nutrition: Calories: 191 Total fat: 8g Protein: 29g Carbs: 0g Fiber: 0g Sugar: 0g Sodium: 86mg

---

332. Mediterranean Turkey Meatloaf

Preparation time: 15 minutes
Cooking time: 55 minutes
Servings: 2

Ingredients:

- For the meatloaf
- Nonstick cooking spray
- 1 pound extra-lean ground turkey
- 1 large egg, lightly beaten
- 1/4 cup whole-wheat Eggplant crumbs
- 1/4 fat-free feta cheese
- 1/4 cup Kalamata olives,
- 1/4 cup chopped fresh parsley
- 1/4 cup minced red onion
- 1/4 cup plus 2 tablespoons hummus, such as Lantana Cucumber Hummus, divided
- 2 teaspoons minced garlic
- 1/2 teaspoon dried basil
- 1/4 teaspoon dried oregano
- For the topping
- 1/2 small cucumber, peeled, seeded, and chopped 1 large tomato, chopped
- 2 to 3 tablespoons minced fresh basil
- Juice of 1/2 lemon
- 1 teaspoon extra-virgin olive oil
- Post-Op Serve.
- 2 ounces
- 2 to 4 ounces

Directions:

To Make the Meatloaf

1. Preheat the oven to 350F. Coat an 8-by-4-inch loaf pan with the cooking spray.
2. In a large bowl, combine the ground turkey, egg, Eggplant crumbs, feta cheese, olives, parsley, onion, 2 tablespoons of hummus, garlic, basil, and oregano. Using clean hands, mix until just combined.
3. Place the meatloaf mixture evenly in the loaf pan. Spread the remaining 1/4 cup of hummus over the top of the meatloaf.
4. Bake for 55 minutes.
5. To Make the Topping
6. In a small bowl, merge together the cucumber, tomato, basil, lemon juice, and olive oil. Refrigerate until ready to serve.
7. The meatloaf is processed when it reaches an internal temperature of 165F. Let it sit for 5 minutes before serving, then slice and garnish with the topping

Nutrition: Calories: 232 Total fat: 8g; Protein: 31g Carbs: 10g Fiber: 2g Sugar: 2g Sodium: 370mg

CHAPTER 22:

After 8th Week Breakfast

333. Pumpkin Parfait

Preparation Time: 5 minutes
Cooking Time: 0 minutes
Servings: 2

Ingredients:

- a cup of pumpkin puree
- 1 (1 ounce) package of instant sugar-free vanilla pudding mix 1 teaspoon pumpkin pie spice
- 1 cup of evaporated skim milk
- 1 cup of skim milk

Directions:

1. Combine the pumpkin puree, vanilla pudding mix, pumpkin pie spice, evaporated milk, and skim milk in a mixing dish. Blend everything together until it's completely smooth.
2. Chill until set, then serve in parfait glasses.

Nutrition: Serving size: 1/2 cup Calories: 71.7kcal Fat: 0.2 g Carbohydrates: 12.7 g Fiber: 0.6 g Protein: 4.9 g Sugar: 7.3 g

334. Carrot-Apple Muffin

Preparation Time: 20 minutes
Cooking Time: 20 minutes
Servings: 2

Ingredients:

- 1 ½ cups all-purpose flour
- ½ cup old-fashioned oats
- ¼ cup brown sugar
- 1 ½ teaspoons baking powder
- 1 ½ teaspoons ground cinnamon
- ½ teaspoon baking soda
- ¼ teaspoon salt
- ¼ teaspoon ground nutmeg
- 1 cup low-fat vanilla Greek yogurt
- ⅓ cup buttermilk
- ¼ cup vegetable oil
- 1 large egg, lightly beaten
- 1 teaspoon vanilla extract
- ¾ cup peeled and grated apple
- ¾ cup peeled and grated carrots ⅓ cup chopped walnuts, lightly toasted

Directions:

1. Preheat the oven to 350 degrees F (175 degrees C). Grease a 12-cup muffin tin or line cups with paper liners.
2. Stir together flour, oats, brown sugar, baking powder, cinnamon, baking soda, salt, and nutmeg together in a large bowl. Whisk together yogurt, buttermilk, oil, egg, and vanilla extract in a second bowl. Fold flour mixture into yogurt mixture, mixing just until combined and flour disappears. Stir together apple, carrot, and walnuts in a separate bowl; gently fold into the batter. Divide batter evenly among the muffin cups.
3. Bake muffins in the preheated oven until golden brown or a toothpick inserted in the center comes out clean, 17 to 19 minutes.
4. Cool muffins in the tin for 5 minutes. Transfer to a wire rack to cool completely.

Nutrition: Calories: 180 kcal Fat: 7.6 g Carbohydrates: 23.7 g Fiber: 1.5 g Protein: 5 g Sugar: 7.9 g

335. Honey Nut Granola

Preparation Time: 10 minutes
Cooking Time: 20 minutes
Servings: 2

Ingredients:

- 4 cups rolled oats
- 1 cup sliced almonds
- 1 cup chopped pecans
- 1 cup raw sunflower seeds
- ⅓ cup canola oil
- ½ cup honey
- 1 teaspoon vanilla extract
- 1 tablespoon ground cinnamon

Directions:

1. Preheat oven to 300 degrees F (150 degrees C).
2. In a large bowl, stir oats, nuts and sunflower kernels together. In a separate bowl, mix together oil, honey, vanilla and cinnamon. Add to dry ingredients; mix well. Spread mixture onto two ungreased baking sheets.
3. Bake in preheated oven, for 10 minutes, remove from oven and stir.

4. Return to oven and continue baking until golden, about 10 minutes.
5. Remove from oven and let cool completely before storing.

Nutrition: Calories: 188 kcal Fat: 11.1 g Carbohydrates: 19.9 g Fiber: 2.8 g Protein: 3.7 g Sugar: 7.5 g

336. Spinach Quiche

Preparation Time: 20 minutes
Cooking Time: 40 minutes
Total time: 1 hour
Servings: 2

Ingredients:

- ½ cup butter
- 3 cloves garlic, chopped
- 1 small onion, chopped
- 1 (10 ounce) package frozen chopped spinach thawed and drained.
- 1 (4.5 ounce) can mushrooms, drained
- 1 (6 ounce) package herb and garlic feta, crumbled.
- 1 (8 ounce) package shredded Cheddar cheese
- salt and pepper to taste
- 1 (9 inch) unbaked deep dish pie crust
- 4 eggs, beaten
- 1 cup milk
- salt and pepper to taste

Directions:

1. Preheat oven to 375 degrees F (190 degrees C).
2. In a medium skillet, melt butter over medium heat. Sauté garlic and onion in butter until lightly browned, about 7 minutes. Stir in spinach, mushrooms, feta and 1/2 cup Cheddar cheese. Season with salt and pepper. Spoon mixture into pie crust.
3. In a medium bowl, whisk together eggs and milk. Season with salt and pepper. Pour into the pastry shell, allowing egg mixture to combine with spinach mixture thoroughly.
4. Bake in preheated oven for 15 minutes. Sprinkle top with remaining Cheddar cheese, and bake an additional 35 to 40 minutes, until set in center. Allow to stand 10 minutes before serving.

Nutrition: Calories: 612 kcal Fat: 48.2 g Carbohydrates: 23.9 g Fiber: 2.8 g Protein: 22.9 g Sugar: 6 g

337. Sausage Egg Roll in Bowl

Preparation Time: 15 minutes
Cooking Time: 12 minutes
Servings: 2

Ingredients:

- 1 pound ground pork sausage
- 6 cups coleslaw mix
- 2 carrots, peeled and grated
- ¼ cup chopped green onions
- 4 cloves garlic, minced
- 1 tablespoon low-sodium soy sauce
- 1 tablespoon sesame oil
- 2 tablespoons shelled sunflower seeds (Optional) 1 tablespoon grated ginger root

Directions:

1. Heat a large skillet over medium-high heat. Cook and stir pork sausage in the hot skillet until browned and crumbly, 5 to 7 minutes.
2. Add coleslaw mix, carrots, green onions, garlic, soy sauce, and sesame oil. Cook and stir until tender, 7 to 10 minutes.
3. Add ginger and sunflower seeds.
4. Stir to combine.

Nutrition: Calories: 310 kcal Fat: 22.4 g Carbohydrates: 14.4 g Fiber: 2 g Protein: 12.5 g Sugar: 0.7 g

338. Easy Asparagus Frittata

Preparation Time: 10 minutes
Cooking Time: 20 minutes
Total time: 30 minutes
Servings: 2

Ingredients:

- 1 tbsp olive oil
- 2 tsp butter
- ½ pound asparagus, trimmed, cut into 1-inch pieces.
- 8 eggs
- ½ cup of grated Parmesan cheese, or more to taste. - 7 tbsp milk
- salt and freshly ground black pepper to taste.
- 1 tbsp chopped fresh parsley (Optional)

Directions

1. Cook asparagus in a 9-inch nonstick pan with olive oil and butter over medium heat, tossing periodically, until tender but still firm to the bite, 10 to 15 minutes.
2. In a mixing dish, whisk the eggs until they are foamy. Season with salt and pepper and stir in the Parmesan cheese and milk. Pour the egg mixture over the asparagus and heat for 10 to 15 minutes, or until the eggs are set.
3. Invert the frittata onto a platter and sprinkle parsley on top.

Nutrition: Calories: 242 kcal Fat: 17.6 g Carbohydrates: 4.6 g Protein: 17.1 g Sugar: 3.1 g

339. Reuben Sandwich

Preparation Time: 15 minutes
Cooking Time: 10 minutes
Servings: 2

Ingredients:

- 8 slices rye Eggplant

- ¾ cup thousand island dressing
- 1 (16 ounce) can sauerkraut, drained
- 8 slices Swiss cheese
- 8 slices pastrami
- ¼ cup margarine, softened

Directions:

1. Spread each slice of Eggplant with thousand island dressing. Top 4 of the Eggplant slices with sauerkraut, cheese and pastrami. Place remaining Eggplant slices on sandwich. Spread margarine on the outsides of each sandwich.
2. Heat a large skillet over medium high heat. Grill until browned, then turn and grill until heated through, and cheese is melted.

Nutrition: Calories: 792.6 kcal Fat: 51.7 g Carbohydrates: 50.2 g Fiber: 6.7 g Protein: 34.2 g Sugar: 14.8 g

340. Muffin Pan Frittatas

Preparation Time: 10 minutes
Cooking Time: 25 minutes
Servings: 2
Ingredients:

- cooking spray - 1 tablespoon olive oil
- 1 cup chopped fresh asparagus
- ¼ cup chopped green bell pepper
- 2 tablespoons chopped red onion
- 6 eggs - ½ cup milk
- ¼ teaspoon salt
- ⅛ teaspoon ground black pepper
- 1 cup shredded Cheddar cheese

Directions:

1. Preheat oven to 350 degrees F (175 degrees C). Spray 12 muffin cups with cooking spray.
2. Heat olive oil in a skillet over medium heat; cook and stir asparagus, green bell pepper, and onion in the hot oil until softened, 5 to 10 minutes.
3. Whisk eggs, milk, salt, and black pepper together in a bowl. Mix cooked vegetables and Cheddar cheese into egg mixture. Spoon about 1/4 cup mixture into each muffin cup.
4. Bake in the preheated oven until frittatas are set in the middle and lightly browned, about 20 minutes.

Nutrition: Calories: 92.5 kcal Fat: 7 g Carbohydrates: 1.5 g Fiber: 0.3 g Protein: 6.1 g Sugar: 1.1 g

341. Yogurt Protein Bowl

Preparation Time: 5 minutes
Cooking Time: 0 minutes
Servings: 1
Ingredients:

- ¼ cup Greek yogurt

- 1 tablespoon peanut butter
- ½ chocolate protein bar, cut into small pieces.
- 5 fresh strawberries, sliced

Directions:

1. Combine Greek yogurt and peanut butter in a bowl and whip together until smooth. Top with protein bar pieces and strawberries.

Nutrition: Serving size: 1 cup Calories: 304.9 kcal Fat: 14 carbohydrates: 34.6 g Fiber: 4.8 g Protein: 12.9 g Sugar: 7.9 g

342. Pumpkin Spice Protein Drink

Preparation Time: 10 minutes
Cooking Time: 0 minutes
Servings: 2
Ingredients:

- 1 cup unsweetened almond milk
- 2 Avocados, sliced and frozen
- ½ cup canned pumpkin
- 2 dates, pitted
- 1 scoop vanilla protein powder
- ½ teaspoon vanilla extract
- 1 pinch ground nutmeg
- 1 pinch ground cinnamon
- 1 pinch ground cloves
- 1 pinch ground ginger

Directions:

1. Blend almond milk, Avocados, pumpkin, dates, protein powder, vanilla extract, nutmeg, cinnamon, cloves, and ginger together in a blender until smooth.

Nutrition: Serving size: 1 cup Calories: 279.5 kcal Fat: 3 g Carbohydrates: 45.6 g Fiber: 7.5 g Protein: 22 g Sugar: 26.5 g

343. Grapefruit Smoothie

Preparation Time: 10 minutes
Cooking Time: 0 minutes
Servings: 2
Ingredients:

- 3 grapefruit, peeled and sectioned
- 1 cup cold water
- 3 ounces fresh spinach
- 6 ice cubes
- 1 (1/2 inch) piece peeled fresh ginger
- 1 teaspoon flax seeds

Directions:

1. Blend grapefruit, water, spinach, ice cubes, ginger, and flax seeds in a blender until smooth.

Nutrition: Serving size: 1 cup Calories: 202 kcal Fat: 1 g Carbohydrates: 47.4 g Fiber: 7.5 g Protein:4.6 g Sugar: 33.2 g

344. Vegan Nut and Date Millet Porridge

Preparation Time: 10 minutes
Cooking Time: 30 minutes
Servings: 2
Ingredients:

- ½ cup hulled millet
- 2 tablespoons slivered almonds
- 2 tablespoons pumpkin seeds
- 2 tablespoons shredded unsweetened coconut
- 1 tablespoon flax seeds
- 2 cups unsweetened almond milk, divided
- 3 Medjool dates, pitted and diced
- ½ teaspoon ground cinnamon
- ¼ tsp ground nutmeg

Directions:

2. In a blender or food processor, pulse millet until it resembles coarse ground coffee. Remove from the equation.
3. Over medium-high heat, heat a nonstick saucepan. Toast the almonds for about 2 minutes, stirring periodically, until golden brown. Continue to stir and toast the pepitas until golden brown, about 3 minutes. Toss in the coconut and flax seeds and toast for another 5 minutes, or until golden. Place the mixture in a mixing dish and put it aside.
4. In the same pan, add the millet that has been ground. Toast for 3 minutes, or until aromatic. 1 1/2 cups almond milk, stirred thoroughly to guarantee no lumps. Bring to a boil and then add the dates. Reduce the heat to low and continue to cook, stirring periodically.
5. Toss 2 teaspoons of the toasted seed mixture into the porridge and stir well.
6. Mix in the cinnamon and nutmeg. Stir everything together thoroughly. Cook for another 6 to 10 minutes, or until the sauce has thickened.
7. Divide the porridge between two bowls. Serve the remaining seed mixture and 1/2 cup almond milk in separate dishes.

Nutrition: Serving size: 1 cup Calories: 412.1kcal Fat: 18 g Carbohydrates: 58.2 g Fiber: 8.9 g Protein: 11.5 g Sugar: 8.5 g

345. Raw Chia Porridge

Preparation Time: 10 minutes
Cooking Time: 15 minutes
Servings: 1
Ingredients:

- ¼ cup chia seeds
- 1 Avocado
- 2 dates, pitted
- 1 cup almond milk
- ¼ teaspoon ground cinnamon
- salt to taste
- ¼ cup fresh blueberries, or more to taste

Directions:

1. Place chia seeds in a bowl.
2. Layer Avocado and dates in a blender; add almond milk, cinnamon, and salt. Blend mixture until smooth and pour over chia seeds, stirring well. Let mixture sit until thickened, at least 15 minutes.
3. Stir chia 'porridge' and top with blueberries.

Tips: The porridge will be softer if you let sit in refrigerator overnight.
Nutrition: Serving size: 1 bowl Calories: 385 kcal Fat: 12.5 g Carbohydrates: 66.8 g Fiber: 17.9 g Protein: 7.7 g Sugar: 36 g

346. Quinoa Prune Breakfast Porridge

Preparation Time: 10 minutes
Cooking Time: 15 minutes
Servings: 2
Ingredients:

- 2 cups water
- ½ teaspoon salt
- 1 cup quinoa, rinsed and drained
- 1 cup chopped pitted prunes
- 2 tablespoons crunchy peanut butter
- 1 cup unsweetened vanilla-flavored almond milk
  ½ teaspoon ground cinnamon
- ¼ teaspoon freshly grated nutmeg

Directions:

1. Boil water and salt in a saucepan. Stir in quinoa; cover, reduce heat
2. to low, and simmer until tender, about 10 minutes.
3. Stir in chopped prunes, peanut butter, almond milk, cinnamon, and nutmeg. Cover and simmer 5 more minutes.

Nutrition: Serving size: 1 cup Calories: 328.3 kcal Fat: 7.5 g Carbohydrates: 59.8 g Fiber: 7.7 g Protein: 9 g Sugar: 23 g

347. Quick Chicken Marsala

Preparation Time: 5 minutes
Cooking Time: 20 minutes
Total time: 25 minutes
Servings: 2
Ingredients:

- 1 tbsp of butter
- 6 skinless, boneless chicken breasts
- 1 (10.75 ounce) can condensed golden mushroom soup.
- 1 ¼ cups of Marsala wine

Directions:

Sauté the chicken breasts in butter in a large skillet. Add the soup (undiluted) and Marsala wine once the chicken is lightly cooked on all sides. Cover and cook for 20 minutes, or until the chicken is no longer pink on the inside. It's time to eat!

Nutrition: Calories: 262 kcal Fat: 4.8 g Carbohydrates: 11.1 g Fiber: 0.4 g Protein: 28.2 g Sugar: 4.4 g

348. Vegan Spinach Artichoke Dip

Preparation Time: 10 minutes
Cooking Time: 25 minutes
Servings: 2
Ingredients:

- 1 (8 ounce) can artichoke hearts, drained and chopped.
- 1 (8 ounce) container cream cheese-style spread, room temperature.
- ½ (6 ounce) package fresh spinach, chopped
- 2 tablespoons all-purpose flour
- ¾ teaspoon garlic salt
- ¼ teaspoon thyme leaves
- ¼ teaspoon red pepper flakes
- cooking spray
- 1 cup grated Parmesan-style vegan cheese.

Directions:

1. Preheat the oven to 350 degrees F (175 degrees C).
2. Mix artichoke hearts, cream cheese spread, spinach, flour, garlic salt, thyme, and red pepper flakes together in a large bowl.
3. Coat a large nonstick baking pan with cooking spray, fill pan with the artichoke mixture.
4. Bake in the preheated oven until center is hot and dip is bubbling, about 25 minutes.
5. Sprinkle the top of the dip with Parmesan-style cheese.

Nutrition: Calories: 176.8 kcal Fat: 12.9 g Carbohydrates: 10.1 g Fiber: 5.7 g Protein: 8.2 g

349. Apple Strawberry Blueberry Smoothie

Preparation Time: 5 minutes
Cooking Time: 0 minutes
Total time: 5 minutes
Servings: 1
Ingredients:

- 0.5 cup Blueberries, fresh
- 1 cup, halves Strawberries, fresh
- 1 cup Lactaid Fat Free Milk
- 3 serving Truvia Natural Sweetener
- 1 cup Ice cubes

Directions:

1. Blend all of the ingredients together in blender or with an immersion blender.
2. Enjoy!

Nutrition: Serving size: 1 cup Calories: 176.2kcal Fat: 0.6 g Carbohydrates: 42.9 g Fiber: 5.5 g Protein: 9.4 g Sugar: 20 g

350. Squash Hash

Preparation Time: 2 minutes
Cooking Time: 10 minutes
Servings: 2
Ingredients:

- 1 tsp. onion powder
- 1/2 cup finely chopped onion
- 2 cups spaghetti squash
- 1/2 tsp. sea salt

Directions:

1. Using paper towels, squeeze extra moisture from spaghetti squash.
2. Place the squash into a bowl, then add the salt, onion, and the onion powder.
3. Stir properly to mix them. Spray a non-stick cooking skillet with cooking spray, then place it over moderate heat. Add the spaghetti squash to the pan.
4. Cook the squash for about 5 minutes. Flip the hash browns using a spatula. Cook for 5 minutes until the desired crispness is reached.
5. Serve.

Nutrition: Calories: 44kcal Fat: 0.6 g Carbohydrates: 9.7 g Fiber: 5.5 g Protein: 0.9 g Sugar: 8 g

351. Chocolate Cherry Crunch Granola

Preparation Time: 10 minutes
Cooking Time: 20 minutes
Total time: 30 minutes
Servings: 2
Ingredients:

- 3 cups rolled oats.
- 2 cups assorted seeds, such as sesame, chia, sunflower, and pepitas (hulled pumpkin seeds)
- 1 cup sliced almonds.
- 1 cup unsweetened coconut flakes
- 2 teaspoons vanilla extract
- 2 teaspoons ground cinnamon
- 1 teaspoon fine sea salt
- ½ cup of cocoa powder
- ½ cup pure maple syrup
- ¼ cup coconut oil or canola oil
- 1 cup dried cherries (unsweetened, if possible) 1 cup of chocolate chips

Directions:

1. Warm oven to 350 F. Spread 2 large baking sheets with parchment paper.
2. Stir the oats, seeds, almonds, and coconut in a large bowl. Add the vanilla, cinnamon, salt, and cocoa powder. Stir to combine.
3. In a frying pan on low, heat the maple syrup and coconut oil. Pour the warm syrup and oil over the oat mixture and stir to coat. On the prepared baking sheets, spread the granola in even layers.
4. Bake for 15 to 18 minutes, scraping and mixing occasionally, then remove from the oven.
5. Put in the dried cherries and chocolate chips, then return to the oven, now turned off but still warm, and let the granola cool and dry thoroughly.

Nutrition: Calories: 570 kcal Fat: 31 g Carbohydrates: 72 g Protein: 12 g Sugar: 57 g

352. Omelet with Tomatoes and Spring Onions

Preparation Time: 5 minutes
Cooking Time: 20 minutes
Servings: 2

Ingredients:

- 6 eggs - 2 tomatoes
- 2 spring onions - 1 shallot - 2 tbsp. butter
- 1 tbsp. olive oil
- 1 pinch of nutmeg
- salt - pepper

Directions:

1. Whisk the eggs in a bowl. Mix them and season them with salt and pepper. Peel the shallot and chop it up.
2. Clean the onions and cut them into rings. Wash the tomatoes and cut them into pieces—heat butter and oil in a pan.
3. Braise half of the shallots in it, then add half the egg mixture. Let everything set over medium heat. Scatter a few tomatoes and onion rings on top.
4. Repeat with the second half of the egg mixture. In the end, spread the grated nutmeg over the whole thing.

Nutrition: Calories: 263 kcal Fat: 24 g Carbohydrates: 8 g Fiber: 1 g Protein: 20.3 g Sugar: 2.4 g

353. Coconut Chia Pudding with Berries

Preparation Time: 40 minutes
Cooking Time: 0 minutes
Servings: 2

Ingredients:

- 150 g raspberries and blueberries
- 60 g chia seeds
- 500 ml of coconut milk
- 1 teaspoon agave syrup
- ½ teaspoon ground bourbon vanilla

Directions:

1. Put the chia seeds, agave syrup, and vanilla in a bowl. Pour in the coconut milk. Mix thoroughly and let it soak for 30 minutes.
2. Meanwhile, wash the berries and let them drain well. Divide the coconut chia pudding between two glasses. Put the berries on top.

Nutrition: Serving size: 1 serving Calories: 165 kcal Fat: 8 g Carbohydrates: 18 g Fiber: 10 g Protein: 6 g Sugar: 6 g

354. Avocado Chicken Salad

Preparation Time: 5 minutes
Cooking Time: 10 minutes
Servings: 2

Ingredients:

- 10 oz. diced cooked chicken.
- ½ cup 2% Plain Greek yogurt
- 3 oz. chopped avocado
- 12 tsp garlic powder
- ¼ tsp salt - 1/8 tsp pepper
- 1 tbsp. + 1 tsp lime juice
- ¼ cup fresh cilantro, chopped.

Directions:

1. Combine all ingredients in a medium-sized bowl. Refrigerate until ready to serve. Cut the chicken salad in half and serve with your favorite greens.

Nutrition: Calories: 265 kcal Fat: 13 g Carbohydrates: 5 g Fiber: 3 g Protein: 35 g Sugar: 1 g

355. Amaranth Porridge

Preparation Time: 5 minutes
Cooking Time: 30 minutes
Servings: 2

Ingredients:

- 2 cups of coconut milk
- 2 cups alkaline water
- 1 cup amaranth - 2 tbsps. coconut oil
- 1 tbsp. ground cinnamon

Directions:

1. In a saucepan, mix the milk with water, then boil the mixture. You stir in the amaranth, then reduce the heat to medium.
2. Cook on medium heat then simmers for at least 30 minutes as you stir it occasionally. Turn off the heat. Add in cinnamon and coconut oil, then stir. Serve.

Nutrition: Calories: 434 kcal Fat: 35 g Carbohydrates: 27 g Fiber: 7.6 g Protein: 6 g Sugar: 1.4 g

356. Crunchy Quinoa Meal

Preparation Time: 5 minutes
Cooking Time: 25 minutes
Servings: 2
Ingredients:

- 3 cups of coconut milk
- 1 cup rinsed quinoa.
- 1/8 tsp. ground cinnamon
- 1 cup raspberry
- 1/2 cup chopped coconuts.

Directions:

1. In a pan, pour milk and bring to a boil over moderate heat.
2. Add the quinoa to the milk, and then bring it to a boil once more.
3. You then let it simmer for at least 15 minutes on medium heat until the milk is reduced. Stir in the cinnamon, then mix properly.
4. Cover it, then cook it for 8 minutes until the milk is completely absorbed. Add the raspberry and cook the meal for 30 seconds.
5. Serve and enjoy.

Nutrition: Calories: 271 kcal Fat: 3.7 g Carbohydrates: 54 g Protein: 6.5 g

357. Avocado Barley Porridge

Preparation Time: 15 minutes
Cooking Time: 5 minutes
Servings: 2
Ingredients:

- 1 cup divided unsweetened coconut milk.
- 1 small peeled and sliced Avocado
- 1/2 cup barley
- 3 drops liquid stevia.
- 1/4 cup chopped coconuts.

Directions:

1. In a bowl, properly mix barley with half of the coconut milk and stevia. Cover the mixing bowl, then refrigerate for about 6 hours.
2. In a saucepan, mix the barley mixture with coconut milk.
3. Cook for about 5 minutes on moderate heat. Then top it with the chopped coconuts and the Avocado slices. Serve

Nutrition: Serving size: 1 cup Calories: 159 kcal Fat: 8.4 g Carbohydrates: 19.8 g Fiber: 12.2 g Protein: 4.6 g Sugar: 11 g

358. Zucchini Muffins

Preparation Time: 10 minutes
Cooking Time: 25 minutes
Servings: 2
Ingredients:

- 1 tbsp. ground flaxseed

- 3 tbsps. alkaline water
- 1/4 cup walnut butter
- 3 medium over-ripe Avocados
- 2 small, grated zucchinis
- 1/2 cup coconut milk
- 1 tsp. vanilla extract
- 2 cups coconut flour
- 1 tbsp. baking powder
- 1 tsp. cinnamon
- 1/4 tsp. sea salt

Directions:

1. Tune the temperature of your oven to 375°F. Grease the muffin tray with the cooking spray.
2. In a medium bowl, combine the flaxseed with water. In a glass bowl, mash the Avocados, then stir in the remaining ingredients.
3. Properly mix and then divide the mixture into the muffin tray. Bake it for 25 minutes. Serve.

Nutrition: Calories: 220 kcal Fat: 9 g Carbohydrates: 32 g Fiber: 1 g Protein: 4 g Sugar: 14 g Snacks

359. Bacon Cheeseburger

Preparation Time: 10 Minutes
Cooking Time: 30 Minutes
Servings: 2
Ingredients:

- 1 lb. lean ground beef
- 1/4 cup chopped yellow onion.
- 1 garlic clove, minced.
- 1 tbsp. yellow mustard
- 1 tbsp. Worcestershire sauce
- 1/2 tsp. salt
- cooking spray
- 4 ultra-thin slices of cheddar cheese cut into six equal-sized rectangular pieces.
- 3 pieces of turkey bacon, each cut into eight evenly sized rectangular pieces.
- 24 dill pickle chips
- 4-6 green leaf
- lettuce leaves, torn into 24 small square-shaped pieces.
- 12 cherry tomatoes sliced in half.

Directions:

1. Pre-heat oven to 400°F. Combine the garlic, salt, onion, Worcestershire sauce, and beef in a medium-sized bowl, and mix well.
2. Form mixture into 24 small meatballs. Put meatballs onto a foil-lined baking sheet and cook for 12-15 minutes. Leave oven on.
3. Top every meatball with a piece of cheese, then go back to the oven until cheese melts for about 2 to 3 minutes. Let meatballs cool.

4. To assemble the bites: on a toothpick layer, a cheese-covered meatball, piece of bacon, piece of lettuce, pickle chip, and a tomato half.

Nutrition: Calories: 500 Carbs: 29g Fat: 30g Protein: 27g

360. Cheeseburger Pie

Preparation Time: 20 Minutes
Cooking Time: 90 Minutes
Servings: 2

Ingredients:

- 1 large spaghetti squash
- 1 lb. lean ground beef
- 1/4 cup diced onion.
- 2 eggs
- 1/3 cup low-fat, plain Greek yogurt
- 2 tbsp. tomato sauce
- 1/2 tsp. Worcestershire sauce
- 2/3 cup reduced fat, shredded cheddar cheese.
- 2 oz. dill pickle slices
- Cooking spray

Directions:

1. Preheat oven to 400°F. Slice spaghetti squash in half lengthwise; dismiss pulp and seeds. Spray insides with cooking spray.
2. Place squash halves cut-side-down onto a foil-lined baking sheet and bake for 30 minutes. Once cooked, let calm before scraping squash flesh with a fork to remove spaghetti-like strands; set aside.
3. Push squash strands in the bottom and up sides of the greased pie pan, creating an even layer.
4. Meanwhile, set up pie filling. In a lightly greased, medium-sized skillet, cook beef and onion over medium heat for 8 to 10 minutes, sometimes stirring, until meat is brown. Drain and remove from heat.
5. In a medium-sized bowl, whisk together eggs, tomato paste, Greek yogurt, and Worcestershire sauce. Stir in ground beef mixture.
6. Pour pie filling over squash crust. Sprinkle meat filling with cheese, and then top with dill pickle slices.
7. Bake for 40 minutes. Serve.

Nutrition: Calories: 409 Fat: 24.49g Carbohydrates: 15.06g Protein: 30.69g

361. Pizza Biscuit

Preparation Time: 5 Minutes
Cooking Time: 15 Minutes
Servings: 1

Ingredients:

- buttermilk cheddar herb biscuit
- 2 tbsp cold water
- cooking spray

- 2 tbsp no-sugar-added tomato sauce.
- 1/4 cup reduced fat shredded cheese.

Directions:

1. Preheat oven to 350°F. Mix biscuit and water, and spread mixture into a small, circular crust shape onto a greased, foil-lined baking sheet.
2. Bake for 10 minutes. Top with tomato sauce and cheese, and cook till cheese is melted, about 5 minutes.

Nutrition: Calories: 500 Carbs: 31g Fat: 25g Protein: 11g

362. Chicken and Mushrooms

Preparation Time: 10 Minutes
Cooking Time: 15 Minutes
Servings: 2

Ingredients:

- 2 breasts of chicken
- 1 cup of sliced white champignons
- 1 cup of sliced green chilies
- 1/2 cup scallions hacked.
- 1 teaspoon of chopped garlic
- 1 cup of low-fat cheddar shredded cheese (1-1,5 lb. grams fat / ounce)
- 1 tablespoon of olive oil
- 1 tablespoon of butter

Directions:

1. Fry the chicken breasts with olive oil. When needed, add salt and pepper. Grill breasts of chicken on a plate with grill.
2. Weigh 4 ounces of chicken for every serving.
3. In a buttered pan, stir in mushrooms, green peppers, scallions, and garlic until smooth and a little dark. Place the chicken on a baking platter.
4. Cover with the mushroom combination top on ham. Place the cheese in a 350C oven until it melts.

Nutrition: Calories: 258 Carbs: 13g Fat: 12g Protein: 0g

363. Chicken Enchilada Bake

Preparation Time: 20 Minutes
Cooking Time: 50 Minutes
Servings: 2

Ingredients:

- 5 oz. shredded chicken breast or 99 percent fat-free white chicken can be used in a pan.
- 1 can tomatoes paste
- 1 low sodium chicken broth can be fat-free.
- 1/4 cup-cheese with low-fat mozzarella
- 1 tablespoon -oil
- 1 tbsp of salt
- ground cumin, chili powder, garlic powder, oregano, and onion powder (all to taste).

- 1 to 2 zucchinis sliced longways.
- Sliced olives

Directions:

1. Prepare Enchilada Sauce: add olive oil in a saucepan over medium/high heat, stir in tomato paste and seasonings, and heat in chicken broth for 2-3 minutes.
2. Stirring regularly to boil, turn heat to low for 15 minutes. Set aside
3. & cool to ambient temperature.
4. Pull-strip of Zucchini thorough enchilada sauce and lay flat on the pan's bottom in a small baking pan, spray with Pam.
5. Add the chicken a little less than 1/4 cup of enchilada sauce and mix it. Stick the chicken to the lids, side to side of the baking dish.
6. Sprinkle over chicken with some bacon. Add another layer of the pulled zucchini via enchilada sauce.
7. When needed, cover with the remaining cheese and olives on top.
8. Bake it for 35 to 40 minutes. When the cheese begins burning, cover with foil.

Nutrition: Calories: 312 Carbohydrates: 21.3g Protein: 27g Fat: 10.2g

364. Jalapeno Lentil Burgerg with Avocado Mango Pico

Preparation Time: 15 Minutes
Cooking Time: 10 Minutes
Servings: 2
Ingredients:

- ½ cup dried red lentils, rinsed.
- 1 can chickpeas; rinsed.
- 1 tsp ground cumin
- 1 tsp chili powder
- 1 tsp sea salt
- ½ cup packed cilantro
- garlic cloves minced.
- jalapeno finely chopped.
- ½ red onion, small, minced.
- red bell pepper
- carrot, shredded.
- ¼ cup oat bran/oat flour (gluten-free)
- lettuce/hamburger buns

For Pico:

- 1 ripe mango, diced.
- 1 ripe avocado, diced.
- ½ red onion, small, finely diced.
- ½ cup chopped cilantro.
- ½ tsp fresh lime juice
- sea salt

Directions:

1. Put all fixings in a large bowl and mix. Stir in the salt to taste. Put a medium saucepan on medium heat, add lentils plus 1 1/2 cups of water, then bring water to a boil, cover it afterward, lower the heat
2. to low, and then simmer lentils until the water is absorbed. Drain, and set aside some extra water.
3. In a food processor, put the cooked lentils, chickpeas, garlic, sea salt, cilantro, chili powder, and cumin, and blend until the beans and lentils are smooth.
4. Add tomato, red pepper, jalapeno, and carrot to compare. Divide into six equal parts and use your hands to create dense patties.
5. Heat skillet over a medium-high flame; apply 1/2 tablespoon of olive oil. Place a few burgers in at a time and cook on either side for a couple of minutes, just until crisp and golden brown.
6. Repeat with remaining patties and add olive oil whenever desired.
7. Place the patties in a bun or lettuce and finish with mango avocado Pico.

Nutrition: Calories: 225 Carbs: 35g Fat: 6g Protein: 10g

365. Lettuce Power Pack

Preparation time: 15 min
Cooking time: 15 min
Servings: 1
Ingredients:

- 1 egg, large
- 1 white of an egg, large
- 125 ml baby spinach leaves, small pieces
- 2 tbsp fat-free feta, crumbled
- 2 tomato, roam, small pieces
- Pinch of salt, kosher or sea
- Black pepper
- 1 large lettuce leaf, preferably not iceberg

Directions:

1. Place the first seven ingredients in a bowl and whisk well. Have a nonstick pan heating on medium heat, add the combined mixture, and cook to the consistency of your choice. Place the cooked ingredients on one end of the leaf and roll up.

366. Greek Egg Muffins

Preparation time: 5 min
Cooking time: 10 min
Servings: 2
Ingredients:

- 5 eggs large
- 10 cherry tomatoes, quartered
- 5 artichoke hearts, marinated and diced
- 125 ml mozzarella cheese, low-fat and shredded

- 2 tbsp basil, fresh and minced Pepper and salt for taste
- Cooking time spray for the muffin tin

Directions:
1. While the oven is preheating to 350 degrees, break the eggs into a bowl and whisk well until smooth.
2. Combine the rest of the ingredients to the eggs and stir gently together.
3. Coat the muffin tin cups lightly with the cooking time spray.
4. Spoon the egg mixture into six cups, dividing it equally.
5. Bake for twenty min or 'til the eggs is set.
6. Let cool for a minute before savoring or store in the fridge to be enjoyed later.

Nutrition: Calories 106 Fats 6g Protein 10g

367. Black Beans Puree With Scrambled Eggs

Preparation time: 20 min
Cooking time: 30 min
Servings: 1

Ingredients:
- For making the scrambled egg part of the recipe 1/8 teaspoon salt
- 1 egg
- 1/8 teaspoon pepper
- Black beans puree
- 3 tablespoons enchilada sauce (green)
- 1/2 cup rinsed black beans
- 2 tablespoon vegetable or chicken broth
- 1 tablespoon protein powder

Directions:
Black beans puree:
1. Put the beans in some small sized saucepan on medium heat. Then put the enchilada sauce. Heat for 2 min. Keep stirring all the time. Then add the chicken broth.
2. Shift the mixture to one blender or use one hand blender to make a smooth mixture. Transfer it into one bowl.
3. Let it cool a bit and then mix the protein powder. Stir well. Cover it to keep it warm till you cook the egg.
4. Keep the leftovers in the fridge so that you can eat them at some other time.

Scrambled egg:
1. Heat one non-stick pan on medium heat. In the meantime, put the egg in one small bowl and whisk it well to incorporate air into it.
2. Pour the egg into the heated pan. Sprinkle pepper and salt. Use one rubber spatula for moving the egg in the pan while it is getting cooked. When it is almost done and still has a

slightly liquid texture, you should fold it and take it out on a plate.
3. Put 1 tablespoon of the black beans puree. Also, put 1 teaspoon of enchilada sauce (green).

Note: it provides approximately 5 grams of fat, 11 grams of proteins, and 6 grams of carbohydrates.

368. Ricotta Baked In The Oven

Preparation time: 10 min
Cooking time: 30 min
Serving: 2

Ingredients:
- 1/4th cup parmesan cheese (grated)
- 1/2 cup ricotta cheese (low fat)
- 1 teaspoon Dijon mustard
- 1 teaspoon thyme (ground)
- 1/4th cup cheddar cheese (shredded)
- 1 egg

Directions:
1. Heat the oven to a temperature of 400f.
2. Put all the ingredients in one bowl. Stir and mix them well. The mixture will appear to be gritty and slightly brown. But it must be smooth.
3. Use one cookie scoop and divide the mixture into 4 wells of the muffin pan.
4. You can use muffin pans made of silicone as you can use them easily and clean them quickly.
5. Bake it for about 20 min. Then remove from the oven and let it cool a bit. It is ready to be servings.

Note: this recipe is for making four ricotta muffins. Every muffin provides approximately 4 grams of fat, 4 grams of carbohydrates and 8 grams of proteins

369. Make-ahead breakfast burritos

Preparation time: 15 min
Cooking time: 20 min
Serving: 2

Ingredients:
- 10 large eggs
- ¼ cup low-fat milk
- 1 cup canned black beans, drained and rinsed 8 (7- to 8-inch) whole wheat tortillas
- ½ cup shredded cheddar cheese
- 1 tsp extra-virgin olive oil
- ½ small yellow onion, diced
- 1 small green bell pepper, seeded and diced
- 7 ounces of salsa

Directions
1. Whisk the eggs and milk together in a large mixing dish.
2. Heat the oil in a large skillet over medium heat. Combine the onion, bell pepper, and black beans in a large mixing bowl.

3. Transfer to a platter after 5 minutes of sautéing until the onion is transparent.
4. Fill the skillet halfway with the egg mixture and gently swirl until the eggs are frothy and hard. Turn off the heat.
5. Top the tortillas with the eggs and onion mixture, followed by the cheese and salsa.
6. Roll tightly to close with both sides of the first tortilla tucked in. Carry on with the remaining tortillas in the same manner.
7. Serve right away or freeze for up to three months. If freezing, wrap the burritos in paper towels and store them snugly wrapped in aluminum foil.
8. Suggestions for post-op meals
9. If you can't handle doughy textures after surgery, omit the tortilla and put the mixture into a bowl instead.

Nutrition: calories: 264; total fat: 12g; protein: 21g; carbohydrates: 24g; fiber: 11g; sugar: 3g; sodium: 593mg.

CHAPTER 23:

Snacks

370. Almond Light-as-Air Cookies

Preparation Time: 5 minutes
Cooking Time: 10 minutes
Servings: 2

Ingredients:

- 8 tablespoons almond flour
- 1 tablespoon low-sugar vanilla whey protein powder 1 tablespoon whipped butter
- 2 teaspoons vanilla extract
- 1 teaspoon baking powder
- 1 teaspoon finely granulated pure cane sugar ½ teaspoon stevia or no-calorie sweetener
- ¼ teaspoon salt

Directions:

1. Preheat the oven to 350°F. Line a large baking sheet with parchment paper.
2. In a large bowl, combine the almond flour, protein powder, whipped butter, vanilla extract, baking powder, sugar, stevia, and salt and mix well until fully incorporated.
3. Scoop heaping tablespoons of the mixture onto the baking sheet about an inch apart. Using a spatula, flatten the batter slightly into about 2-inch circles.
4. This should yield 8 cookies.
5. Bake for 7 to 9 minutes, or until the edges of cookies are slightly golden brown. Keep a close eye on the cookies since as soon as this happens, you will want to remove the cookies from the oven to prevent overcooking.
6. Allow the cookies to cool slightly before serving.

Nutrition: (2 COOKIES): Calories: 117; Protein: 6g; Fat: 9g; Carbohydrates: 5g; Fiber: 2g; Sugar: 2g; Sodium: 288mg

371. Strawberry Gelatin Tea

Preparation Time: 5 minutes
Cooking Time: 5 minutes
Servings: 1

Ingredients:

- ½ cup frozen sliced strawberries
- ¼ teaspoon stevia or no-calorie sweetener
- ½ cup hot water
- 2 tablespoons plain gelatin powder

Directions:

1. In a small saucepan, cook the strawberries over medium heat for 3 minutes, stirring frequently, until softened.
2. Stir in the stevia. Remove the pan from the heat and set aside.
3. Pour the hot water into a mug. Mix in the gelatin powder a bit at a time while continuously stirring with a fork. Keep stirring as you add in the cooked strawberries.
4. Blend the mixture in a blender for about 30 seconds, until frothy.
5. Pour into a mug. Sip once cooled and enjoy as a tea within about 15 minutes or so before it starts to set.

Nutrition: (¾ CUP OR 12 TABLESPOONS): Calories: 89; Protein: 12g; Fat: 0g; Carbohydrates: 10g; Fiber: 2g; Sugar: 5g; Sodium: 47mg

372. Caprese Snack

Preparation time: 5 min
Cooking time: 10 min
Servings: 2

Ingredients:

- 8 oz. Mozzarella, mini cheese balls
- 8 oz. Cherry tomatoes
- 2 tablespoons green pesto
- Salt and black pepper, to taste
- 1 tablespoon garlic powder

Directions:

1. Slice the mozzarella balls and tomatoes in half.
2. Stir in the green pesto and season with garlic powder, salt and pepper to servings.

Nutrition: Calories 407 Total fat 34.5g Saturated fat 7.4g Cholesterol 30mg Sodium 343mg Total carbohydrate 6.3g Dietary fiber 0.9g Total sugars 2g Protein 19.4g

373. Almond Flour Crackers

Preparation time: 25 min
Cooking time: 20 min
Servings: 2
Ingredients:

- 2 tablespoons sunflower seeds
- 1 cup almond flour
- ¾ teaspoon sea salt
- 1 tablespoon whole psyllium husks
- 1 tablespoon coconut oil

Directions:

1. Preheat the oven to 3500f and grease baking sheet lightly.
2. Mix together sunflower seeds, almond flour, sea salt, coconut oil, psyllium husks and 2 tablespoons of water in a bowl.
3. Transfer into a blender and blend until smooth.
4. Form a dough out of this mixture and roll it on the parchment paper until 1/16 inch thick.
5. Slice into 1-inch squares and season with some sea salt.
6. Arrange the squares on the baking sheet and transfer to the oven.
7. Bake for about 15 min until edges are crisp and brown.
8. Allow to cool and separate into squares to servings.

Nutrition: Calories 141 Total fat 11.6g Saturated fat 2.7g Cholesterol 0mg Sodium 241mg Total carbohydrate 5.2g Dietary fiber 3.1g Total sugars 0g Protein 4.2g

374. Crispy Baked Zucchini Fries

Preparation time: 30 min
Cooking time: 23 min
Servings: 2
Ingredients:

- ¾ cup parmesan cheese, grated
- 2 medium zucchinis, chopped into small ticks 1 large egg - ¼ teaspoon black pepper
- ¼ teaspoon garlic powder

Directions:

1. Preheat the oven to 4250f and grease a baking sheet lightly. Whisk egg in one bowl and mix together parmesan cheese, black pepper and garlic powder in another bowl.
2. Dip each zucchini stick in the egg and then dredge in the dry mixture.
3. Transfer to the baking sheet and place in the oven.
4. Bake for about 20 min until golden and broil for 3 min to servings.

Nutrition: Calories 102 Total fat 5.9g Saturated fat 3.4g Cholesterol 62mg Sodium 222mg Total carbohydrate 4.3g Dietary fiber 1.1g Total sugars 1.8g Protein 9.6g

375. Low Carb Onion Rings

Preparation time: 30 min
Cooking time: 15 min
Servings: 2
Ingredients:

- 2 medium white onions, sliced into ½ inch thick rings Ingredients:
- ½ cup coconut flour
- 4 large eggs
- 4 oz pork rinds
- 1 cup parmesan cheese, grated

Directions:

1. Preheat an air fryer to 3900f and grease a fryer basket.
2. Put coconut flour in one bowl, eggs in the second bowl and pork rinds and parmesan cheese in the third bowl.
3. Coat the onion rings through the three bowls one by one and repeat.
4. Place the coated onion rings in the fryer basket and cook for about 15 min.
5. Dish out to a platter and Servings: with your favorite low carb sauce.

Nutrition: Calories 270 Total fat 15.1g Saturated fat 7.1g Cholesterol 164mg Sodium 586mg Total carbohydrate 11g Dietary fiber 4.8g Total sugars 1.8g Protein 24.1g

376. Broccoli fritters with cheddar cheese

Preparation time: 20 min
Cooking time: 25 minutes
Servings: 2
Ingredients:

- 1 cup cheddar cheese, shredded
- 8 ounces broccoli, chopped, steamed and drained
- 2 large eggs, beaten
- 1 tablespoon avocado oil
- 2 tablespoons oat fiber

Directions:

1. Mix together broccoli with cheddar cheese, eggs and oat fiber in a bowl.
2. Heat avocado oil over medium heat in a nonstick pan and add the broccoli mixture in small chunks.
3. Cook for about 5 min on both sides until browned and dish onto a platter to servings.

Nutrition: Total fat 12.6g Saturated fat 6.8g Cholesterol 123mg Sodium 236mg Total carbohydrate 5.3g Dietary fiber 2g Total sugars 1.4g Protein 12.1g

377. Cheesy low carb creamed spinach Servings8

Preparation time: 25 min
Cooking time: 30 min
Servings: 2

Ingredients:

- 2 (10 oz) packages frozen chopped spinach, thawed 3 tablespoons butter
- 6 ounces cream cheese
- Onion powder, salt and black pepper
- ½ cup parmesan cheese, grated

Directions:

1. Mix together 2 tablespoons of butter with cream cheese, parmesan cheese, salt and black pepper in a bowl.
2. Heat the rest of the butter on medium heat in a small pan and add onion powder.
3. Sauté for about 1 minute and add spinach.
4. Cover and cook on low heat for about 5 min.
5. Stir in the cheese mixture and cook for about 3 min.
6. Dish into a bowl and Servings: hot.

Nutrition: Calories 141 Total fat 12.8g Saturated fat 8g Cholesterol 37mg Sodium 182mg Total carbohydrate 3.5g Dietary fiber 1.6g Total sugars 0.5g Protein 4.8g

378. Jicama Fries

Preparation time: 20 min
Cooking time: 20 min
Servings: 2

Ingredients:

- 2 tablespoons avocado oil
- 1 jicama, cut into fries
- 1 tablespoon garlic powder ½ cup parmesan cheese, grated
- Salt and black pepper, to taste

Directions:

1. Preheat the air fryer to 4000f and grease the fryer basket.
2. Boil jicama fries for about 10 min and drain well.
3. Mix jicama fries with garlic powder, salt and black pepper in a bowl.

4. Place in the fryer basket and cook for about 10 min.
5. Dish onto a platter and Servings: warm.

Nutrition: Calories 145 Total fat 7.8g Saturated fat 4.4g Cholesterol 20mg Sodium 262mg Total carbohydrate 10.4g Dietary fiber 4g Total sugars 2.6g Protein 10.4g

379. Spicy Tuna Rolls

Preparation time: 15 min
Cooking time: 10 minutes
Servings: 2

Ingredients:

- 1 pouch Star-Kist selects a.s.a.p. Wild caught yellowfin tuna 1 medium cucumber, thinly sliced lengthwise 1 teaspoon hot sauce
- 2 slices avocado, diced
- Cayenne, salt and black pepper

Directions:

1. Mix together tuna with hot sauce, cayenne, salt and black pepper in a bowl until combined.
2. Put the tuna mixture on the cucumber slices and top with avocado.
3. Roll up the cucumber and secure with 2 toothpicks to servings.

Nutrition: Calories 139 Total fat 6.5g Saturated fat 1.2g Cholesterol 22mg Sodium 86mg Total carbohydrate 8.4g Dietary fiber 2.9g Total sugars 2.8g

380. Classic Tuna Salad

Preparation Time: 10 minutes
Cooking Time: 10 minutes
Servings: 2

Ingredients

- 1/2 cup of mayonnaise
- 1 tbsp dijon mustard
- 2 tbsp sweet relish
- 1/4 tsp coarse ground black pepper
- 1 tbsp lemon juice
- 18 ounces tuna drained well
- 1/2 cup of minced celery

Directions:

Note: Click on the timings in the directions to start a kitchen timer while cooking.

1. In a big mixing bowl, combine the mustard, mayonnaise, relish, pepper, and lemon juice before adding the tuna and celery and mixing well again.
2. Before eating, chill for at least one hour.

Nutrition Amount per serving: 315 calories, Calories: 315g, Carbohydrates: 3g, Protein: 25g, Fat: 22g, Cholesterol: 57mg, Sodium: 606mg, Potassium: 261mg, Sugar: 3g;

381. Edamame And Avocado Dip

Preparation Time: 10 Mins
Cooking Time: 10 Mins
Servings: 2

Ingredients

- 12 to 16 ounces shelled edamame, fresh or frozen 1/2 cup of, packed, roughly chopped fresh cilantro, including stems
- 1/2 cup of plain yogurt
- 1 avocado, peeled, pitted, roughly chopped
- 1/2 cup of water
- 1/4 cup lime or lemon juice
- 1-2 tsp salt
- 5 shakes of Tabasco (less or more as need)
- 3 drops of dark sesame oil (more as need)

Directions

Cook the edamame:

1. Bring 2 quarts of well-salted water to a boil (2 tbsp salt). Add the edamame that has been shelled. Return to a low heat and prepare for another 5 minutes, or until the chicken is fully cooked and soft. Using cold water, drain. **Blend the edamame with the remaining ingredients:**
2. In a food processor, combine cooked edamame that has been drained. Pulse a few of times. Add the cilantro, chopped. Pulse once more.
3. Pulse in the other ingredients until they are fully puréed. If you want a smoother consistency, add additional water. Sprinkle with salt and pepper as needed (salt, Tabasco, lime, sesame oil).
4. Serve with pita, chips, crostini, or a tray of vegetables.

382. Chicken And Spinach Salad

Preparation Time: 5m
Cooking Time: 15m
Servings: 2

Ingredients

- 1 lb chicken breasts, grilled/fully cooked
- kosher salt
- fresh cracked black pepper
- 1/2 tsp turmeric
- 2 tbsp extra virgin olive oil
- 5 ounces baby spinach
- 1/2 small red onion, thinly sliced
- 1 cup of grape tomatoes, sliced into half
- 1/3 cup of whole almonds
- 1 small avocado, sliced
- 1/2 cup of Honey
- 2 tbsp apple cider vinegar
- 2 tbsp extra virgin olive oil

- 1 tbsp garlic paste/minced garlic
- kosher salt
- fresh cracked black pepper
- 2–3 tbsp water, to thin

Directions

1. Season the chicken bosoms with pepper, salt, and turmeric. Season the chicken with the spices.
2. Heat the olive oil in a large pan over medium-high heat. Cook chicken breasts for 5-6 minutes on all sides, or until they are thoroughly cooked through. Grilling or baking chicken in the oven (at 350°F for at least 1 hour) are other options. After that, leave the chicken aside.
3. In a mason jar, combine the mustard, apple cider vinegar, olive oil, garlic, and salt/pepper. To thin out the dressing, add a tbsp of water at a time until it reaches the appropriate consistency; around 2-3 tbsp should sufficient.

Nutrition Calories 119; Fat 4g; Carbohydrates 18g; Fiber 6g; Sugar 7g; Protein 5g.

383. Brussels Sprouts With Pomegranates

Preparation Time: 5 minutes
Cooking Time: 30 minutes
Servings: 2

Ingredients

- 2 pounds brussels sprouts, stem removed and cut in half 3 tbsp balsamic vinegar
- 1 1/2 tbsp coconut oil
- 2 tsp ground ginger
- 1 tbsp lemon juice
- 1/2 cup of pomegranate arils
- salt and pepper, as need
- lemon zest, as need

Directions

1. Heat the oven 375 degrees F. Using parchment paper, line 1-2 baking sheets.
2. In a small bowl, combine balsamic vinegar, coconut oil, ginger, lemon juice, and salt & pepper. Toss the brussels sprouts in a large mixing bowl. Stir in the balsamic mixture until well combined. Roast for 30 minutes, stirring halfway through, on baking pans, spreading them out evenly.
3. Add the pomegranates and lemon zest to a serving bowl. Combine well.
4. Enjoy!

Nutrition Calories 119; Fat 4g; Carbohydrates 18g; Fiber 6g; Sugar 7g; Protein 5g.

384. Nutella Protein Bars

Preparation Time: 5 minutes
Cooking Time: 30 minutes
Servings: 2

Ingredients

- 4 serving (serving = 1/4 cup of) Bob's Red Mill Hazelnut Meal/Flour
- 3 serving (serving = 1 scoop) Wegmans Natural Whey Protein Powder - Chocolate
- 0.3 cup of Cocoa Powder (Unsweetened)
- 2 tbsp Honey
- 1/4 serving (serving = 1 cup of) Blue Diamond Almond Breeze Unsweetened Vanilla Milk

Directions

1. Combine 1 cup hazelnut flour, 3 scoops chocolate protein powder, 1/3 cup cocoa powder, 2 tablespoons honey, and 1/4 cup milk in a mixing bowl (I recommend unsweetened almond milk). Combine the ingredients and, if necessary, add an extra tablespoon of milk. Fill a small tined pan halfway with the ingredients and freeze until firm. Refrigerate after chopping into slices.

Nutrition Calories 120; Total Fat 7.69; Polyunsaturated Fat 0.01; Monounsaturated Fat 0.12; Cholesterol 6.00; Sodium 17.24; Potassium 106.28; Total Carbohydrate 7.49; Dietary Fiber 2.38; Sugars 3.90; Protein 7.54.

385. Zucchini Eggplant

Preparation Time: 15 minutes
Cook Time: 50 minutes
Servings: 2 slices

Ingredients

- 1 1/2 cups of grated zucchini - lightly packed - do not drain liquid 1 cup of granulated sugar
- 1/4 cup packed light brown sugar 1/2 cup of unsweetened applesauce
- 1/3 cup of vegetable oil -or your preferred cooking oil 2 large eggs
- 1 tsp vanilla extract
- 1 1/2 cups of all-purpose flour
- 1/2 tsp baking powder
- 1/2 tsp baking soda
- 1/2 tsp salt
- 1/2 tsp ground cinnamon

Directions

1. Preheat the oven to 350 degrees Fahrenheit. Using cooking spray, coat a 9x5 inch loaf pan.
2. Combine the grated zucchini, sugar, brown sugar, applesauce, oil, eggs, and vanilla in a large mixing bowl. Using a whisk, combine all of the items until they are thoroughly combined.
3. Combine the flour, baking powder, baking soda, salt, and cinnamon in a large mixing bowl. Stir

just until no dry flour remains, taking care not to overmix.

4. Fill the loaf pan halfway with batter. Heat the oven 350°F and bake for 50–54 minutes. When a toothpick is placed into the center of the Eggplant, moist crumbs should emerge.
5. Allow 10 minutes to cool in the pan. Remove from the pan and cool fully before slicing on a wire cooling rack.
6. Refrigerate in an airtight container.
7. It's ideal to serve this Eggplant after it's been in the fridge for at least 12 hours.

Nutrition Calories: 213kcal Carbohydrates: 35g Protein: 3g Fat: 7g Saturated Cholesterol: 31mg Sodium: 158mg Potassium: 135mg Sugar: 22g

386. Rice Cooker Quinoa

Preparation time: 5 mins
Cooking time: 30 mins
Servings: 2

Ingredients

- 1 cup of quinoa
- 2 cups of water or broth
- 1/2 tsp salt (optional)

Directions

1. Rinse the quinoa well.
2. In a rice cooker, combine the quinoa with the broth or water. If you're not sure what you're going to do with it, you may simply use water. If you know what you're going to do in the future, broth is an excellent way to add flavor.
3. Turn on the rice cooker and add the salt.
4. In most cases, cooking will be completed in under 30 minutes.
5. Wait a few minutes after it's finished cooking before fluffing it with a fork.
6. It will yield around 3-4 cups of quinoa.

Nutrition Calories: 213kcal Carbohydrates: 35g Protein: 3g Fat: 7g Saturated Cholesterol: 31mg Sodium: 158mg Potassium: 135mg Sugar: 22g

387. Parsley Sautéed Mushrooms

Preparation time: 20 mins
Cooking time: 20 mins
Servings: 2

Ingredients

- 1 tbsp unsalted butter
- 1 tbsp extra-virgin olive oil
- 1 1/2 pounds mixed mushrooms, such as button, stemmed shiitake and oyster, sliced 1/4 inch thick
- 1 small minced garlic clove
- Chopped flat-leaf parsley
- Kosher salt and freshly ground pepper

Directions

1. Melt the butter and olive oil in a large skillet. Cook, without stirring, until the mushrooms are browned on the bottom, about 3 minutes over moderately high heat. Cook, stirring occasionally, for another 6 minutes or until the mushrooms are browned and soft.
2. Cook for 1 minute, or until the garlic is aromatic.
3. Add the chopped parsley and mix well. Using salt and pepper, season the mushrooms. Serve warm in a bowl.

388. Spinach Dip

Preparation time: 15 mins
Cooking time: 6 hrs.
Servings: 2
Ingredients

- 1 cup of mayonnaise
- 1 (16-ounce) sour cream
- container
- 1 dry leek soup mix package (1.8 oz.)
- 1 (4 ounce) can drained and chopped water chestnuts ½ (10 ounce) package thawed and drained frozen chopped
- spinach
- 1 (1 pound) loaf round sourdough Eggplant

Directions

1. Combine mayonnaise, sour cream, dried leek soup mix, water chestnuts, and chopped spinach in a medium mixing bowl. Refrigerate for at any rate 6 hours or overnight.
2. Remove the sourdough Eggplant's top and interior. Fill to the brim with the mayonnaise mixture. Remove the Eggplant portions and tear them into pieces for dipping.

Nutrition 682 calories; protein 13.3g; carbohydrates 53.2g; fat 47.4g; cholesterol 48.3mg; sodium 1183.4mg.

389. Thai 'Rice Noodle' Salad

Preparation time: 20 mins
Cooking time: 10 mins
Servings: 2
Ingredients

- 1 (8 ounce) package dried rice noodles
- 1 tbsp olive oil
- ¼ head chopped romaine lettuce,
- ¼ red bell pepper, diced
- ¼ cup of chopped red onion
- 3 green chopped onions
- ¼ diced cucumber,
- 2 tbsp chopped fresh basil, or as need
- 2 tbsp chopped fresh cilantro, or as need
- 1 (1 inch) piece fresh minced ginger root

- ¼ seeded and minced jalapeno pepper,
- 2 cloves minced garlic,

Sauce:

- ⅓ cup of olive oil
- ¼ cup of rice vinegar
- ¼ cup of soy sauce
- ¼ cup of white sugar
- 1 lemon, juiced
- 1 lime, juiced
- 1 tsp salt
- ¼ tsp ground turmeric
- ¼ tsp paprika

Directions

1. Toss the rice noodles in a bowl half-filled with boiling water. Cover bowl and set aside for 10 minutes, or until noodles are softened. Drain the water. Toss in 1 tablespoon olive oil to coat.
2. Toss rice noodles with romaine lettuce, red bell pepper, red onion, green onions, cucumber, basil, cilantro, ginger root, jalapeño pepper, and garlic.
3. In a mixing bowl, whisk together 1/3 cup olive oil, rice vinegar, soy sauce, white sugar, lemon juice, lime juice, salt, turmeric, and paprika; pour over rice noodle mixture and toss to coat.

Nutrition 472 calories; protein 3.9g; carbohydrates 65.2g; fat 21.9g; sodium 1591.5mg.

390. Pickle Rollups

Preparation Time: 10 minutes
Cooking Time: 1 minute
Servings: 2
Ingredients

- 8 slices beef lunch meat
- 4 oz cream cheese softened
- 4 med dill pickles

Directions

1. Place the meat in two-by-two piles on a firm surface.
2. Using 1 ounce of cream cheese, spread 1 ounce of cream cheese on each stack. Place a pickle in the center of each one. Cut each roll into four equal sections after wrapping the beef around the pickles.

Notes Ham or turkey can be substituted for beef lunch meat.
Nutrition Calories: 286kcal Carbohydrates: 4g Protein: 10g Fat: 26g Cholesterol: 74mg Sodium: 946mg Potassium: 285mg | Sugar: 1g .

391. Baked Zucchini Fries

Preparation time: 15 Minutes
Cooking time: 20 Minutes
Servings: 2
Ingredients:

- 1 cup of Panko
- 1/2 cup freshly grated Parmesan cheese
- 1 tsp Italian seasoning
- Kosher salt and black pepper, as need
- 4 zucchini, quartered lengthwise
- 1/2 cup of all-purpose flour
- 2 large beaten eggs
- 2 tbsp chopped fresh parsley leaves

Directions:

1. Preheat the oven to 425 degrees Fahrenheit. Set aside a cooling rack that has been sprayed with nonstick cooking spray and placed on a baking sheet.
2. Combine Panko, Parmesan, and Italian seasoning in a large mixing bowl; season with salt and pepper as needed. Remove from the equation.
3. Dredge zucchini in flour, dip in eggs, then dredge in Panko mixture, pressing to coat in batches.
4. Place the zucchini on the baking sheet that has been prepared. Preheat oven to 200°F and bake for 20-22 minutes, until golden brown and crisp.
5. If preferred, garnish with parsley before serving.

Notes: Panko is a Japanese-style Eggplant crumb that may be found at your local grocery store's Asian department.
Nutrition Calories 135.4; Total Fat 4.5g; Trans Fat 0g; Cholesterol 76.8mg; Sodium 181.0mg; Total Carbohydrate 15.6g; Dietary Fiber 0.4g; Sugars 0.5g; Protein 7.8g

392. Spicy Mango Chutney

Preparation Time: 10 mins
Cooking Time: 20 mins
Servings: 2
Ingredients

- 2 tbsp vegetable oil
- 1 small sweet chopped onion
- 1 medium chopped red bell pepper
- 2 serrano chopped peppers
- 1 tsp chopped fresh ginger
- 1 tbsp yellow curry powder
- 1 tsp turmeric - 1 tsp paprika
- 3 cups of fresh chopped mango
- Juice from half an orange
- 1 tbsp apple cider vinegar
- 1 tbsp sugar - Pinch of sea salt

Directions

1. In a medium-sized pot, heat the olive oil on medium.
2. Cook for 5 minutes, or until the onion, peppers, and ginger have softened.
3. Cook for another minute while tossing in the spices.
4. Combine the mango, orange juice, apple cider vinegar, sugar, and a sprinkle of salt in a mixing bowl. Decrease the heat to low and cook for 20 minutes or until the mango chutney has softened and become delicious.
5. Enjoy!

Notes Heat Factor: Hotter or milder peppers, as well as chili flakes and powders, can simply be used to vary the heat level. Keep sealed containers in the fridge. It should be good for approximately a month.
This recipe yields around 2 cups of soup.
Nutrition Calories: 24kcal Carbohydrates: 3g Sodium: 1mg Potassium: 53mg Sugar: 3g Vitamin A: 320IU Vitamin C: 11.1mg Calcium: 5mg Iron: 0.2mg

393. Tomato, Basil And Cucumber Salad

Preparation Time: 10 mins
Cooking Time: 15 mins
Servings: 2
Ingredients

- 1 ¾ pounds ripe heirloom tomatoes, cut into chunks 8 ounces cherry and teardrop-shaped tomatoes, halved ¾ English cucumber, peeled in alternating strips and cut into chunks
- 10 large basil leaves, torn into pieces
- 2 tbsp red wine vinegar
- ¼ cup of extra-virgin olive oil
- 1 tsp sea salt such as sel gris ¼ tsp pepper

Directions

1. In a bowl, gently combine the ingredients and let aside for a few minutes.
2. Toss once more.

Nutrition 89 calories; calories from fat 70%; protein 1.1g; fat 7.3g; saturated fat 1g; carbohydrates 6.4g; fiber 1.5g; sodium 196mg.

394. Cauliflower Rice

Preparation Time: 7 mins
Cooking Time: 3 mins
Servings: 2
Ingredients

- 1 medium head of cauliflower
- 1 tsp olive oil
- 1/2 cup of chopped scallions
- juice of 1/2 lime
- sea salt and freshly ground black pepper

Directions

1. Before cooking, make sure your cauliflower is completely dry. Cauliflower should be chopped into big chunks. The cores can be kept, but the leaves should be discarded or saved for another time. Grind the cauliflower pieces in a mixing bowl until they have the texture of rice. If necessary, work in batches, and don't over process or the mixture will become mushy. Riced cauliflower may be used in any recipe that asks for it. Continue to follow the recipe's directions.

2. If you want to serve your cauliflower as a side dish or substitute it for ordinary rice, briefly heat it and season it to remove the raw taste. 1 tsp olive oil, heated in a big skillet over medium heat. Sauté the onions and cauliflower for 3 to 5 minutes, or until cooked through. To help eliminate any bitterness from the raw cauliflower, season with salt, pepper, and a squeeze of lime juice.

Nutrition 89 calories; calories from fat 70%; protein 1.1g; fat 7.3g; saturated fat 1g; carbohydrates 6.4g; fiber 1.5g; sodium 196mg.

395. Pumpkin Pancakes

Preparation time: 5 minutes
Cooking time: 20 minutes
Servings: 2

Ingredients:

- 1 large egg, beaten
- ¼ cup vanilla yogurt
- ¾ cup of milk
- ¾ cup canned pumpkin
- 2 tbsp. melted butter
- 1 cup. whole flour
- ¼ tsp. salt
- 2 tbsp. stevia
- 2 tsp. baking powder
- ½ tsp. baking soda
- ½ tsp. cinnamon
- ¼ tsp. nutmeg
- ½ tsp. powdered ginger

Directions:

1. In a bowl, combine egg, milk, pumpkin, yogurt, and melted butter, mix well.

2. Add flour, salt, stevia, baking powder, baking soda, and spices; stir or whisk just until dry ingredients are moistened and a few lumps remain.

3. Pour or spoon batter into buttered skillet to make pancakes; when bubbles begin to form and the underside is browned, turn over to brown another side.

4. Remove cooked pancakes and repeat the process with the remaining batter.

Nutrition: Calories: 221.7, Fat: 3.6 g, Carbs: 37.2 g, Protein: 12 g.

CHAPTER 24:

Lunch

396. Cauliflower Fried Rice

Preparation time: 15 min
Cooking time: 15 min
Servings: 2

Ingredients

- 1 teaspoon sesame oil, plus 1 tablespoon
- 2 large eggs, beaten
- 4 cups cauliflower rice (or florets of 1 head of cauliflower riced in a food processor)
- 1 cup frozen mixed vegetables
- 2 garlic cloves, minced
- 2 tablespoons low-sodium soy sauce
- 2 scallions, diced

Directions:

1. In a large skillet over medium heat, heat 1 teaspoon of sesame oil. Add the eggs, and stir until they are cooked. Set aside.
2. In the same skillet over medium heat, heat the remaining tablespoon of oil.
3. Add the cauliflower rice, mixed vegetables, garlic, soy sauce, scallions, and eggs. Cook, stirring, until well combined and the cauliflower is soft, about 4 min, and servings. Make sure not to overcook the cauliflower or it will become soggy.
4. Ingredient tip: you should be able to find fresh or frozen cauliflower rice at your local grocery store. If not, remove the florets from a head of cauliflower and pulse in a food processor until the pieces are rice-size.

Nutrition: calories: 121; total fat: 7g; protein: 6g; carbohydrates: 9g; fiber: 3g; sugar: 3g; sodium: 357mg.

397. Roasted Garden Vegetables

Preparation time: 5 min
Cooking time: 30 min
Servings: 2

Ingredients

1. 1 medium bell pepper, cut into strips
2. 1 small onion, halved then sliced
3. 1 small zucchini, sliced into rounds
4. 1 pint grape tomatoes
5. 2 tablespoons extra-virgin olive oil
6. Salt
7. Freshly ground black pepper

Directions:

1. Preheat the oven to 400 degrees Fahrenheit.
2. Arrange the vegetables on 1 or 2 big baking pans so that they are lying flat and lightly touching each other.
3. Pour the olive oil evenly over the vegetables and toss gently to coat, either with a spoon or your hands. Season to taste with salt and pepper.
4. Roast for 20 to 30 minutes, stirring halfway through, or until soft and gently charred, and serve.
5. Cauliflower, brussels sprouts, asparagus, sweet celeriac, broccoli, summer squash, butternut squash, and carrots are seasonal vegetables that provide variation throughout the year. Using the same manner, set a timer for preparation, bearing in mind that harder vegetables, such as butternut squash, may require more time in the oven.

Nutrition: calories: 75; total fat: 5g; protein: 0g; carbohydrates: 8g; fiber: 1g; sugar: 4g; sodium: 2mg.

398. Asian Peanut Cabbage Slaw

Preparation time: 10 min
Cooking time: 10 min
Servings: 2

Ingredients

- 1 (14-ounce) package coleslaw
- 1 red bell pepper, thinly sliced
- 2 big carrot, grated
- ¼ cup diced scallions
- ¼ cup sliced fresh cilantr
- ¼ cup chopped peanuts
- ⅓ cup spicy peanut dressing or more

Directions:

1. Combine coleslaw, bell pepper, carrot, scallions, cilantro, and peanuts in a large mixing bowl. Toss with the dressing, season with salt and pepper to taste, and serve.
2. Powdered peanut butter is created by dehydrating and grinding raw peanuts into a fine powder. This lowers the fat content, but Protein and taste preservation In any recipe that calls for regular peanut butter, use powdered peanut butter to get the same excellent flavor.

3. Powdered peanut butter can be found in the nut butter section of your local supermarket..

Nutrition: calories: 123; total fat: 6g; protein: 6g; carbohydrates: 16g; fiber: 6g; sugar: 6g; sodium: 198mg.

399. Roasted Vegetable Quinoa Salad with Chickpeas

Preparation time: 15 minutes
Cooking time: 30 minutes
Servings: 2
Ingredients:

- 1 small eggplant, diced
- 1 small zucchini, diced
- 1 small yellow summer squash, diced
- ½ cup grape tomatoes halved
- 1 (15-ounces) can chickpeas, drained and rinsed
- 3 tbsp. extra-virgin olive oil, divided
- 1/2 cup packaged quinoa
- 1 cup low-sodium vegetable or chicken broth
- 2 tbsp. freshly squeezed lemon juice
- 1 tsp. minced fresh garlic or 1 garlic clove, minced
- 1 tbsp. dried basil
- 1 tsp. dried oregano

Directions:

1. Preheat the oven to 425 degrees Fahrenheit. Using parchment paper, line a 9-by-13-inch baking pan.
2. Toss the eggplant, zucchini, yellow squash, tomatoes, and chickpeas with 1 tablespoon of olive oil and spread them out on the baking sheet.
3. Preheat oven to 350°F and bake for 30 minutes, stirring halfway through. The final vegetables and tomatoes should be soft and moist. The chickpeas will be crunchy and firm.
4. In a small saucepan over medium-high heat, combine the quinoa and broth while the vegetables and chickpeas are roasting. Bring to a boil, covered. Reduce the heat to low and continue to cook for another 15 minutes.
5. minutes, or until the drink has been absorbed completely. Remove the skillet from the heat and use a fork to fluff the quinoa. (If not, follow the package directions for quinoa preparation.)
6. Whisk together the lemon juice, garlic, and the remaining 2 tablespoons olive oil in a small bowl. Combine the basil and oregano in a bowl.
7. Combine the quinoa, roasted veggies with chickpeas, and dressing in a large serving bowl. To blend, gently whisk everything together.

8. Serve and have fun!

Nutrition: Calories: 200, Total Fat: 9 g, Protein: 7 g, Carbs: 27 g, Fiber: 8 g, Sugar: 4 g, Sodium: 160 mg.

400. Mexican Stuffed Summer Squash

Preparation time: 5 minutes
Cooking time: 33 minutes
Servings: 2
Ingredients:

- Nonstick cooking spray
- 1 yellow summer squash
- ½ cup Refried Black Beans or canned Fat:-free refried pinto beans with 1 tsp. taco seasoning mixed in (for flavor)
- ½ cup cooked quinoa
- ¼ cup shredded Colby Jack cheese
- 1 small tomato, diced
- 2 tbsp. sliced black olives
- 2 scallions, chopped, for garnish

Directions:

1. Preheat the oven to 400 degrees Fahrenheit. Using the cooking spray, coat an 8-by-8-inch baking dish.
2. Remove the ends of the summer squash and toss them out. Cut lengthwise, then extract and discard the seeds with a spoon.
3. Place the squash halves in the baking dish cut-side down. To vent the squash, gently poke a couple of holes in it. 1 tbsp. water added to the dish 3 minutes in the microwave, or until somewhat tender.
4. Any remaining water should be discarded.
5. Turn the squash skin-side down and evenly distributed in the dish once it has cooled enough to handle.
6. 14 cup beans are layered in each squash, followed by 14 cup quinoa.
7. Colby Jack cheese should be sprinkled over everything. Bake for 25 minutes, covered in aluminum foil. Remove the foil and bake for another 5 minutes, or until the squash is soft and the cheese is bubbling.
8. Just before serving, garnish each squash with tomatoes, olives, and scallions.

Nutrition: Calories: 190, Total Fat: 8 g, Protein: 9 g, Carbs: 21 g, Fiber: 4 g, Sugar: 3 g, Sodium: 40 mg.

401. Tomato Bruschetta

Preparation time: 15 minutes
Cooking time: 5 minutes
Servings: 2
Ingredients:

- ½ finely chopped small red onion

- 8 medium coarsely chopped and drained tomatoes (about 500 g)
- 2-3 crushed garlic cloves
- 6-8 leaves of finely chopped fresh basil
- 30 ml balsamic vinegar
- 60-80ml extra virgin olive oil
- 1 crusty loaf of Eggplant

Directions:

1. Mix the onions, tomatoes, garlic, and basil in a big bowl, taking care not to crush or break the tomatoes up too much. Balsamic vinegar and extra virgin olive oil should be added. As need, add salt and pepper. Again, combination. For at least an hour, cover and relax. This will make it easier to soak and mix the flavors.
2. Slice the baguette loaf into 12 thick slices diagonally and lightly toast them until both sides are light brown. On the warm Eggplant slices, serve the mixture. Take out from the frozen half an hour before serving if you like the mix at room temperature.

Nutrition: Calories: 310, Fat: 12 g, Carbs: 42 g, Sugar: 6 g, Fiber: 3 g, Protein: 8 g, Salt: 0.72 g.

402. Zucchini with Tomatoes

Preparation time: 15 minutes
Cooking time: 18 minutes
Servings: 2
Ingredients:

- 2 zucchini cut in half lengthwise, then cut into 1/2-inch half-moons
- 2 cups quartered ripe tomatoes
- ½ onion, minced - 3 cloves garlic, minced
- ½ tsp. crushed red pepper flakes
- ¼ cup of olive oil Salt and pepper as need
- ½ cup of grated Parmesan cheese
- 1 tbsp. chopped fresh basil

Directions:

1. Heat the oven to 450 °F. Lightly grease a baking dish measuring 9x13 inches.
2. In the prepared baking dish, combine the zucchini, tomatoes, and onion, garlic, and red pepper flakes. Add the olive oil and sprinkle, season with salt and pepper, and blend well.
3. Set in a preheated oven. Roast for about 18 minutes until the vegetables are tender and slightly golden. Remove from the oven; sprinkle with basil and Parmesan cheese.

Nutrition: Calories: 204, Protein: 5.9 g, Carbs: 9.5 g, Fat: 16.8 g, Cholesterol: 8.8 mg, Sodium: 165.2 mg.

403. Broiled Fish Fillet

Preparation time: 5 minutes
Cooking time: 10 minutes
Servings: 2
Ingredients:

- 2 cod fish fillets
- 1/8 tsp. curry powder
- 2 tsp. butter
- 1/4 tsp. paprika
- 1/8 tsp. pepper
- 1/8 tsp. salt

Directions:

1. Preheat the broiler.
2. Spray broiler pan with cooking spray and set aside.
3. In a small bowl, mix together paprika, curry powder, pepper, and salt.
4. Coat fish fillet with paprika mixture and place on broiler pan.
5. Broil fish for 10-12 minutes.
6. Top with butter and serve.

Nutrition: Calories: 224, Fat: 5.4 g, Carbs: 0.3 g, Sugar: 0 g, Protein: 41.2 g, Cholesterol: 109 mg.

404. Baked Lemon Tilapia

Preparation time: 10 minutes
Cooking time: 12 minutes
Servings: 2
Ingredients:

- 4 tilapia fillets
- 2 tbsp. fresh lemon juice
- 1 tsp. garlic, minced
- 1/4 cup olive oil
- 2 tbsp. fresh parsley, chopped
- 1 lemon zest
- Pepper
- Salt

Directions:

1. Preheat the oven to 425 °F/ 220 °C.
2. Spray a baking dish with cooking spray and set it aside.
3. In a small bowl, whisk together olive oil, lemon zest, lemon juice, and garlic.
4. Season fish fillets with pepper and salt and place them in the baking dish.
5. Pour olive oil mixture over fish fillets. Bake fish fillets in the oven for 10-12 minutes.
6. Garnish with parsley and serve.

Nutrition: Calories: 252, Fat: 14.7 g, Carbs: 0.5 g, Sugar: 0.2 g, Protein: 32.2g, Cholesterol: 85 mg.

405. Acorn Squash - Stuffed With Cheese

Preparation time: 5 minutes
Cooking time: 40 minutes
Servings: 2
Ingredients:

- 1 Pound ground turkey breast (extra-lean)
- 3 acorn squash
- 1 can (8 ounces) tomato sauce
- 1 Cup Each:
- Sliced fresh mushrooms
- Chopped onion
- Diced celery
- 1 Tsp. Each:
- Garlic powder
- Basil
- Oregano

Directions

1. 1 pinch black pepper
2. 1/8 tsp. salt
3. 1 cup shredded cheddar cheese (reduced-fat) Directions:
1. Program the oven temperature to 350 °F.
2. Slice the squash in half and remove the seeds. Arrange the squash, cut side down, in a dish, and microwave on high for 20 minutes.
3. Brown the turkey in a skillet and add the onion and celery. Sauté two to three minutes. Blend in the mushrooms, and add the sauce and seasonings. Divide into quarters and spoon into the squash.
4. Cover and bake for 15 minutes.
5. Garnish with the cheese and bake until the cheese has melted.

Nutrition: Calories: 299, Protein: 30 g, Fat: 4 g, Carbs: 38 g.

406. Broccoli Casserole

Preparation time: 1 minute
Cooking time: 20 minutes
Servings: 2
Ingredients:

- 4 cups cut-up broccoli
- Sleeve Ritz crackers
- Cups cheddar cheese

Directions:

1. Add the casserole ingredients into a Pyrex dish with the crumbled crackers on top.
2. Bake long enough to melt the cheese at 375 °F.

Nutrition: Calories: 90.5, Protein: 10.3 g, Carbs: 9.8 g, Fat: 2.3 g.

407. Chickpea and Feta Salad

Preparation time: 7 minutes
Cooking time: 0 minute
Servings: 2
Ingredients:

- ¾ cup chopped raw vegetables
- ¼ Cup Each:
- Can/fresh chickpeas
- Crumbled feta cheese
- Tbsp. lemon juice
- Tbsp. olive oil
- 1 tsp. dried oregano
- Dash Each of:
- Pepper
- Salt

Directions:

1. Use your imagination for the chopped veggies. Include peppers, avocado, tomatoes, onions, and celery or your favorites.
2. Rinse and drain the chickpeas.
3. Combine all of the ingredients and chill in the fridge until ready to serve.

Nutrition: Calories: 285.2, Protein: 10.2 g, Carbs: 22.2 g, Fat: 18.4 g.

408. Eggplant Pesto Mini Pizza

Preparation time: 10 minutes
Cooking time: 45 minutes
Servings: 2
Ingredients:

- 1 Each Chopped:
- Bell pepper
- Tomato
- Eggplant
- 1 medium sliced red onion
- 1/8 tsp. salt
- 3 cloves of garlic
- Pinch of oregano
- ¼ Cup Each:
- Extra-virgin olive oil
- Pesto sauce
- Humus
- Vegan Parmesan cheese
- Sandwich thins — Arnold Or wheat used
- Optional: Pepper flakes

Directions:

1. Set the oven to 400 °F.
2. Chop the vegetables and combine the oil, pepper, salt, oregano, and pepper flakes if desired. Arrange on a baking tin and toast for approximately 30 to 45 minutes or until they are done the way you like them.

3. Toast the buns and spread the hummus on them, add the veggies, and a bit of pesto sauce. Sprinkle with the vegan cheese and enjoy.

Nutrition: Calories: 405, Protein: 11.4 g, Carbs: 40.6 g, Fat: 24.5 g.

409. Lentil Vegetarian Loaf

Preparation time: 5 minutes
Cooking time: 1 hour 30 minutes
Servings: 2
Ingredients:

- ½ cup rinsed — dried lentils
- 1 medium yellow onion
- ½ cup cooked brown rice
- 2 tbsp. canola/olive oil
- ½ cup ketchup
- 1 can tomato paste (6 ounces)
- 1 tsp. Each of:
- Marjoram
- Garlic powder
- Sage
- ½ cup quartered cherry tomatoes
- ¾ cup tomato/pasta sauce
- To Taste:
- Salt
- More ketchup

Directions:

1. Preheat the oven to 350 °F.
2. Rinse and cook the lentils in 3 to 4 cups of water for approximately 30 minutes.
3. Drain and slightly mash the lentils.
4. Peel and chop the onions. Cook in the oil until golden.
5. Combine the onions, lentils, tomato paste, rice, tomatoes, sauce, and spices into a large pot. Mix well.
6. Press the mixture into a well-greased baking dish with ½ cup of ketchup over the top.
7. Bake for one hour.

Nutrition: Calories: 254.2, Protein: 10.9 g, Carbs: 44.9 g, Fat: 4.4 g.

410. Shrimp Spring Rolls

Preparation time: 10 minutes
Cooking time: 25 minutes
Servings: 2
Ingredients:

- ½ cup deveined raw shrimp, chopped & peeled.
- 2 and 1/2 tbsp olive oil
- 1 cup matchstick carrots
- 1 cup slices of red bell pepper
- 1/4 teaspoon red pepper, crushed.
- 3/4 cup slices of snow peas
- 2 cups shredded cabbage.
- 1 tablespoon lime juice
- 1/2 cup sweet chili sauce
- 2 teaspoons fish sauce
- 8 spring rolls (wrappers)

Directions:

1. In a skillet, add one and a half tbsp of olive until smoking lightly.
2. Stir in bell pepper, cabbage, carrots, and cook for two minutes.
3. Turn off the heat, take out in a dish and cool for five minutes.
4. In a bowl, add shrimp, lime juice, cabbage mixture, crushed red pepper, fish sauce, and snow peas. Mix well.
5. Lay spring roll wrappers on a plate. Add 1/4 cup of filling in the middle of each wrapper. Fold tightly with water. Brush the olive oil over folded rolls.
6. Put spring rolls in the air fryer basket and cook for 6 to 7 minutes at 390°F until light brown and crispy. You may serve with sweet chili sauce.

Nutrition: Calories 180 Fat 9g Protein 17g Carbohydrate 9g

411. Scallops with Tomato Cream Sauce

Preparation time: 5 minutes
Cooking time: 10 minutes
Servings: 2
Ingredients:

- 8 sea scallops, jumbo
- 1 tbsp tomato paste
- 1 tbsp chopped fresh basil.
- 3/4 cup of low-fat whipping cream
- ½ tsp kosher salt
- ½ tsp ground freshly black pepper
- 1 tsp minced garlic
- ½ cup frozen spinach, thawed.
- oil spray

Directions:

1. Take a seven-inch pan(heatproof) and add spinach in a single layer at the bottom. Rub olive oil on both sides of scallops, season with kosher salt and pepper.
2. Place the seasoned scallops on top of the spinach. Put the pan in the air fryer and cook for ten minutes at 350F, until scallops are cooked thoroughly, and internal temperature reaches 135F. Serve immediately.

Nutrition: Calories: 259 Carbohydrates: 6g Protein: 19g Fat: 13g

412. Sriracha & Honey Tossed Calamari

Preparation time: 10 minutes
Cooking time: 20 minutes
Servings: 2

Ingredients:

- 1 cup club soda
- 1-2 tbsp sriracha
- 2 cups calamari tubes
- 1 cup flour
- pinches of salt
- ground black pepper
- red pepper flakes
- red pepper
- 1/2 cup honey

Directions:

1. Cut the calamari tubes into rings. Submerge them with club soda.
2. Let it rest for ten minutes. Put freshly ground black pepper, flour, red pepper, kosher salt in a bowl, and mix well.
3. Drain the calamari and pat dry with a paper towel. Coat the calamari well in the flour mix and set aside. Spray oil in the air fryer basket and put calamari in one single layer.
4. Cook at 375 for 11 minutes. Toss the rings twice while cooking.
5. Meanwhile, to make sauce honey, red pepper flakes, and sriracha in a bowl, well.
6. Take calamari out from the basket, mix with sauce cook for another two minutes more. Serve with salad green.

Nutrition: Cal 252 Fat: 38g Carbs: 3.1g Protein: 41g

413. Southern Style Catfish with Green Beans

Preparation time: 10 minutes
Cooking time: 20 minutes
Servings: 2

Ingredients:

- 2 pieces catfish fillets
- ½ cup green beans, trimmed.
- 2 tsp honey
- ground black pepper
- salt
- ½ crushed red pepper.
- ¼ cup flour
- 1 egg, lightly beaten.
- 3/4 teaspoon dill pickle relish
- ½ tsp apple cider vinegar
- 1/3 cup whole-wheat Eggplant crumbs
- 2 tablespoons mayonnaise
- dill
- lemon wedges

Directions:

1. In a bowl, add green beans, spray them with cooking oil. Coat with crushed red pepper, 1/8 teaspoon of kosher salt, and half tsp of honey and cook in the air fryer at 400 F until soft and browned, for 12 minutes. Take out from fryer and cover with aluminum foil.
2. In the meantime, coat catfish in flour. Then dip in egg to coat, then in Eggplant crumbs. Place fish in an air fryer basket and spray with cooking oil.
3. Cook for 8 minutes, at 400°F, until cooked through and golden brown. Sprinkle with pepper and salt. In the meantime, mix vinegar, dill, relish, mayonnaise, and honey in a bowl. Serve the sauce with fish and green beans.

Nutrition: Cal 243 Fat 18 g Carbs 18 g Protein 33 g

414. Roasted Salmon with Fennel Salad

Preparation time: 15 minutes
Cooking time: 10 minutes
Servings: 2

Ingredients:

- 4 salmon fillets, skinless and center-cut
- 1 teaspoon lemon juice, fresh
- 2 teaspoons parsley, chopped.
- 1 teaspoon salt, divided.
- 2 tablespoons olive oil
- 1 teaspoon chopped thyme.
- 4 cups fennel heads thinly sliced.
- 1 clove of minced garlic
- 2 tablespoons fresh dill, chopped.
- 2 tablespoons orange juice, fresh
- 2/3 cup Greek yogurt, reduced fat.

Directions:

1. Mix half a teaspoon of salt, parsley, and thyme in a bowl. Rub oil over salmon, and sprinkle with thyme mixture.
2. Put salmon fillets in the air fryer basket, cook for ten minutes at 350°F. In the meantime, mix garlic, fennel, orange juice, yogurt, half tsp of salt, dill, lemon juice in a bowl. Serve with fennel salad.

Nutrition: Calories 364 Fat 30g Protein 38g Carbohydrate 9g

415. Catfish with Cajun Seasoning

Preparation time: 5 minutes
Cooking time: 20 minutes
Servings: 2

Ingredients:

- 3 teaspoons Cajun seasoning

- 3/4 cup oatmeal
- 4 catfish fillets

Directions:

1. Put Cajun seasoning and oatmeal in a zip lock bag. Wash and pat dry the catfish fillets. Add them to the zip lock bag.
2. Coat well the fillets with seasoning. Put catfish fillets in the air fryer. And cook within 15 minutes at 390 F, turn fillets halfway thorough.
3. To get a golden color on the fillets, cook for more 5 minutes.
4. Serve with lemon wedges and spicy tartar sauce.

Nutrition: Cal 324 Fat: 13.9g Carbohydrates: 15.6g Protein: 26.3g

416. Sushi Roll

Preparation time: 1 hour 30 minutes
Cooking time: 10 minutes
Servings: 2

Ingredients:

For the Kale Salad:

- ½ tsp rice vinegar
- 1 and 1/2 cups chopped kale.
- 1/8 teaspoon garlic powder
- 1 tablespoon sesame seeds
- 3/4 teaspoon toasted sesame oil
- 1/4 teaspoon ground ginger
- 3/4 teaspoon

Soy sauce:

- sushi rolls
- 1/2 avocado, sliced.
- cooked sushi rice cooled.
- ½ cup whole wheat Eggplant crumbs
- 3 sheets of sushi

Directions:

1. In a bowl, add vinegar, garlic powder, kale, soy sauce, sesame oil, and ground ginger. With your hands, mix with sesame seeds and set them aside.
2. Lay a sheet of sushi on a flat surface. With damp fingertips, add a tablespoon of rice, and spread it on the sheet. Cover the sheet with rice leaving a half-inch space at one end.
3. Add kale salad with avocado slices. Roll up the sushi, use water if needed. Add the Eggplant crumbs to a bowl. Coat the sushi roll with Sriracha Mayo, then in Eggplant crumbs.
4. Add the rolls to the air fryer. Cook for ten minutes at 390 F, shake the basket halfway thorough. Take out from the fryer, and let them cool, then cut with a sharp knife. Serve with soy sauce.

Nutrition: Calories: 369 Fat: 13.9g Carbohydrates: 15g Protein: 26.3g

417. Garlic-Lime Shrimp Kebabs

Preparation time: 5 minutes
Cooking time: 18 minutes
Servings: 2

Ingredients:

- 1 lime
- 1 cup raw shrimp
- 1/8 tsp Salt
- 1 clove of garlic
- Freshly ground black pepper

Directions:

1. In water, let wooden skewers soak for 20 minutes. Let the Air fryer preheat to 350F. In a bowl, mix shrimp, minced garlic, lime juice, kosher salt, and pepper. Add shrimp on skewers.
2. Place skewers in the air fryer and cook for 8 minutes. Turn halfway over. Top with cilantro and your favorite dip.

Nutrition: Calories: 76 Carbohydrates: 4g Protein: 13g Fat 9 g

418. Fish Finger Sandwich

Preparation time: 10 minutes
Cooking time: 20 minutes
Servings: 2

Ingredients:

- 1 tbsp Greek yogurt
- 4 cod fillets, without skin
- 2 tbsp flour
- 5 tbsp whole-wheat Eggplant crumbs
- kosher salt and pepper, to taste
- 10-12 capers
- ¾ cup frozen peas
- lemon juice

Directions:

1. Let the air fryer preheat. Sprinkle kosher salt and pepper on the cod fillets, and coat in flour, then in Eggplant crumbs 2. Spray the fryer basket with oil. Put the cod fillets in the basket.
2. Cook for 15 minutes at 200 C. In the meantime, cook the peas in boiling water for a few minutes. Take out from the water and blend with Greek yogurt, lemon juice, and capers until well combined. On a bun, add cooked fish with pea puree. Add lettuce and tomato.

Nutrition: Cal 240 Fat: 12g Carbs: 7g Protein: 20g

419. Healthy Tuna Patties

Preparation time: 15 minutes
Cooking time: 10 minutes
Servings: 1

Ingredients:

- ½ cup whole wheat Eggplant crumbs

- 4 cups fresh tuna, diced.
- lemon zest
- 1 tbsp lemon juice
- 1 egg
- 3 tbsp grated parmesan cheese
- 1 chopped stalk celery
- ½ tsp garlic powder
- ½ tsp dried herbs
- 3 tbsp minced onion
- salt, to taste
- freshly ground black pepper

Directions:
1. In a bowl, add lemon zest, Eggplant crumbs, salt, pepper, celery, eggs,
2. dried herbs, lemon juice, garlic powder, parmesan cheese, and onion. Mix everything.
3. Then add in tuna gently. Shape into patties, and if the mixture is too loose, cool in the refrigerator. Add air fryer baking paper in the air fryer basket. Spray the baking paper with cooking spray.
4. Spray the patties with oil.
5. Cook for ten minutes at 360°F. Turn the patties halfway over.
6. Serve with lemon slices and microgreens.

Nutrition: Cal 214 Fat: 15g Carbs: 6g Protein: 22g

420. Egg planted Air Fried Shrimp with Bang-Bang Sauce

Preparation time: 10 minutes
Cooking time: 20 minutes
Servings: 2
Ingredients:

- 3/4 cup whole wheat Eggplant crumbs
- 4 cups raw Shrimp, deveined, peeled.
- 1 tsp ½ cup flour
- 1 tsp paprika
- chicken seasoning, to taste
- 2 tbsp. of one egg white
- kosher salt and pepper to taste
- Bang-Bang Sauce:
- ¼ cup sweet chili sauce
- 1/3 cup plain Greek yogurt
- 2 tbsp sriracha

Directions:
1. Let the Air Fryer preheat to 400 degrees. Add the seasonings to Shrimp and coat well. In three separate bowls, add flour, Eggplant crumbs, and egg whites.
2. First coat the Shrimp in flour, dab lightly in egg whites, then in the
3. Eggplant crumbs. With cooking oil, spray the Shrimp.

4. Place the Shrimps in an air fryer, cook for four minutes, turn the Shrimp over, and cook for another four minutes. In a small bowl, mix all the bang-bang ingredients. Serve with micro green and bang-bang sauce.

Nutrition: Calories 229 Fat 10g Carbohydrates 13g Protein 22g

421. Crispy Fish Sandwich

Preparation time: 15 minutes
Cooking time: 10 minutes
Servings: 2
Ingredients:

- 2 fillets cod
- 2 tbsp all-purpose flour
- ¼ tsp pepper
- 1 tbsp lemon juice
- ¼ tsp salt
- ½ tsp garlic powder
- 1 egg
- ½ tbsp mayo
- ½ cup whole wheat Eggplant crumbs

Directions:
1. In a bowl, add salt, flour, pepper, and garlic powder. In a separate bowl, add lemon juice, mayo, and egg. In another bowl, add the Eggplant crumbs.
2. Coat the fish in flour, then in egg, then in Eggplant crumbs. With cooking oil, spray the basket and put the fish in the basket.
3. Also, spray the fish with cooking oil. Cook at 400 F for ten minutes. This fish is soft, be careful if you flip.

Nutrition: Cal 218 Carbs:7g Fat:12g Protein: 22g

422. Shrimp Egg Rolls

Preparation time: 20 minutes
Cooking time: 20 minutes
Servings: 2
Ingredients:

- 2-3 cloves of minced garlic
- 12-14 egg roll wrappers
- 2-3 cloves of minced garlic
- 4 cups raw Shrimp, roughly chopped, peeled, and deveined.
- 3 cups coleslaw mix
- 1 ½ tsp sesame oil
- 1 tbsp soy sauce
- 1 tsp fish sauce
- salt, pepper to taste
- ½ tsp grated ginger
- 2 green onions, chopped.
- 1 cup water

Directions:

1. In a skillet, add Shrimp with garlic, kosher salt, and pepper, spray with cooking oil and sauté until Shrimp is pink. Set it aside.
2. In a bowl, add coleslaw mix, cooked Shrimp, green onions, fish sauce, soy sauce, sesame oil, and ginger. Mix well.
3. Add two tbsp of filling to each wrapper, seal tightly with water.
4. With cooking oil, spray the air fryer basket. Put the egg rolls in a single layer in the basket. Spray with cooking oil.
5. Cook for 7 minutes at 400 degrees. Flip the rolls, then cook for 5
6. minutes more. Serve with a microgreen salad.

Nutrition: Calories 228 Fat 11g Carbs 11g Protein 20g

423. Easy Baked Salmon

Preparation Time: 10 Minutes
Cooking Time: 15 Minutes
Servings: 2
Ingredients:

- 4 salmon fillets
- 1 lemon zest
- 1 tsp. sea salt
- 3 oz. olive oil
- 1 garlic clove, minced
- 1 tsp. fresh dill, chopped
- 1 tbsp. fresh parsley, chopped
- 1/8 tsp. white pepper

Directions:

1. Preheat the oven at 200 C.
2. Place all ingredients except salmon fillet in microwave safe bowl and microwave for 45 seconds.
3. Stir well until combine.
4. Place salmon fillets on parchment lined baking dish.
5. Spread evenly olive oil and herb mixture over each salmon fillet.
6. Place in preheated oven and bake for 15 minutes.
7. Serve and enjoy.

Nutrition Net carbs 0.5 g Fiber 3.1 g Fats 30.9 g Sugar 1 g Calories 408

424. Wild Salmon Salad

Preparation Time: 10 Minutes
Cooking Time: 15 Minutes
Servings: 2
Ingredients:

- 2 medium-sized cucumbers, sliced
- A handful of iceberg lettuce, torn
- 1 large tomato, roughly chopped
- 8 oz. smoked wild salmon, sliced

- 4 tbsp. freshly squeezed orange juice

Dressing:

- 1 1/4 cup liquid yogurt, 2% fat
- 1 tbsp. fresh mint, finely chopped
- 2 garlic cloves, crushed
- 1 tbsp. sesame seeds

Directions:

1. Combine vegetables in a large bowl. Drizzle with orange juice and top with salmon slices. Set aside.
2. In another bowl, whisk together yogurt, mint, crushed garlic, and sesame seeds.
3. Drizzle over salad and toss to combine. Serve cold.

Nutrition Net carbs 32.8 g Fiber 3.2 g Fats 11 g Sugar 2 g Calories 249

425. Herbed Salmon

Preparation Time: 10 Minutes
Cooking Time: 15 Minutes
Servings: 2
Ingredients:

- 2 salmon fillets
- 1/2 teaspoon onion powder
- 1/2 teaspoon garlic powder
- Salt and freshly ground black pepper
- 1 tablespoon olive oil
- 1 can diced tomatoes
- 1 teaspoon Italian herb seasoning
- 2 tablespoons finely grated Parmesan cheese

Directions:

1. Warmth a medium nonstick skillet over medium heat. Brush salmon fillets with olive oil, sprinkle with onion and garlic powder and season to taste with salt and pepper. Sear fillets until browned on both sides, turning as necessary, 3 to 4 minutes 2. Pour undrained tomatoes over salmon fillets, sprinkle with herb seasoning and season to taste with salt and pepper. Heat to a boil, then reduce heat, cover and simmer until salmon is cooked through, 6 to 8 minutes.
2. Transfer salmon with sauce onto plates and sprinkle with Parmesan cheese to serve.
3. Enjoy!

Nutrition Net carbs 7 g Fiber 2 g Fats 10 g Sugar 1 g Calories 227

426. Slowly Roasted Pesto Salmon

Preparation Time: 10 Minutes
Cooking Time: 20 Minutes
Servings: 2
Ingredients:

- 4 salmon fillets
- 1 teaspoon extra-virgin olive oil
- 4 tablespoons basil pesto

Directions

1. Pre-heat your oven to 275 degrees F.
2. Set a rimmed baking sheet with foil and brush with olive oil.
3. Transfer salmon fillets skin-side down on a baking sheet and spread 1 tablespoon pesto on each fillet.
4. Roast for 20 minutes.
5. Serve and enjoy!

Nutrition: Net carbs 1 g Fiber 2 g Fats 10 g Sugar 3 g Calories 182

427. Grilled Lemon Shrimps

Preparation Time: 1 hour
Cooking Time: 15 Minutes
Servings: 2

Ingredients:

- 1 lb. fresh shrimps, cleaned
- 1 tbsp. fresh rosemary
- 4 tbsp. extra-virgin olive oil
- 1 tsp. garlic powder
- 2 tbsp. lemon juice, freshly squeezed
- 1/2 tsp. salt
- 1/2 tsp. black pepper, freshly ground
- 1/2 tsp. dried thyme, ground
- 1/2 tsp. dried oregano, ground
- 1 organic lemon, sliced into wedges

Directions:

1. Combine olive oil, garlic, lemon juice, salt, pepper, thyme, and oregano in a medium bowl and mix until well incorporated. Place the shrimp and coat evenly with the marinade mixture. Cover the bowl and chill for at least 1 hour to marinate the shrimps.
2. Preheat the grill to a medium-high temperature. Brush the grill grids with some oil.
3. Insert 2 to 3 shrimps on each skewer, brush with marinade and grill for 3 minutes. Set and grill the other side for another 3 minutes. Transfer to a serving platter.
4. Serve warm with lemons wedges and sprinkle with chopped parsley.

Nutrition Net carbs 6.2 g Fiber 2 g Fats 21.6 g Sugar 3 g Calories 357

428. Marinated Tuna

Preparation Time: 2 hours 10 Minutes
Cooking Time: 15 Minutes
Servings: 2

Ingredients:

- 2 lbs. tuna steaks, boneless
- 1/4 cup fresh coriander, chopped
- 2 garlic cloves, minced
- 2 tablespoons lemon juice

- 1 cup olive oil
- 1/2 tsp. smoked paprika
- 1/2 tsp. cumin, ground
- 1/2 tsp. chili pepper, ground
- 1/2 tsp. salt
- 1/4 tsp. black pepper, ground

Directions:

1. Add the coriander, garlic, paprika, cumin, chili and lemon juice in a food processor and pulse to combine. Gradually add in the oil and mix the ingredients until a smooth mixture.
2. Transfer the mixture into a bowl, add the fish and gently toss to coat the fish evenly with sauce. Chill for at least 2 hours to allow the flavors to penetrate into the fish.
3. Remove the fish from the chiller and preheat the grill. Lightly brush the grid with oil, place the fish on the grid, and grill for about 3 to 4 minutes on each side.
4. Remove the fish from the grill, transfer to a serving plate and serve with lemon wedges or some vegetables.

Nutrition Net carbs 0.7 g Fiber 1 g Fats 11.9 g Sugar 4 g Calories 303

429. Broiled White Fish Parmesan

Preparation Time: 10 Minutes
Cooking Time: 15 Minutes
Servings: 2

Ingredients:

- 3 ounces, Codfish
- 1/4 cup, Parmesan cheese, grated
- 2 tablespoons, Light margarine, softened
- 1/8 teaspoon, Garlic salt
- 1/8 teaspoon, Ground black pepper
- 1 tablespoon, Lemon juice
- 1 tablespoon and 11/2 teaspoons, Mayonnaise
- 1/8 teaspoon, Dried basil
- 1/8teaspoon, Onion powder
- Cooking spray

Directions:

1. Set the grill on high temperature and preheat before start cooking.
2. Grease the broiling pot with cooking spray.
3. Combine butter, Parmesan cheese, lemon juice and mayonnaise.
4. Season it with pepper, onion powder, dried basil, and garlic salt.
5. Mix it well and keep ready to use.
6. Layer the fillets on the broiler pan and broil for 2-3 minutes.
7. Set it and cook for another 2-3 minutes.
8. Remove the baked fillets from the grill onto a plate and transfer the Parmesan mixture over it.

9. Again, broil it for a couple of minutes until the topping becomes brown.
10. Serve hot, when the flakes can easily remove.

Nutrition: Net carbs 1 g Fiber 1 g Fats 8.2 g Sugar 2 g Calories 197.1 g

430. Grilled Mediterranean Ahi Tuna

Preparation Time: 10 Minutes
Cooking Time: 15 Minutes
Servings: 2
Ingredients:

- 41/2 ounces, Ahi tuna steaks, Fresh
- 1 tablespoon, Extra virgin olive oil
- 1/2 teaspoon Salt
- 1/2 teaspoon, Lemon juice
- 1/4 teaspoon, Cracked black pepper
- 1/2 teaspoon, Oregano, finely chopped
- 1/4 teaspoon, Red pepper, ground
- 1 teaspoon, Basil, finely chopped
- 1 clove Garlic, finely minced

Directions:

1. Set the charcoal grill on high heat for 30 minutes before you start grilling the tuna steak.
2. Wash and clean the tuna.
3. Pat dry before marinating and put in a shallow bowl.
4. In a small bowl mix all the spices with oil and lemon juice.
5. Allow the mixture to have a rest for 5 minutes so that everything blends well. If you are sensitive to spices, use a fork/spoon to mix the spices.
6. Now, marinate the tuna steaks applying the mixture with a brush.
7. Allow it to settle for 5 minutes.
8. Grill all the steaks on a hot grill at least for 3-5 minutes for both sides to get the desired result.
9. When the fish grilled well, it will turn to pinkish at the center.
10. Don't overcook.

Nutrition: Net carbs 0.5 g Fiber 0.1 g Fats 5.3 g Sugar 4 g Calories 229.2

431. Herb-Crusted Salmon Fillets

Preparation Time: 10 Minutes
Cooking Time: 10 Minutes
Servings: 2
Ingredients:

- 16 ounces, Atlantic salmon
- 2 tablespoons, Chives, roughly chopped
- 2 tablespoons, Parsley, chopped
- 1 cup, Eggplant crumbs, whole-grain
- 1/2 teaspoon, Garlic powder
- 1/2 teaspoon, Onion powder
- 1 teaspoon, Lemon peel, grated

- 1/4 cup, Lemon juice
- 1/4 teaspoon, Salt
- 1/2 teaspoon, Pepper
- Cooking spray.

Directions

1. Preheat the oven on high heat at 400F.
2. Line the baking tray with a baking paper and spray some cooking oil.
3. Season the salmon fillets with pepper and salt.
4. Place the salmon on the baking tray, skin side down facing the baking liner.
5. Put all the ingredients except lemon juice in mixer bowl.
6. Combine well until it becomes a smooth mix.
7. Drizzle some lemon juice on the salmon fillets and spread the Eggplant crumb mixture over the salmon fillets.
8. Spray evenly with cooking spray, and bake it at least for 10 - 15
9. minutes.
10. Serve hot.

Nutrition: Net carbs 7.2 g Fiber 1.1 g Fats 14.4 g Sugar 2 g Calories 259.5

432. Honey and Soy Glazed Salmon

Preparation Time: 10 Minutes
Cooking Time: 7 Minutes
Servings: 2
Ingredients:

- 2 filets, Salmon
- 2 tablespoons, Honey
- 11/2 tablespoons, Lime juice
- 2 tablespoons, Soy sauce, low sodium
- 2 tablespoons, Vegetable oil
- 2 teaspoons, Mustard
- 1 tablespoon, Water

Directions

1. In a medium bowl, set honey, soy sauce, mustard, lime juice, and water.
2. Pour vegetable oil into a non-stick skillet and bring to high heat.
3. Roast the filets at least for 2 to 3 minutes and flip sides and continue roasting for another 2-3 minutes, until it becomes brown.
4. Transfer filets into a serving plate.
5. Add some honey glaze to the skillet and heat for one minute.
6. Pour the honey glaze over salmon and serve hot.

Nutrition: Net carbs 21.3 g Fiber 0.7 g Fats 11.2 g Sugar 2 g Calories 277.3 g

433. Lemon Garlic Tilapia

Preparation Time: 10 Minutes
Cooking Time: 30 Minutes
Servings: 2
Ingredients:

- 4 fillets, Tilapia
- 1 tablespoon, Olive oil
- 1 tablespoon, Margarine
- 1 tablespoon, Lemon juice
- 1/4 teaspoon, Salt
- 1 teaspoon, Garlic salt
- 1 teaspoon, Parsley flakes, dried
- 1/4 teaspoon, Cayenne pepper
- Cooking spray

Directions:

1. Set the temperature of the oven at 400F and start preheating.
2. Spray nonstick cooking oil onto the baking tray.
3. Put the butter into a nonstick saucepan and melt it on low-medium heat.
4. Add some lemon juice, salt, olive oil, garlic powder, and parsley into it and sauté for 3-4 minutes.
5. Place the tilapia fillets in the baking tray and pour the preparation on the top of the fillets.
6. Now sprinkle some cayenne pepper on the fish.
7. Put in the oven and bake for about 12-13 minutes.
8. Flip sides and cook it for extra time.
9. Serve hot

Nutrition: Net carbs 1.8 g Fiber 0.3 g Fats 7.3 g Sugar 3 g Calories 175.2

434. Lime Shrimp

Preparation Time: 10 Minutes
Cooking Time: 10 Minutes
Servings: 2
Ingredients:

- 28 Shrimps, ready to cook
- 1 tablespoon, Lime juice
- 1/8 teaspoon, Salt
- 3/4 teaspoon, Black pepper
- 2 tablespoons, Chopped onion
- Cooking spray

Directions:

1. Spray some cooking oil into the skillet.
2. Bring the skillet to medium heat.
3. When the skillet becomes hot, put all the ingredients and sauté occasionally until the onions and shrimps get cooked well.
4. Serve hot

Nutrition: Net carbs 2.2 g Fiber 0.4 g Fats 0.9 g Sugar 1 g

435. Shrimp Gazpacho-Style Soup

Preparation Time: 10 Minutes
Cooking Time: 15 Minutes
Servings: 2
Ingredients:

- 1 tablespoon extra-virgin olive oil
- 1 cup chopped yellow onion
- 1/2 cup diced bell pepper
- 3 cups chopped tomato
- 4 teaspoons freshly squeezed lemon juice
- 1/2 teaspoon salt
- 11/2 cups cooked shrimp

Directions:

1. Coat a medium skillet with the oil and heat over medium heat.
2. Add the onion and pepper, and cook for 5 to 7 minutes, stirring occasionally, until the onion is slightly translucent.
3. Add the cooked onion and pepper, tomato, lemon juice, and salt to a blender. Blend for 1 to 2 minutes on high or until mixture is smooth.
4. Pour the soup into a bowl and add the shrimp. Enjoy.

Nutrition: Calories: 109 Protein: 11g Fat: 4g Carbohydrates: 9g Fiber: 3g Sugar: 7g Sodium: 484mg

436. Shrimp Cauliflower Chowder

Preparation Time: 10 Minutes
Cooking Time: 25 Minutes
Servings: 2
Ingredients:

- 1 tablespoon extra-virgin olive oil
- 1 cup diced yellow onion
- 1 cup cauliflower rice
- 1/2 cup water - 1/4 teaspoon salt
- 1/2 cup unsweetened light canned coconut milk
- 1/2 unsweetened almond milk
- 4 tablespoons nutritional yeast
- Dash freshly ground black pepper
- 11/2 cups peeled raw small salad shrimp

Directions

1. In a medium saucepan, warm the oil over medium heat. Cook the onion stirring frequently, or until the onion is slightly translucent.
2. Add the cauliflower rice, water, and salt. Cook for 6 to 8 minutes, stirring occasionally, until cauliflower is softened and the water is absorbed.
3. Add the coconut milk, almond milk, nutritional yeast, and pepper to the pot and stir well. Simmer on low-to-medium heat for 1 to 2
4. minutes. Remove from heat.

5. Pour the mixture into a blender and blend for 1 to 2 minutes on low until the mixture is smooth.

6. Pour the mixture back into the pot and add the shrimp. Simmer on low to medium heat for 5 to 7 minutes, until the shrimp are pink and cooked through. Remove from heat and serve.

Nutrition Calories: 133 Protein: 14g Fat: 6g Carbohydrates: 6g Fiber: 3g Sugar: 3g Sodium: 358mg

437. Shrimp Toast–Style Low-Carb Seafood Cakes

Preparation Time: 10 Minutes
Cooking Time: 15 Minutes
Servings: 2
Ingredients:

- 1/2 cup canned baby shrimp
- 4 tablespoons almond flour
- 2 tablespoons coconut aminos, plus more for dipping 2 tablespoons unsweetened almond milk
- 2 tablespoons light unsweetened canned coconut milk 1 large egg
- 1/2 teaspoon garlic powder
- 1/2 teaspoon ginger powder
- 1/2 teaspoon chopped parsley or dried
- 1/4 teaspoon salt
- 1 tablespoon extra-virgin olive oil
- 1/3 cup finely diced yellow onion
- Nonstick cooking spray (optional)

Directions:

1. In a large mixing bowl, merge the shrimp, almond flour, coconut aminos, almond milk, coconut milk, egg, garlic powder, ginger powder, parsley, and salt. Mix well and set aside.

2. In a medium skillet, warmth the oil over medium heat. Cook the onion for about 5 minutes or until slightly translucent. Detach from the heat and add to the shrimp mixture. Incorporate well.

3. Scoop a heaping tablespoon or two of the shrimp mixture into the same skillet and flatten with the back of a spoon. Repeat with the remaining shrimp mixture to make 8 cakes.

4. Cook the shrimp cakes for 3 to 4 minutes on each side, or until each side is a little more than golden brown, working in batches if needed. If the cakes stick to the skillet, spray lightly with cooking spray to prevent sticking.

5. Remove the cakes from the heat and enjoy with additional coconut aminos on the side for dipping.

Nutrition: Calories: 124 Protein: 7g Fat: 9g Carbohydrates: 5g Fiber: 1g Sugar: 2g Sodium: 445mg

438. Roasted Vegetable and Shrimp Salad

Preparation Time: 10 Minutes
Cooking Time: 20 Minutes
Servings: 2
Ingredients:

- Nonstick cooking spray
- 1/4 cup diced yellow or red onion
- 1/4 cup diced bell pepper
- 2 teaspoons extra-virgin olive oil, divided
- 11/2 cups canned baby shrimp
- 2 tablespoons nonfat plain Greek yogurt
- 1 teaspoon apple cider vinegar
- 1/2 teaspoon garlic powder
- 1/2 teaspoon ground cumin

Directions:

1. Preheat the oven to 400F. Set a baking sheet with parchment paper or aluminum foil and spray with nonstick cooking spray.

2. Arrange the onion and pepper on the baking sheet and drizzle with 1 tablespoon of oil. Toss the vegetables with the oil and coat well.

3. Bake for about 20 minutes, until all the vegetables are softened and lightly browned. Remove from heat.

4. In a large mixing bowl, merge the onion and pepper with the shrimp, yogurt, remaining oil, vinegar, garlic powder, and cumin.

5. Serve warm or chill in the refrigerator before serving.

Nutrition: Calories: 71 Protein: 10g Fat: 3g Carbohydrates: 2 Fiber: 1g Sugar: 1g Sodium: 189mg

439. Tuna Noodle-Less Casserole

Preparation Time: 15 minutes
Cooking Time: 40 minutes
Servings: 1
Ingredients:

- Nonstick cooking spray
- 1 medium red onion, chopped
- 1 red bell pepper, chopped
- 1½ cups diced tomato
- 3 cups fresh green beans
- ⅓ cup olive oil-based mayonnaise
- 1 (14.5-ounce) can condensed cream of mushroom soup ½ cup low-fat milk
- 1 cup shredded Cheddar cheese
- ½ teaspoon freshly ground black pepper
- 8 (5-ounce) cans water-packed albacore tuna, drained

Directions:

1. Preheat the oven to 425°F.

2. Coat a large skillet with the cooking spray and place it over medium heat. Add the onion, red bell pepper, and tomatoes and sauté for about 5 minutes, or until the vegetables are tender and the tomatoes start to soften. Remove the skillet from the heat and set aside.

3. Cut off the stem ends of the green beans, and snap them into 3- to 4-inch pieces.

4. Fill a large saucepot ⅓ full with water, and place a steamer basket inside. Place the pot over high heat, and bring the water to a boil.

5. Add the green beans to the steamer basket, cover the pot, and reduce the heat to medium. Steam the green beans for 5 minutes.

6. Immediately remove them from the heat, drain, and set aside.

7. Coat a 9-by-13-inch baking dish with the cooking spray.

8. In a large bowl, mix together the mayonnaise, condensed soup, milk, and cheese. Season the mixture with the black pepper.

9. Add the tuna, green beans, and sautéed vegetables to the bowl, and mix to combine. Pour the mixture into the baking dish.

10. Serve after baking for 30 minutes and brown.

11. Cooking tip: It's easy to shake up this standby recipe. To boost protein and reduce fat, add ½ cup of nonfat cottage cheese and reduce the mayonnaise to 2 tablespoons. Use an immersion blender to puree until smooth. To change the flavor profile, first sauté the diced tomatoes in 1 teaspoon of extra-virgin olive oil for 5 minutes before cooking the rest of the vegetables.

12. Set the sautéed tomatoes aside and mix them in with the tuna. Then follow the rest of directions to put together the casserole. The tomatoes become almost like sun-dried and help attenuate some of the fishiness of the tuna.

Nutrition: Per Serving (1 cup): Calories: 147 Total fat: 7g Protein: 15g Carbs: 6g Fiber: 2gSugar: 2g Sodium: 318mg

440. Slow-Roasted Pesto Salmon

Preparation Time: 5 minutes
Cooking Time: 20 minutes
Servings: 2

Ingredients:

- 4 (6-ounce) salmon fillets
- 1 teaspoon extra-virgin olive oil
- 4 tablespoons Perfect Basil Pesto

Directions:

1. Preheat the oven to 275°F. Brush the foil with the olive oil.

2. Place the salmon fillets skin-side down on the baking sheet.

3. Spread 1 tablespoon of pesto on each fillet.

4. Roast the salmon for about 20 minutes, or just until opaque in the center.

5. Serve immediately.

6. Cooking tip: Enjoy a gourmet meal any night of the week by keeping a bag of freshly frozen wild Alaskan salmon fillets on hand. Look for the kind that are perfectly portioned into individual fillets for easy meal prep—just thaw in the fridge a day or two before needed.

Nutrition Calories: 182 Total fat: 10g Protein: 20g Carbs: 1g Fiber: 0g Sugar: 0g Sodium: 90mg

CHAPTER 25:

Snack

441. Cannellini Bean and Bell Pepper Burger

Preparation time: 15 minutes
Cooking time: 35 minutes
Servings: 2

Ingredients:

- ¾ cup quinoa
- 1½ cups water
- 2 (15-ounce / 425-g) cans cannellini beans, rinsed and drained ½ cup ground flaxseeds
- 1 cup walnuts, finely chopped
- 1 tablespoon ground cumin
- 3 tablespoons Italian seasoning
- 1 tablespoon minced garlic
- 2 tablespoons almond butter
- 1 teaspoon salt (optional)
- ½ teaspoon freshly ground black pepper
- 3 tablespoons Dijon mustard
- 1½ tablespoons avocado oil (optional)
- 4 to 5 large red bell peppers cut into thirds

Topping:

- 1 cucumber, sliced
- 2 to 3 tomatoes, sliced
- ½ small red onion, sliced

Directions:

1. In a saucepan, combine the quinoa and water. Bring to a boil over high heat, then cover and reduce heat to medium-low. Simmer for 20
1. minutes or until all the water has absorbed. Set aside.
2. On a large cutting board, spread out the beans. Pat dry with paper towels. Then press down firmly with the beans between the paper
3. towel and cutting board, using your knuckles to mash them. When you remove the paper towel, you should have a layer of semi-smashed beans. Using a chef's knife, chop the beans a little bit more, leaving a few larger chunks.
4. Transfer the mashed beans to a medium bowl. Add the cooked quinoa, flaxseeds, walnuts, cumin, Italian seasoning, garlic, almond butter, salt (if desired), pepper, and mustard. Mix until well combined.

5. Dip your fingers in water to prevent the burger mixture from sticking and form 12 burger patties.
6. In a nonstick skillet, heat ½ tablespoon olive oil (if desired) over medium heat. Once hot, add 4 patties. Cook for 3 minutes, then flip to the other side and cook for 3 minutes more.
7. To serve, cutting bell peppers into thirds and sandwiching a burger patty between two pieces of pepper. Top with sliced cucumber, tomatoes, and onion.

Nutrition: Calories: 304 fat: 16.1g carbs: 27.9g protein: 12.2g fiber: 11.8g

442. Oil-Free Mushroom and Tofu Burritos

Preparation time: 15 minutes
Cooking time: 28 to 45 minutes
Servings: 2

Ingredients:

- 1½ cups shiitake mushrooms, stemmed and sliced
- 2 large leeks, white and light green parts only, diced 1 medium red bell pepper, diced
- 3 cloves garlic, minced
- 3 tablespoons nutritional yeast
- 2 tablespoons low-sodium soy sauce
- 2 teaspoons ground coriander
- 2 teaspoons turmeric
- 2 teaspoons ground cumin
- Black pepper, to taste
- 1 pound (454 g) lite firm tofu, pressed and mashed ½ cup chopped cilantro
- 4 whole-wheat tortillas
- 1 cup salsa

Directions

1. Preheat the oven to 350°F (180°C). Line a baking pan with the parchment paper.
1. Add the mushrooms, leeks and red bell pepper to a saucepan over medium-high heat. Sauté for 8 to 10 minutes, or until the vegetables are softened.

2. Add the garlic, nutritional yeast, soy sauce, coriander, turmeric, cumin and black pepper to the saucepan. Reduce the heat to medium-low. Sauté for 5 minutes. Stir in the tofu mash.

3. Spread the mixture in an even layer in the prepared pan. Bake for 25

4. to 30 minutes. Transfer the mixture to a large bowl and mix with the cilantro to combine well.

5. On a clean work surface, lay the tortillas. Spoon the mixture into the tortillas and spread all over. Drizzle the salsa over the filling. Roll up the tortillas tightly.

6. Serve immediately.

Nutrition: Calories: 411 | fat: 15.1g | carbs: 48.9g | protein: 28.1g | fiber: 12.4g

443. Tempeh and Vegetable Wraps

Preparation time: 10 minutes
Cooking time: 16 minutes
Servings: 2

Ingredients:

- 1 pound (454 g) tempeh
- 1 cup water
- ¼ cup maple syrup (optional)
- 2 teaspoons extra-virgin olive oil (optional)
- 1 teaspoon low-sodium soy sauce
- 1 teaspoon ground cayenne pepper
- ⅛ Teaspoon liquid smoke
- Cooking spray (optional)
- 4 whole-wheat tortillas
- 2 large tomatoes cut into 8 slices total
- 8 lettuce leaves
- ½ cup almond butter

Directions:

1. Heat the water in a pot over medium heat and bring to a boil. Put a steam basket in the pot and place the tempeh in the basket.

2. Cover and steam for 10 minutes. Transfer the tempeh to a plate and let rest for 5 minutes. Slice into 16 strips. Set aside.

3. Stir together the maple syrup (if desired), olive oil (if desired), soy sauce, cayenne pepper and liquid smoke in a small bowl.

4. Spritz a pan over medium-high heat with cooking spray. Place the tempeh slices in the pan. Spread the sauce over the tempeh and cook for 6 minutes, flipping halfway through. Transfer the tempeh back to the plate.

1. On a clean work surface, lay the tortillas. Place 4 tempeh slices, tomato slices, 2 lettuce leaves and 2 tablespoons of almond butter on each tortilla. Roll up tightly and serve.

Nutrition: Calories: 433 fat: 22.8g carbs: 40.9g protein: 23.2g fiber: 3.1g

444. Sumptuous Black and Veggie Tacos

Preparation time: 15 minutes
Cooking time: 10 minutes
Servings: 2

Ingredients:

- 2 (15-ounce / 425-g) cans black beans, drained and rinsed ¼ cup ground flaxseeds
- 1 teaspoon paprika
- 1 teaspoon dried oregano
- 1 teaspoon ground cumin
- 1 teaspoon salt (optional)
- 1 teaspoon freshly ground black pepper
- 1 tablespoon coconut oil (optional)
- 1 medium tomato, diced (about 7 ounces / 198 g in total) ¼ cup chopped cilantro
- ½ yellow onion, diced (about 3½ ounces / 99 g in total) 3 romaine lettuce leaves, sliced into thin ribbons 2 avocados, sliced
- 4 lime wedges

Directions:

1. Pour the black beans in a food processor, then pulse to mash the beans until chunky.

2. Sprinkle the flaxseeds, paprika, oregano, cumin, salt (if desired), and ground black pepper over the mashed beans, then pulse to mix thoroughly.

3. Heat the coconut oil (if desired) in a skillet over medium heat.

4. Add the bean mixture to a single layer in the skillet and level with a spatula. Cook for 2 minutes or until the bottom of the mixture starts to brown. Flip the mixture and cook for 2 minutes to brown the other

2. side. Turn off the heat and allow to cool.

5. Unfold the tortillas among 4 plates, then divide the cooked bean mixture, tomato, cilantro, onion, lettuce, and avocado over the tortillas. Squeeze the lime wedges over and serve immediately.

Nutrition: Calories: 578 fat: 22.0g carbs: 75.0g protein: 20.0g fiber: 20.0g

445. Refried Bean Taquitos

Preparation time: 5 minutes
Cooking time: 21 to 22 minutes
Servings: 2

Ingredients:

- 2 cups pinto beans, cooked
- 1 teaspoon chili powder
- 1 teaspoon ground cumin
- ½ teaspoon garlic powder
- ½ teaspoon onion powder
- ¼ teaspoon red pepper flakes

- 12 tortillas

Directions:

1. Preheat the oven to 400°F (205°C). Line a baking pan with the parchment paper.
2. In a blender, combine all the ingredients, except for the tortillas, and blend until creamy and smooth.
3. Arrange the tortillas in the baking pan and bake for 1 to 2 minutes, or until softened and pliable.
4. Transfer the tortillas to a clean work surface. Spoon the mashed beans into the center of each tortilla and spread over. Roll up tightly and secure with toothpicks.
5. Arrange the stuffed tortillas in the baking pan and bake for 20
6. minutes, or until golden brown and crispy, flipping halfway through.
7. Let rest for 5 minutes before serving.

Nutrition: Calories: 285 fat: 13.1g carbs: 5.8g protein: 12.2g fiber: 12.9g

446. Avocado and Dulse Pitas

Preparation time: 15 minutes
Cooking time: 10 minutes
Servings: 2
Ingredients:

- 2 teaspoons coconut oil (optional)
- ½ cup dulse
- ¼ teaspoon liquid smoke
- Salt and ground black pepper, to taste (optional) 2 avocados, sliced
- ¼ cup chopped cilantro
- 2 scallions, white and light green parts, sliced 2 tablespoons lime juice
- 4 (8-inch) whole wheat pitas, sliced in half
- 4 cups chopped romaine
- 4 plum tomatoes, sliced

Directions:

1. Heat the coconut oil (if desired) in a skillet over medium heat.
2. Add the dulse and drizzle with liquid smoke. Cook for 5 minutes or until crispy. Stir constantly. Turn off the heat and sprinkle with ground black pepper. Transfer on a plate and set aside.
3. Put the avocado, cilantro, and scallions in a food processor, then drizzle with lime juice and sprinkle with salt (if desired) and ground black pepper. Pulse to combine well and mash the avocado.
4. Toast the pita halves in the skillet for 4 minutes or until lightly browned on both sides. Set aside until cool enough to handle.
5. Stuff the pita halves with the avocado mixture, romaine, plum tomatoes, and crispy dulse. Serve immediately.

Nutrition: Calories: 434 fat: 18.9g carbs: 61.0g protein: 9.6g fiber: 13.5g

447. Creamy Cauliflower Chipotle Spread

Preparation time: 10 minutes
Cooking time: 20 minutes
Servings: Makes 1 cup 1½ cups cauliflower florets
Ingredients:

- 2 chipotle peppers in adobo sauce
- ½ cup low-sodium vegetable soup
- Sea salt and black pepper, to taste (optional)
- 3 shallots, minced
- 2 cloves garlic, minced
- ¼ cup dry white wine

Directions:

1. Cook the cauliflower in a steamer for 10 minutes or until soft.
2. Transfer the cauliflower in a food processor. Add the chipotle peppers, then pour in the vegetable soup and sprinkle with salt (if desired). Pulse to purée until creamy and smooth. Set aside.
3. Add the shallots in a skillet and sauté over medium heat for 5
1. minutes or until translucent.
4. Add the garlic and sauté for 1 more minute or until fragrant.
5. Pour the wine in the skillet and cook until the liquid is almost absorbed.
6. Reduce the heat to medium-low and pour in the puréed cauliflower and chipotle peppers. Cover and simmer for 5 minutes until it becomes thick. Stir occasionally.
7. Smear on the fillings of the tortillas or pitas to serve.

Nutrition: Calories: 235 fat: 1.8g carbs: 39.7g protein: 8.8g fiber: 8.2g

448. Coriander Mushroom Wraps

Preparation time: 10 minutes
Cooking time: 5 minutes
Servings: 2
Ingredients:

- ½ cup Spicy Cilantro Pesto or Coriander Chutney
- 8 romaine lettuce leaves
- 2 cups cooked brown rice
- batch Grilled Portobello Mushrooms, cut into ¾-inch-wide strips

Directions:

1. Spread 1 tablespoon of the pesto in the bottom of one of the lettuce leaves and top with ¼ cup of the rice and about half of a grilled mushroom.
2. Roll the lettuce leaf up around the filling. Repeat for the remaining lettuce leaves

Nutrition: Calories: 115 fat: 1.39g carbs: 21.92g protein: 6.21

449. Brown Rice Lettuce Wraps

Preparation time: 10 minutes
Cooking time: 5 minutes
Servings: 2

Ingredients

- 1 batch Cauliflower Samosa Filling
- 8 romaine lettuce leaves
- 3 cups cooked brown rice
- Coriander Chutney

Ingredients:

1. Place some of the samosa filling on the bottom of one of the lettuce leaves. Top with some brown rice and a spoonful of the coriander chutney.
2. Roll the leaf up around the filling. Repeat for the remaining lettuce leaves.

Nutrition: Calories: 284 fat: 0.33g carbs: 64.46g protein: 7.45

450. Guacamole Lettuce Wraps

Preparation time: 10 minutes
Cooking time: 0 minutes
Servings: 2

Ingredients

- 1 batch Black Beans and Rice
- 1 large head romaine lettuce leaves separated
- 1 batch Not-So-Fat Guacamole

Directions:

1. Place some of the black beans and rice into the center of one of the lettuce leaves. Top with some of the guacamole.
2. Fold the leaf in from the sides and roll it up like a cigar.
3. Repeat for any remaining lettuce leaves until the beans and rice and guacamole are used up.

Nutrition: Calories: 3586 fat: 357.09g carbs: 19.04g protein: 77.51g

451. Tomato Salad Lettuce Wraps

Preparation time: 10 minutes
Cooking time: 5 minutes
Servings: 2

Ingredients:

- 1½ cups Fava Bean Spread
- 8 romaine lettuce leaves

- 1 batch Tomato, Cucumber and Mint Salad

Directions:

1. Place some of the fava bean spread in the center of one of the lettuce leaves. Top with some of the tomato salad.
2. Fold the leaf in from the sides and roll it up like a cigar.
3. Repeat for the remaining lettuce leaves.

Nutrition: Calories: 789 | fat: 3.69g | carbs: 135.94g | protein: 59.85g

452. Onion Mushroom Wraps

Preparation time: 10 minutes
Cooking time: 5 minutes
Servings: 2

Ingredients:

- 1 tbsp grated ginger
- 2 cloves garlic, peeled and minced
- Zest and juice of 1 lime
- 3 tablespoons low-sodium soy sauce
- 1 tsp crushed red pepper flakes
- 2 big shallots, diced small
- 1 pound Portobello mushrooms, stemmed and finely chopped ½ cup coarsely chopped cilantro
- 2 tbsp finely chopped mint
- 4 green onions (white and green parts), thinly sliced 4 large romaine lettuce leaves or 8 small ones

Directions:

1. Set aside a small bowl containing the ginger, garlic, lime zest and juice, soy sauce, and crushed red pepper flakes.
2. In a large skillet, heat the oil over high heat. Stir in the shallots and mushrooms for 3 to 4 minutes.
3. To avoid the vegetables from sticking to the pan, add 1 to 2 teaspoons of water at a time.
4. Cook for another minute after adding the ginger mixture. Remove from the fire and stir in the cilantro, mint, and green onions.
5. Place some of the mushroom mixture on the bottom of a lettuce leaf and fold the lettuce over the filling to serve. Continue with the remaining lettuce leaves.

Nutrition: Calories: 3225 fat: 62.15g carbs: 541.15g protein: 206.58g

453. Lime Bean Artichoke Wraps

Preparation Time: 10 minutes.
Cooking Time: 10 minutes.
Servings: 2

Ingredients:

- Lima bean spread
- 1 cup cooked baby lima beans

- 2 tablespoons nutritional yeast
- 2 tablespoons parsley, chopped
- ½ teaspoon garlic, minced ½ teaspoon onion powder
- 2 teaspoons fresh lime juice
- 2 teaspoons white balsamic vinegar
- Wraps
- 2 gluten-free vegan wraps
- 1 cup raw broccoli, sliced lengthwise
- 2 whole hearts of palm, sliced lengthwise

Direction:
1. Blend lime beans with yeast, parsley, garlic, onion powder, lime juice and vinegar in a blender until smooth.
2. Spread the beans mixture on top of the wraps and top them with broccoli and hearts of palm.
3. Roll the wraps like a burrito and cut in half.
4. Grill the wraps in the grill over high heat for 5 minutes per side.
5. Serve.

Serving Suggestion: Serve the wraps with roasted veggies on the side.
Variation Tip: Add chopped spinach to filling.
Nutrition: Calories 324 Fat 1g Sodium 236mg Carbs 42g Fiber 0.3g Sugar 0.1g Protein 1

454. Butternut Squash Lasagna

Preparation Time: 10 minutes.
Cooking Time: 1 hour 40 minutes.
Servings: 2
Ingredients:
- 2 tablespoons olive oil
- 2 pounds butternut squash, cubed
- ½ cup water
- 4 amaretti cookies, crumbled
- 8 ounces shiitake mushrooms, sliced
- ¼ cup butter
- ¼ cup whole-wheat flour
- 3½ cups almond milk
- ½ teaspoon ground nutmeg
- 1 cup fresh basil leaves
- 13 ounces DeLillo no-boil lasagna noodles
- 3 cups vegan cheese, shredded
- Salt and black pepper, to taste

Direction:
1. Preheat your oven to 375 °F.
2. Sauté squash with black pepper, salt and oil in a skillet for 5 minutes.
3. Add water to the squash, cover and cook for about 20 minutes on medium heat.
4. Blend the squash with amaretti in a blender until smooth.

5. Sauté mushrooms with oil and ¼ teaspoons salt in a skillet for 10 minutes.
6. Mix butter with flour in a skillet for 1 minute.
7. Pour in milk, mix well until lump-free then boil the mixture.
8. Stir in black pepper, nutmeg and ¼ teaspoons salt.
9. Mix well then cook for about 5 minutes until the sauce thickens.
10. Add basil and blend well with a blender.
11. Grease a 13x9 -inch baking dish with butter.
12. Spread ¾ cup sauce in the baking dish.
13. Arrange the lasagna noodles at the bottom of this dish.
14. Top the noodles with ⅓ squash puree and add ⅓ mushroom on top.
15. Drizzle 1 cup vegan cheese on top.
16. Repeat all the layers and cover this dish with foil sheet.
17. Bake the prepared lasagna for 40 minutes in the oven.
18. Remove the tin foil from the top and bake for another 15 minutes.
19. Serve warm.

Serving Suggestion: Serve the lasagna with mashed cauliflower.
Variation Tip: You can replace lasagna noodles with zucchini slices
Nutrition: Calories 438 Fat 7g Sodium 316mg Carbs 34g Fiber 0.3g Sugar 0.3g Protein 3g

455. Sweet Cauliflower Penne Pasta

Preparation Time: 15 minutes.
Cooking Time: 15 minutes.
Servings: 2
Ingredients:
Sauce:
- ½ cup cashews
- 1 roasted sweet Cauliflower, peeled
- ⅔ cup water
- 2 garlic cloves
- 1 chipotle pepper
- ⅛ teaspoon nutmeg
- ½ teaspoon sea salt
- Black pepper, to taste

Pasta:
- 3 cups of quinoa penne
- Mushrooms
- ½ tablespoon olive oil
- 1 cup baby bella mushrooms, sliced
- ¼ teaspoon garlic powder
- Salt and black pepper, to taste

Direction:

1. Soak cashews in 4 cups water in a bowl for 2 hours then drain.
2. Blend cashews with black pepper, salt, nutmeg, chili pepper, garlic, water, and sweet Cauliflower in a blender until smooth.
3. Boil pasta in a boiling water in a cooking pot as per the package's instructions.
4. Drain the pasta and transfer to the pot.
5. Sauté mushrooms with oil, black pepper, salt and garlic powder in a skillet for 5 minutes.
6. Add the sweet Cauliflower sauce and pasta then mix well.
7. Garnish with sage.
8. Serve warm.

Serving Suggestion: Serve the pasta with roasted broccoli florets.
Variation Tip: Drizzle lemon juice on top before cooking.
Nutrition: Calories 456 Fat 4g |Sodium 634mg Carbs 31g Fiber 1.4g Sugar 1g Protein 3g

456. Roasted Butternut Squash Pasta

Preparation Time: 15 minutes.
Cooking Time: 35 minutes.
Servings: 2
Ingredients:

- ½ tablespoon olive oil
- 4 cups butternut squash, cubed
- 2 garlic cloves, unpeeled
- Salt and black pepper, to taste
- 8 ounces brown rice pasta
- 2 tablespoons vegan cream cheese
- 1 cup almond milk
- ½ cup frozen peas, thawed

Direction:

1. Preheat your oven to 400 °F .
2. Toss butternut squash with oil, black pepper and salt in a baking pan.
3. Add garlic and roast for 30 minutes.
4. Cook the pasta as per the package's instruction then drain.
5. Peel the roasted garlic and add to a blender along with squash, salt, black pepper, almond milk and vegan cream cheese then blend until smooth.
6. Add peas and squash sauce to the pasta and serve.
7. **Serving Suggestion:** Serve the pasta with crumbled tofu on top.

Variation Tip: Add garlic salt on top for more taste.
Nutrition: Calories 449 Fat 31g Sodium 723mg Carbs 32g Fiber 2.5g Sugar 2g Protein 26g

457. Cashew Mac and Cheese

Preparation Time: 15 minutes.
Cooking Time: 10 minutes.
Servings: 2
Ingredients:

- 1½ cups raw cashews
- 2 garlic cloves
- ½ cup nutritional yeast
- 1¼ cups almond milk
- 1 jalapeño, chopped
- ¾ teaspoon ground turmeric
- ¾ teaspoon paprika
- ½ teaspoon onion powder
- 1 teaspoon Dijon mustard
- 1 teaspoon salt
- Black pepper, to taste
- 1-pound shell Conchiglie pasta

Direction:

1. Soak cashews in 4 cups water in a bowl for 2 hours then drain.
2. Drain and blend the cashews with black pepper, salt, mustard, onion powder, paprika, turmeric, jalapeño, almond milk, yeast, and garlic in a blender until smooth.
3. Cook the noodles as per the package's instructions then drain.
4. Mix the noodles with the cashews sauce in a bowl.
5. Garnish with black pepper.
6. Serve warm.

Serving Suggestion: Serve the mac and cheese with mashed sweet celeriac.
Variation Tip: Add a drizzle of taco seasoning on top.
Nutrition: Calories 310 Fat 6g Sodium 220mg Carbs 31g Fiber 2.4g Sugar 1.2g Protein 12g

458. Taco Pasta with oregano

Preparation Time: 15 minutes.
Cooking Time: 10 minutes.
Servings: 2
Ingredients:
Pasta cheese sauce:

- ¾ cup cashews
- ¾ cup water
- 1 garlic clove
- 2 tablespoons lime juice
- 2½ teaspoons cumin
- 2 teaspoons chili powder
- 1 teaspoon dried oregano
- ½ teaspoon paprika
- ⅛ teaspoon cayenne pepper
- ¾ teaspoon salt

Pasta:

8 ounces large elbow noodles
1 (15-ounce) can black beans, rinsed
cooked ¾ cup chunky salsa

Preparation:

1. Soak cashews in 2 cups of water for 2 hours then drain.
2. Blend cashews with paprika, oregano, chili powder, cumin, lime juice, garlic, and ½ cup of water.
3. Boil the pasta as per the package's instruction then drain.
4. Return the pasta to a cooking pot then add cashew sauce, salsa and beans.
5. Mix well and garnish with all the toppings.
6. Serve warm.

Serving Suggestion: Serve the pasta with mashed cauliflower

Variation Tip: Add hot sauce for tangy taste.

Nutrition: Calories 382 Fat 6g Sodium 620mg Carbs 15g Fiber 2g Sugar 1.2g Protein 12g

459. Vegetarian Lentil Loaf

Preparation Time: 15 minutes.
Cooking Time: 1 hr. 23 minutes.
Servings: 2

Ingredients:

- 1 cup dry green lentils
- 4 cups water
- 3 tablespoons flaxseed meal
- ⅓ cup water
- ½ tablespoon olive oil
- 4 garlic cloves, minced
- 1 small white or yellow onion, diced
- 1 red bell pepper, diced
- 1 carrot, diced
- 1 jalapeño, seeded and diced 2 teaspoons cumin
- 1 teaspoon chili powder
- ½ teaspoon paprika
- ½ teaspoon garlic powder
- ½ teaspoon onion powder
- ¼ teaspoon coriander
- ½ cup gluten free rolled oats
- ½ cup gluten free oat flour
- ½ cup fresh cilantro, chopped
- 1 teaspoon salt
- Black pepper, to taste
- Glaze:
- ½ cup ketchup
- ½ teaspoon yellow mustard
- ½ teaspoon apple cider vinegar
- ¼ teaspoon chipotle chili powder

Direction:

1. Rinse and add lentils to a cooking pot with 4 cups of water.
2. Add a dash of salt and cook for 30 minutes on a simmer then drain.
3. Mix ⅓ cup water and flaxseed meal in a bowl.
4. Preheat your oven to 350 °F.
5. Grease a loaf pan with cooking spray.
6. Sauté garlic, jalapeño, cilantro, carrot, bell pepper, onion with oil in a suitable skillet for 7 minutes.
7. Stir in spices and cook for 30 seconds.
8. Blend the 2 cups of cooked lentils in a blender until smooth.
9. Return the lentils to the cooking pot and add the veggies.
10. Stir in the rest of the ingredients then mix well.
11. Prepare the glaze by mixing its ingredients in a bowl.
12. Brush the glaze over the meatloaf.
13. Spread the mixture in a meatloaf pan and bake for 45 minutes.
14. Allow it to cool then slice.
15. Serve warm.

Serving Suggestion: Serve the lentil loaf with roasted vegetables.

Nutrition: Calories 93 Fat 3g Sodium 510mg Carbs 22g Fiber 3g Sugar 4g Protein 4g

460. Black Bean Loaf with Avocado Sauce

Preparation Time: 15 minutes.
Cooking Time: 42 minutes.
Servings: 2

Ingredients:

- 3 tablespoons flaxseed meal
- ½ cup water
- 1 teaspoon olive oil
- 1 small yellow onion
- 3 garlic cloves, minced
- 1 red bell pepper, finely diced
- 1 carrot, shredded
- 1 jalapeño, seeded and diced
- 2 teaspoons cumin
- 1 tablespoon chili powder
- 1 teaspoon dried oregano
- ¼ teaspoon cayenne pepper
- ¼ cup cilantro, diced
- 2 (15-ounce) cans black beans, rinsed
- ½ cup gluten free oats
- ½ cup gluten free oat flour
- Salt and black pepper, to taste

Sauce:

- ⅓ cup salsa Verde green salsa
- ½ avocado, mashed
- 2 tablespoons cilantro, chopped

Direction:

1. Preheat your oven to 350 °F .
2. Layer a 9-inch loaf pan with cooking spray.
3. Mix ½ cup water with flaxseed meal in a bowl then leave for 10m minutes.
4. Sauté garlic, jalapeño, carrots, bell pepper, and onion with 1 teaspoon oil in a skillet for 7 minutes.
5. Blend beans with sautéed veggies, black pepper, salt and rest of the ingredients along with flaxseeds.
6. Spread this meatloaf mixture in the pan and bake for 35 minutes in the oven.
7. Allow the meatloaf to cool then slice.
8. Mix salsa with cilantro and avocado in a bowl.
9. Add this sauce over the meatloaf.
10. Serve warm

Serving Suggestion: Serve the bean loaf with sautéed vegetables on the side.

Variation Tip: Add boiled peas to the bean loaf.

Nutrition: Calories 378 Fat 3.8g Sodium 620mg Carbs 33g Fiber 2.4g Sugar 1.2g Protein 5.4

461. Pineapple Tofu Kabobs

Preparation Time: 10 minutes.
Cooking Time: 10 minutes.
Servings: 2

Ingredients:

- 2 tablespoons tamari
- 1 teaspoon apple cider vinegar
- 2 tablespoons fresh pineapple juice
- 2 teaspoons ginger, grated
- 2 garlic cloves, minced
- ½ teaspoon ground turmeric
- 1 (14-ounce) package Nagoya extra firm tofu
- 2 cups fresh pineapple, cubed

Garnish

Fresh chopped cilantro
Diced onion
Hot sauce

Direction:

1. Pat dry the tofu block with a paper towel and cut into cubes.
2. Mix tamari, turmeric, garlic, ginger, pineapple juice, and apple cider vinegar in a large bowl.
3. Toss in tofu cubes then mix well and cover to marinate for 30 minutes.
4. Set a grill over medium high heat and grease its grilling grates.
5. Thread tofu and pineapple on the skewers and grill the skewers for 5 minutes per side.
6. Garnish with hot sauce, green onion and cilantro.
7. Serve warm.

Serving Suggestion: Serve the tofu kebobs with mashed cauliflower.

Variation Tip: Brush the kebabs with sriracha sauce for seasoning.

Nutrition: Calories 304 Fat 31g Sodium 834mg Carbs 27g Fiber 0.2g Sugar 0.3g Protein 4.6g

462. Lentil Sloppy Joes with Spaghetti Squash

Preparation Time: 10 minutes.
Cooking Time: 4 hours.
Servings: 2

Ingredients:

- 1¼ cups uncooked green lentils, rinsed
- 1 white onion, diced - 1 red pepper, diced
- 1 carrot, sliced - 3 garlic cloves, minced
- 1½ tablespoons chili powder
- 1 teaspoon cumin - ½ teaspoon onion powder
- ¼ teaspoon cayenne pepper
- 1 (15-ounce) can tomato sauce
- 1 (15-ounce) can diced tomatoes
- 1½ cups water
- 2 tablespoons organic ketchup
- 1 teaspoon yellow mustard
- 1 spaghetti squash, halved and seeded
- 1 teaspoon soy sauce
- Salt and black pepper, to taste

Direction:

1. Add all the ingredients except spaghetti squash to a slow cooker.
2. Mix well and place the spaghetti squash on top.
3. Cover and slow-cook on high for 4 hours on High heat.
4. Remove the squash from the top and shred the flesh. Transfer the flesh to a serving plate and then top it with lentils mixture.
5. Garnish with cheese and serve warm.

Serving Suggestion: Serve the sloppy joe with some vegan cheese on top.

Variation Tip: Add cabbage coleslaw to the sloppy joe.

Nutrition: Calories 341 Fat 24g Sodium 547mg Carbs 24g Fiber 1.2g Sugar 1g Protein 10.3g

463. Sesame-Orange Chickpea Stir-Fry

Preparation Time: 15 minutes.
Cooking Time: 25 minutes.
Servings: 2

Ingredients:

Sauce:

- ¾ cup orange juice

- 1 tablespoon honey
- 2 tablespoons soy sauce
- 1 teaspoon ginger, grated
- Zest of 1 orange

Stir-fry:

- 1½ tablespoon toasted sesame oil
- 1 (15-ounce) can chickpeas, rinsed
- ½ red onion, chopped
- 3 garlic cloves, minced
- 1 large red bell pepper, sliced
- 8 ounces green beans, chopped
- Green onion, for garnish
- Toasted sesame seeds, for garnish
- Red pepper flakes
- Cooked Quinoa, for serving

Direction:

1. Mix orange zes, ginger, soy sauce, honey, and orange juice in a large bowl.
2. Set a suitable skillet with 1 tablespoon sesame oil over medium-high heat.
3. Stir in chickpeas then sauté for 5 minutes.
4. Mix well and transfer the chickpeas to a plate.
5. Sauté onion with ½ tablespoons oil in a skillet over medium heat for 4 minutes.
6. Stir in bell pepper and garlic then sauté for 3 minutes.
7. Add green beans then sauté for 4 minutes.
8. Pour in the prepared sauce then mix and cook until the sauce thickens.
9. Add chickpeas and cook on low heat for 4 minutes.
10. Garnish with green onion, red pepper flakes and sesame seeds.
11. Serve warm.

Serving Suggestion: Serve the stir-fry with zucchini noodles or rice.

Variation Tip: Add peas to the stir-fry.

Nutrition: Calories 318 Fat 15.7g Sodium 124mg Carbs 31g Fiber 0.1g Sugar 0.3g Protein 4.9g

464. Sweet Cauliflower Zoodles

Preparation Time: 15 minutes.
Cooking Time: 21 minutes.
Servings: 2

Ingredients:

- 1 teaspoon coconut oil
- 3 garlic cloves, minced
- 2 teaspoons fresh grated ginger
- 1 small white onion, diced
- 1 red pepper, diced
- 2 medium sweet celeriac, peeled and diced
- 1¼ teaspoon ground turmeric

- ½ teaspoon salt
- Black pepper, to taste
- 1 (15-ounce) can light coconut milk
- 2 tablespoons creamy peanut butter
- 2 medium zucchinis, spiralized

Direction:

1. Sauté ginger, and garlic with oil in a suitable skillet for 30 seconds.
2. Stir in sweet celeriac cubes, onion and red pepper then cook for 5 minutes.
3. Add turmeric, coconut milk, black pepper, salt and peanut butter then cook to a boil.
4. Reduce its heat, and cook for 15 minutes.
5. Add zucchini noodles then mix well.
6. Garnish with green onion, cilantro and lime juice.
7. Serve warm.

Serving Suggestion: Serve the zoodles with tofu stir fry.

Variation Tip: Add vegan cheese on top of the zoodles.

Nutrition: Calories 391 Fat 2.2g Sodium 276mg Carbs 27g Fiber 0.9g Sugar 1.4g Protein 8.8g

465. Butternut Squash Chickpea Stew

Preparation Time: 15 minutes.
Cooking Time: 21 minutes.
Servings: 2

Ingredients:

- 1 tablespoon olive oil
- 1 medium white onion, chopped
- 6 garlic cloves, minced
- 2 teaspoons cumin
- 1 teaspoon cinnamon
- 1 teaspoon ground turmeric
- ¼ teaspoon cayenne pepper
- 1 (28-ounce) can crushed tomatoes
- 2½ cups vegetable broth
- 1 (15-ounce) can chickpeas, rinsed
- 4 cups butternut squash, cubed
- 1 cup green lentils, rinsed
- ½ teaspoon salt
- Black pepper, to taste
- fresh juice of ½ lemon
- ⅓ cup cilantro, chopped
- Basil leaves, chopped

Direction:

1. Sauté garlic and onion with oil in a suitable pot over medium high heat for 5 minutes.
2. Stir in cayenne, turmeric, cinnamon and cumin then sauté for 30 seconds.
3. Add black pepper, salt, lentils. Butternut squash, chickpeas, broth and tomatoes.

4. Cook to a boil, reduce its heat then cover and cook for 20 minutes.
5. Add basil, cilantro and lemon juice.
6. Serve warm.

Serving Suggestion: Serve the stew with roasted mushrooms.

Variation Tip: Add lemon zest on top for better taste.

Nutrition: Calories 324 Fat 5g Sodium 432mg Carbs 31g Fiber 0.3g Sugar 1g Protein 5.7g

466. Strawberry and Avocado Smoothie

Preparation time: 5 minutes.
Cooking time: 0 minutes.
Servings: 1
Ingredients:

- 1 cup sliced Avocado, frozen
- 2 tablespoons chia seeds
- 2 cups strawberries, frozen - 2 teaspoons honey
- ¼ teaspoon vanilla extract, unsweetened
- 6 ounces coconut yogurt
- 1 cup almond milk, unsweetened

Directions:

1. Place all the ingredients in the jar of a food processor or blender, and then cover it with the lid.
2. Pulse until smooth and then serve.

Nutrition: Calories: 114 Fat: 2.1g Protein: 3.7g Carbs: 22.3g Fiber: 3.8g

467. Orange Smoothie

Preparation time: 5 minutes.
Cooking time: 0 minutes.
Servings: 1
Ingredients:

- 1 cup slices of oranges
- ½ teaspoon grated ginger
- 1 cup of mango pieces
- 1 cup of coconut water
- 1 cup chopped strawberries
- 1 cup crushed ice

Directions:

1. Place all the ingredients in the jar of a food processor or blender, and then cover it with the lid.
2. Pulse until smooth and then serve.

Nutrition: Calories: 198.7 Fat: 1.2g Protein: 6.1g Carbs: 34.3g Fiber: 0g

468. Pumpkin Chai Smoothie

Preparation time: 5 minutes.
Cooking time: 0 minutes.
Servings: 1
Ingredients:

- 1 cup cooked pumpkin

- ¼ cup pecans
- 1 frozen Avocado
- ¼ teaspoon ground cinnamon
- ¼ teaspoon cardamom
- ¼ teaspoon ground nutmeg
- 2 teaspoons maple syrup
- 1 cup of water, cold
- ½ cup of ice cubes

Directions:

1. Place pecans in a small bowl, cover with water, and then let them soak for 10 minutes.
2. Drain the pecans, add them into a blender, and then add the remaining ingredients.
3. Pulse for 1 minute until smooth and then serve.

Nutrition: Calories: 157.5 Fat: 3.8g Protein: 3g Carbs: 32.3g Fiber: 4.5g

469. Avocado Shake

Preparation time: 5 minutes.
Cooking time: 0 minutes.
Servings: 1
Ingredients:

- 3 medium frozen Avocados
- 1 tablespoon cocoa powder, unsweetened
- 1 teaspoon shredded coconut
- 1 tablespoon maple syrup
- 1 tablespoon peanut butter
- 1 teaspoon vanilla extract, unsweetened
- 2 cups of coconut water
- 1 cup of ice cubes

Directions:

1. Add Avocado in a food processor, add maple syrup and vanilla, pour in water and then add ice.
2. Pulse until smooth and then pour half of the smoothie into a glass.
3. Add butter and cocoa powder into the blender, pulse until smooth, and then add to the smoothie glass.
4. Sprinkle coconut over the smoothie and then serve.

Nutrition: Calories: 301 Fat: 9.3g Protein: 6.8g Carbs: 49g Fiber: 1.9g

470. Green Honeydew Smoothie

Preparation time: 5 minutes.
Cooking time: 15 minutes.
Servings: 2
Ingredients:

- 1 large Avocado
- 6 large leaves of basil
- ½ cup frozen pineapple
- 1 teaspoon lime juice
- 1 cup pieces of Honeydew melon

- 1 teaspoon green tea matcha powder
- ¼ cup almond milk, unsweetened

Directions:
1. Place all the ingredients in the jar of a food processor or blender, and then cover it with the lid.
2. Pulse until smooth and then serve.

Nutrition: Calories: 223.5 Fat: 2.7g Protein: 20.1g Carbs: 32.7g Fiber: 5.2g

471. Summer Salsa

Preparation time: 5 minutes.
Cooking time: 15 minutes.
Servings: 2

Ingredients:
- 1 cup cherry tomatoes chopped
- 1/4 cup chopped cilantro
- 2 tablespoons chopped red onion
- 1 teaspoon minced garlic
- 1 small jalapeno, seeded, chopped
- 1/2 of a lime, juiced
- 1/8 teaspoon salt
- 1 tablespoon olive oil

Directions:
1. Place all the ingredients in the jar of a food processor or blender except for cilantro, and then cover with its lid.
2. Pulse until smooth and then pulse in cilantro until evenly mixed.
3. Tip the salsa into a bowl and then serve with vegetable sticks.

Nutrition: Calories: 51 Fat: 0.1g Protein: 1.7g Carbs: 11.4g Fiber: 3.1g

472. Red Salsa

Preparation time: 35 minutes
Cooking time: 15 minutes
Servings: 2

Ingredients:
- 4 Roma tomatoes, halved
- ¼ cup chopped cilantro
- 1 jalapeno pepper, seeded, halved
- ½ of a medium white onion, peeled, cut into quarters 3 cloves of garlic, peeled
- ½ teaspoon salt
- 1 tablespoon brown sugar
- 1 teaspoon apple cider vinegar

Directions:
1. Switch on the oven, then set it to 425°F and let it preheat.
2. Meanwhile, take a baking sheet, line it with foil and then spread tomato, jalapeno pepper, onion and garlic.

3. Bake the vegetables for 15 minutes until vegetables have cooked and begin to brown, and then let the vegetables cool for 3 minutes.
4. Transfer the roasted vegetables into a blender, add the remaining ingredients and then pulse until smooth.
5. Tip the salsa into a medium bowl and then chill it for 30 minutes before serving with vegetable sticks.

Nutrition: Calories: 240 Fat: 0g Protein: 0g Carbs: 48g Fiber: 16g

473. Pinto Bean Dip

Preparation time: 5 minutes.
Cooking time: 0 minutes.
Servings: 2

Ingredients:
- 15 ounces canned pinto beans
- 1 jalapeno pepper
- 2 teaspoons ground cumin
- 3 tablespoons nutritional yeast
- 1/3 cup basil salsa

Directions:
1. Place all the ingredients in a food processor, cover with the lid and then pulse until smooth.
2. Tip the dip in a bowl and then serve with vegetable slices.

Nutrition: Calories: 360 Fat: 0g Protein: 24g Carbs: 72g Fiber: 24g

474. Smoky Red Pepper Hummus

Preparation time: 5 minutes.
Cooking time: 0 minutes.
Servings: 2

Ingredients:
- 1/4 cup roasted red peppers
- 1 cup cooked chickpeas
- 1/8 teaspoon garlic powder
- 1/2 teaspoon salt
- 1/8 teaspoon ground black pepper
- 1/4 teaspoon ground cumin
- 1/4 teaspoon red chili powder
- 1 tablespoon tahini
- 2 tablespoons water

Directions:
1. Place all the ingredients in the jar of the food processor and then pulse until smooth.
2. Tip the hummus in a bowl and then serve with vegetable slices.

Nutrition: Calories: 489 Fat: 30g Protein: 9g Carbs: 15g Fiber: 6g

475. Tomatillo Salsa

Preparation time: 5 minutes.
Cooking time: 20 minutes.
Servings: 2
Ingredients:
- 5 medium tomatillos, chopped
- 3 cloves of garlic, peeled, chopped
- 3 Roma tomatoes, chopped
- 1 jalapeno, chopped
- ½ of a medium red onion, peeled, chopped
- 1 Anaheim chili
- 2 teaspoons salt
- 1 teaspoon ground cumin
- 1 lime, juiced
- ¼ cup cilantro leaves
- ¾ cup of water

Directions:
1. Take a medium pot, place it over medium heat, pour in water and then add onion, garlic, tomatoes, tomatillo, jalapeno and Anaheim chili.
2. Sauté the vegetables for 15 minutes, remove the pot from heat, add cilantro, cumin and lime juice and then stir in salt.
3. Remove the pot from heat and then pulse by using an immersion blender until smooth.
4. Serve the salsa with chips.

Nutrition: Calories: 317.4 Fat: 0g Protein: 16g Carbs: 64gFiber: 16g

476. Arugula Pesto Couscous

Preparation time: 10 minutes.
Cooking time: 20 minutes.
Servings: 2
Ingredients:
- 8 ounces Israeli couscous
- 3 large tomatoes, chopped
- 3 cups arugula leaves
- ½ cup parsley leaves
- 6 cloves of garlic, peeled
- ½ cup walnuts
- ¾ teaspoon salt
- 1 cup and 1 tablespoon olive oil
- 2 cups vegetable broth

Directions:
1. Take a medium saucepan, place it over medium-high heat, add 1 tablespoon oil and then let it heat.
2. Add couscous, stir until mixed, and then cook for 4 minutes until fragrant and toasted.
3. Pour in the broth, stir until mixed, bring it to a boil, switch heat to medium level and then simmer for 12 minutes until the couscous has been absorbed all the liquid and turn tender.

4. When done, remove the pan from heat, fluff it with a fork, and then set it aside until required.
5. While couscous cooks, prepare the pesto and for this, place walnuts in a blender, add garlic and then pulse until nuts have broken.
6. Add arugula, parsley and salt, pulse until well combined, and then blend in oil until smooth.
7. Transfer couscous to a salad bowl, add tomatoes and the prepared pesto, and then toss until mixed.
8. Serve straight away.

Nutrition: Calories: 73 Fat: 4g Protein: 2g Carbs: 8g Fiber: 2g

477. Oatmeal and Raisin Balls

Preparation time: 40 minutes.
Cooking time: 0 minutes.
Servings: 2
Ingredients:
- 1 cup rolled oats
- ¼ cup raisins
- ½ cup peanut butter

Directions:
1. Place oats in a large bowl, add raisins and peanut butter, and then stir until well combined.
2. Shape the mixture into twelve balls, 1 tablespoon of mixture per ball, and then arrange the balls on a baking sheet.
3. Place the baking sheet into the freezer for 30 minutes until firm and then serve.

Nutrition: Calories: 135 Fat: 6g Protein: 8g Carbs: 13g Fiber: 4g

478. Nacho Cheese

Preparation time: 10 minutes.
Cooking time: 15 minutes.
Servings: 2
Ingredients:
- 1 cup chopped carrots
- ½ teaspoon onion powder
- 2 cups peeled and chopped celeriac
- ½ teaspoon garlic powder
- 1 teaspoon salt
- ½ cup nutritional yeast
- 1 tablespoon lemon juice
- ¼ cup of salsa
- ½ cup of water

Directions:
1. Take a medium pot, place carrots and Cauliflower in it, cover with water and then place the pot over medium-high heat.
2. Boil the vegetables for 10 minutes, drain them and then transfer them into a blender.
3. Add the remaining ingredients and then pulse until smooth.

4. Tip the cheese into a bowl and then serve with vegetable slices.

Nutrition: Calories: 611.7 Fat: 17.2g Protein: 32.1g Carbs: 62.1g Fiber: 12.1g

479. Pico de Gallo

Preparation time: 5 minutes.
Cooking time: 0 minutes.
Servings: 2

Ingredients:

- 1/2 of a medium red onion, peeled, chopped
- 2 cups diced tomato
- 1/2 cup chopped cilantro
- 1 jalapeno pepper, minced
- 1/8 teaspoon salt
- 1/4 teaspoon ground black pepper
- 1/2 of a lime, juiced
- 1 teaspoon olive oil

Directions:

1. Take a large bowl, place all the ingredients in it and then stir until well mixed.
2. Serve the Pico de Gallo with chips.

Nutrition: Calories: 790 Fat: 6.4g Protein: 25.6g Carbs: 195.2g Fiber: 35.2g

480. Beet Balls

Preparation time: 10 minutes.
Cooking time: 0 minutes.
Servings: 2

Ingredients:

- 1/2 cup oats
- 1 medium beet, cooked
- 1/2 cup almond flour
- 1/3 cup shredded coconut and more for coating 3/4 cup Medjool dates, pitted
- 1 tablespoon cocoa powder
- 1/2 cup peanuts
- 1/4 cup chocolate chips, unsweetened

Directions:

1. Place cooked beet in a blender and then pulse until chopped into very small pieces.
2. Add the remaining ingredients and then pulse until the dough comes together.
3. Shape the dough into eighteen balls, coat them in some more coconut and then serve.

Nutrition: Calories: 114.2 Fat: 2.4g Protein: 5g Carbs: 19.6g Fiber: 4.9g

481. Cheesy Crackers

Preparation time: 10 minutes.
Cooking time: 20 minutes.
Servings: 2

Ingredients:

- 1 ¾ cups almond meal

- 3 tablespoons nutritional yeast
- ½ teaspoon and a pinch of sea salt
- 2 tablespoons lemon juice
- 1 tablespoon melted coconut oil
- 1 tablespoon ground flaxseed
- 2 (½) tablespoons water

Directions:

1. Switch on the oven, then set it to 350°F and let it preheat.
2. Meanwhile, take a medium bowl, place flaxseed in it, stir in water and then let the mixture rest for 5 minutes until thickened.
3. Place almond meal in a medium bowl, add sea salt and yeast, and then stir until mixed.
4. Add lemon juice and coconut oil into the flaxseed mixture and then whisk until mixed.
5. Pour the flaxseed mixture into the almond meal mixture, and then stir until the dough comes together.
6. Place a piece of wax paper on a clean working space, place the dough on it, cover with another piece of wax paper, and then roll dough into a 1/8-inch thick crust.
7. Cut the dough into a square shape, sprinkle salt over the top and
8. then bake for 15 to 20 minutes until done.
9. Serve straight away.

Nutrition: Calories: 30 Fat: 1g Protein: 1g Carbs: 5g Fiber: 0g

482. Butterscotch Tart

Preparation Time: 50 Minutes
Cooking time: 20 minutes
Servings: 1

Ingredients:

- Crust:
- ½ Cup Sugar
- ¼ Cup Coconut Oil
- 1 Teaspoon Vanilla Extract, Pure
- ½ Teaspoon Sea Salt
- 2 Cups Almond Meal Flour
- Filling:
- 2/3 Cup Light Brown Sugar, Packed
- 1 Teaspoon Kosher Salt
- ½ Cup Coconut Oil
- 2/3 Cup Coconut Cream, Canned
- Flaked Sea Salt, As Needed
- 1 Green Apple, Sliced

Directions:

1. Preheat the oven to 375 degrees and keep a bowl ready. To make your crust, combine all of the ingredients in a mixing bowl and stir until smooth. Spread the mixture into a nine-inch tart pan. Spread it out as evenly as you can. Freeze

for 10 minutes before baking for fifteen minutes. It should have a golden brown color.

2. Cook for twenty-five minutes in a pot to prepare the filling. Allow it to thicken and chill before using. To prevent it from burning, stir it frequently.

3. After adding this to the tart, chill it for two hours before serving.

Nutrition: Calories: 40 Fat: 1g Protein: 3g Carbs: 5g Fiber: 2g

483. Easy Brownies

Preparation time: 20 minutes
Cooking Time: 25 Minutes
Servings: 2

Ingredients:
- 2 Tablespoons Coconut Oil, Melted
- ½ Cup Peanut Butter, Salted
- ¼ Cup Warm Water
- 2 Cups Dates, Pitted
- 1/3 Cup Dark Chocolate chips
- 1/3 Cup Cocoa Powder
- ½ Cup Raw Walnuts, Chopped

Directions:
1. Preheat the oven to 350 degrees and prepare a loaf pan. Get a food processor out and put parchment paper in it. Blend the dates until they're a fine paste. Add some hot water and combine until the batter is as smooth as possible.

2. Combine the coconut oil, cacao powder, and peanut butter in a large mixing bowl. Blend some more, then fold in the walnuts and chocolate. This should be spread into your loaf pan.

3. Bake for fifteen minutes, then refrigerate until ready to serve.

Nutrition: Calories: 50 Fat: 5g Protein: 4g Carbs: 6g Fiber: 0g

CHAPTER 26:

Dinner

484. Steak Fajitas

Preparation time: 15 minutes
Cooking time: 30 minutes
Servings: 2
Ingredients:

- Salsa:
- 1 onion cut into strips
- 1 green bell cut into strips
- ½ tsp. dried thyme
- ½ tsp. mustard powder
- 1 tsp. black pepper - 1 tsp. cumin
- 2 tsp. dried rosemary
- 2 tsp. chili powder
- 2 packets natural sweetener
- 1 tbsp. paprika - 1 tbsp. sea salt
- 1 pound lean sirloin steak, cut into strips

Directions:

1. Place the salt, paprika, sweetener, chili powder, dried rosemary, cumin, pepper, mustard powder, and dried thyme into a bowl and mix well to combine. Take out one tsp. of this mixture and reserve.
1. Rub the steak slices really well with the spice mixture that you just made. Cover the steak and allow it to marinate until you are ready to cook it.
2. Place a large skillet on the stove and heat to medium-high. Add the onion and pepper to the skillet along with the spice mixture that you set to the side earlier. You need to cook the onion and peppers until they have softened up and the onions turn translucent. Take off heat and place in a bowl. Cover to keep warm.
3. Into the same skillet, add half the seasoned steak and cook for about two minutes per side or until done to your liking. Place cooked steak onto a clean plate and cover until the rest of the steak gets done.
4. Once all the steak strips are done, add everything back into the skillet and warm everything up for a few minutes. Spoon onto plates and enjoy.

Nutrition: Calories: 663, Fat: 22.1 g, Protein: 104.7 Carb: 6 g.

485. Greek Yogurt Chicken

Preparation time: 10 minutes
Cooking time: 45 minutes
Servings: 2
Ingredients:

- 1 tsp. garlic powder
- ½ tsp. pepper
- 1 ½ tsp. seasoning salt
- ½ cup parmesan cheese
- 1 cup Greek yogurt
- 4 skinless, boneless chicken breasts

Directions:

1. Start by setting your oven to 375 °F.
2. Mix together the seasonings, cheese, and Greek yogurt.
3. Lay some tin foil on a baking sheet and spritz it with some nonstick spray.
4. Spread the Greek yogurt mixture over the chicken breasts and lay them on the prepared baking sheet.
5. Slide them into the oven and let them cook for 45 minutes.

Nutrition: Calories: 266, Fat: 4 g, Protein: 46 g, Carb: 3 g.

486. Taco Beef

Preparation time: 15 minutes
Cooking time: 8 hours
Servings: 2
Ingredients:

- 1 chipotle pepper in adobo sauce, minced
- 5 garlic cloves minced
- 2 tsp. chili powder
- 1 small white onion, diced
- 2 lb. chuck tender roast
- 2 tbsp. tomato paste
- 1 cup beef broth, low sodium
- ½ tsp. paprika
- 1 tsp. cumin
- 2 tsp. olive oil

Directions:

1. Place the paprika, cumin, and chili powder into a small bowl and mix everything together. Rub this mixture into the chuck roast.

1. Make sure that you cover the chuck roast well.
2. Set a large pan on top of the stove and warm it to medium-high.
3. Add in the olive oil and let it get hot. Place beef into the skillet and sear for two minutes. Turn the roast and sear every side. Take the beef out of the skillet and put it into the bottom of the slow cooker.
4. Add the diced onion into the skillet you seared the beef in and cook for three minutes until onions become soft and translucent.
5. Mix in the garlic, cooking until fragrant. Pour the beef broth into the skillet and scrape with a wooden spoon to deglaze the pan.
5. Add the minced chipotle and tomato paste into the skillet and using a whisk, stir until everything is combined. Allow the mixture to come up to a boil and then turn the heat down until it simmers.
6. Let it simmer for five minutes, or until it has thickened. Take off heat and pour over beef in the bottom of the slow cooker.
6. Place lid on the slow cooker and set on low. Cook for eight hours until the beef will shred easily with a fork.
7. When beef is done, take it out of the cooker and shred it up. Mix it back into the juices so that it is well coated.
8. Use as you would any meat mixture in your favorite Mexican dishes or eat as is.

Nutrition: Calories: 292, Fat: 11.1 g, Protein: 42.3 g, Carb: 4 g.

487. Chicken Chili with Jalapeno and Cheddar

Preparation time: 10 minutes
Cooking time: 40 minutes
Servings: 2
Ingredients:
- 1 cup diced carrots
- 1 tbsp. cumin
- ½ cup shredded pepper jack cheese
- ¼ cup low-fat cream cheese
- ½ cup chicken broth

Directions
1. 1 tsp. oregano
2. 1 tbsp. chili powder
3. 1/2 cup diced jarred jalapeno slices
4. 1 pound skinless, boneless chicken breast
Directions:
1. Spray a Dutch oven with cooking spray. Place the Dutch oven over medium-high heat.
2. Add in the diced chicken along with the diced jalapenos. Cook until chicken turns opaque.

3. Add oregano, chili powder, and cumin to the chicken and jalapenos. Stir everything together so that it is well combined.
4. Mix in the carrots and chicken broth. Stir to combine. Bring to a boil. Once boiling, turn the heat down to low and cover.
5. Allow this mixture to simmer for 20 minutes until the carrots are soft.
6. Add in pepper jack and cream cheese. Stir until mixed well and cheese are melted. Allow it to simmer for five minutes more.
7. Divide evenly into bowls.
8. Serve and enjoy.

Nutrition: Calories: 450, Fat: 18.2 g, Protein: 61.7 g, Carb: 7.9 g.

488. One-Pan Pork Chops with Apples and Red Onion

Preparation time: 10 minutes
Cooking time: 30 minutes
Servings: 2
Ingredients:
- 2 tsp. extra-virgin olive oil, divided
- 4 boneless center-cut thin pork chops
- 2 small apples, thinly sliced
- Small red onion, thinly sliced
- 1 cup low-Sodium: chicken broth
- 1 tsp. Dijon mustard
- 1 tsp. dried sage
- 1 tsp. dried thyme

Directions:
1. Place a large nonstick frying pan over high heat and add 1 tsp. of olive oil. When the oil is hot, add the pork chops and reduce the heat to medium. Sear the chops for 3 minutes on one side, flip, and sear the other side for 3 minutes, 6 minutes Total. Put the chops by the side.
2. In the same pan, add the remaining 1 tsp. of olive oil. Add the apples and onion. Cook for 5 minutes or until tender, stirring frequently to prevent burning.
3. While the apples and onion cook, mix together the broth and Dijon mustard in a small bowl.
4. Add the sage and thyme to the pan and stir to coat the onion and apples. Stir in the broth mixture and return the pork chops to the pan. Cover the pan and simmer for 10 to 15 minutes.
5. Let pork chops rest for 2 minutes before cutting.

Nutrition: Per Serving (1 pork chop): Calories: 234, Total Fat: 11 g, Protein: 20 g, Carbs: 13 g, Fiber: 3 g, Sugar: 9 g, Sodium: 290 mg.

489. Slow Cooker Pork with Red Peppers and Pineapple

Preparation time: 10 minutes
Cooking time: 5 hours
Servings: 2
Ingredients:

- ¼ cup low-sodium soy sauce or Bragg Liquid Aminos
- ½ lemon juice
- 1 tsp. garlic powder
- 1 tsp. ground cumin
- ½ tsp. cayenne pepper
- ¼ tsp. ground coriander
- 1½ pounds boneless pork tenderloin
- 2 red bell peppers, thinly sliced
- 2 (20-ounces) cans pineapple chunks in 100% natural juice or water, drained

Directions:

1. In a small bowl, mix together the soy sauce, lemon juice, garlic powder, cumin, cayenne pepper, and coriander.
2. Place the pork tenderloin in the slow cooker and add the red bell pepper slices. Cover with the pineapple chunks and their juices.
1. Pour the soy sauce mixture on top.
2. Cover the slow cooker and turn on low for about 5 hours.
3. Shred the pork with a fork and tongs and continue to cook on low for 20 minutes more, or until juices are absorbed.
4. Serve and enjoy!
5. Ingredient tip: If you're not familiar with Bragg Liquid Aminos, it is a liquid Protein: concentrate, derived from soybeans. It contains all 16 amino acids and has a taste that's very similar to soy sauce.

Nutrition: Per Serving (3 ounces): Calories: 131, Total Fat: 2 g, Protein: 17 g, Carbs: 11 g; Fiber: 2 g, Sugar: 8 g, Sodium: 431 mg.

490. Pork, White Bean, and Spinach Soup

Preparation time: 10 minutes
Cooking time: 40 minutes
Servings: 2
Ingredients:

- 1 tsp. extra-virgin olive oil
- 1 medium onion, chopped
- 2 (4-ounces) boneless pork chops, cut into 1-inch cubes
- 1 (14.5 ounces) can diced tomatoes
- 3 cups low-sodium chicken broth
- ½ tsp. dried thyme
- ¼ tsp. crushed red pepper flakes
- 1 (15-ounces) can great northern beans, drained and rinsed
- 8 ounces fresh spinach leaves

Directions:

1. Place a large soup pot or Dutch oven over medium heat and heat the olive oil.
2. Add the onion and sauté for 2 to 3 minutes, or until tender. Add the pork and brown it for 4 to 5 minutes on each side.
3. Mix in the tomatoes, broth, thyme, red pepper flakes, and beans.
1. Boil and minimize heat to simmer, covered, for 30 minutes.
4. Add the spinach and stir until wilted, about 5 minutes, and serve immediately.
5. Did You Know? Pork (and all meats, eggs, and dairy) is an excellent source of vitamin B12, which is important for preventing anemia and is crucial for nerve function. Because of changes in the absorption of vitamin B12 and the risk of its deficiency after bariatric surgery, many patients need a B12 supplement in the form of a pill or injection. Eating foods that are high in vitamin B12 is a good way to keep those levels topped up.

Nutrition: Per Serving (1 cup): Calories: 156, Total Fat: 4 g, Protein: 17 g, Carbs: 17 g, Fiber: 4 g, Sugar: 6 g, Sodium: 600 mg.

491. Pork Egg Roll Bowl

Preparation time: 10 min
Cooking time: 10 min
Servings: 2
Ingredients

- 1 lb. Ground pork
- 3 tbsp soy sauce
- 1 tbsp sesame oil
- 1/2 onion, sliced
- 1 medium cabbage head, sliced
- 2 tbsp green onion, chopped
- 2 tbsp chicken broth
- 1 tsp ground ginger
- 2 garlic cloves, minced
- Pepper
- Salt

Directions

1. Brown meat in a pan over medium heat.
2. Add oil and onion to the pan with meat. Mix well and cook over medium heat.
3. In a small bowl, mix together soy sauce, ginger, and garlic.
4. Add soy sauce mixture to the pan.
5. Add cabbage to the pan and toss to coat.

6. Add broth to the pan and mix well.
7. Cook over medium heat for 3 min.
8. Season with pepper and salt.
9. Garnish with green onion and servings.

Nutrition Calories 171 Fat 5 g Carbohydrates 10 g Sugar 5 g Protein 23 g Cholesterol 56 mg

492. Onion Paprika Pork Tenderloin

Preparation time: 10 min
Cooking time: 30 min
Servings: 2

Ingredients

- 2 lbs. Pork tenderloin
- For rub
- 1 1/2 tbsp smoked paprika
- 1 tbsp garlic powder
- 1 1/2 tbsp onion powder
- ½ tbsp salt

Directions

1. Preheat the oven to 425 f.
2. In a small bowl, mix together all rub ingredients and rub over pork tenderloin.
3. Spray pan with cooking time spray and heat over medium-high heat.
4. Sear pork on all sides until lightly golden brown.
5. Place pan into the oven and roast for about 25-30 min.
6. Sliced and servings.

Nutrition Calories 225 Fat 5 g Carbohydrates 2 g Sugar 1 g Protein 41 g Cholesterol 45 mg

493. Stuff Cheese Pork Chops

Preparation time: 10 min
Cooking time: 25 min
Servings: 2

Ingredients

- 4 pork chops, boneless and thick cut
- 2 tbsp olives, chopped
- 2 tbsp sun-dried tomatoes, chopped
- ½ cup feta cheese, crumbled
- 2 garlic cloves, minced
- 2 tbsp fresh parsley, chopped

Directions

1. Preheat the oven to 375 f.
2. In a bowl, mix together feta cheese, garlic, parsley, olives, and sun-dried tomatoes.
3. Stuff feta cheese mixture in the pork chops. Season with pepper and salt.
4. Bake for 35 min.
5. Servings: and enjoy.

Nutrition Calories 316 Fat 25 g Carbohydrates 2 g Sugar 1 g Protein 21 g Cholesterol 75 mg

494. Herb Pork Chops

Preparation time: 10 min
Cooking time: 30 min
Servings: 2

Ingredients

- 4 pork chops, boneless
- 1 tbsp olive oil
- 2 garlic cloves, minced
- 1 tsp dried rosemary, crushed
- 1 tsp oregano
- ½ tsp thyme
- 1 tbsp fresh rosemary, chopped
- ¼ tsp pepper
- ¼ tsp salt

Directions

1. Preheat the oven 425 f.
2. Season pork chops with pepper and salt and set aside.
3. In a small bowl, mix together garlic, oil, rosemary, oregano, thyme, and fresh rosemary and rub over pork chops.
4. Place pork chops on baking tray and roast for 10 min.
5. Turn heat to 350 f and roast for 25 min more.
6. Servings: and enjoy.

Nutrition Calories 260 Fat 22 g Carbohydrates 2.5 g Sugar 0 g Protein 19 g Cholesterol 65 mg

495. Delicious Seafood Dip

Preparation time: 10 min
Cooking time: 30 min
Servings: 2

Ingredients

- 1/2 lb. Shrimp, cooked
- 4 oz can green chilies
- 2 cups pepper jack cheese
- 4 oz cream cheese
- 1/2 tsp old bay seasoning
- 2 garlic cloves, minced
- 1/2 cup spinach, minced
- 1/2 cup onion, minced
- 2 tbsp butter
- 4 oz crab meat

Directions

1. Preheat the oven to 425 f.
2. Melt butter in a pan over medium heat.
3. Add garlic, old bay seasoning, spinach, crab meat, chilies, and shrimp and cook for 4-5 min.
4. Add 1 cup pepper jack cheese and cream cheese.

5. Top with remaining cheese and bake for 20 min.
6. Servings: and enjoy.

Nutrition Calories 63 Fat 4 g Carbohydrates 1 g Sugar 0.2 g Protein 5 g Cholesterol 45 mg

496. Spinach Shrimp Alfredo

Preparation time: 10 min
Cooking time: 15 min
Servings: 2

Ingredients

- 1/2 lb. Shrimp, deveined
- 2 garlic cloves, minced
- 2 tbsp onion, chopped
- 1 cup fresh spinach, chopped
- 1/2 cup heavy cream
- 1 tbsp butter
- Pepper
- Salt

Directions

1. Melt butter in a pan over medium heat.
2. Add onion, garlic and shrimp in the pan and sauté for 3 min.
3. Add remaining ingredients and simmer for 7 min or until cooked.
4. Servings: and enjoy.

Nutrition Calories 300 Fat 19 g Carbohydrates 5 g Sugar 0.5 g Protein 27 g Cholesterol 295 mg

497. Shrimp Scampi

Preparation time: 10 min
Cooking time: 10 min
Servings: 2

Ingredients

- 1 lb. Shrimp
- 1/4 tsp red pepper flakes
- 1 tbsp fresh lemon juice
- 1/4 cup butter
- 1/2 cup chicken broth
- 2 garlic cloves, minced
- 1 shallot, sliced
- 3 tbsp olive oil
- 3 tbsp parsley, chopped
- Pepper
- Salt

Directions

1. Heat oil in a pan over medium heat.
2. Add garlic and shallots and cook for 3 min.
3. Add broth, lemon juice, and butter and cook for 5 min.
4. Add red pepper flakes, parsley, pepper, and salt. Stir.

5. Add shrimp and cook for 3 min.
6. Servings: and enjoy.

Nutrition Calories 336 Fat 24 g Carbohydrates 3 g Sugar 0.2 g Protein 26 g Cholesterol 269 mg

498. Crab Cakes

Preparation time: 10 min
Cooking time: 15 min
Servings: 2

Ingredients

- 1 egg
- 2 tbsp butter
- 1 tbsp cilantro, chopped
- 1/2 cup almond flour
- 4 tbsp pork rinds
- 1 lb. Crab meat
- 3 tsp ginger garlic paste
- 2 tsp sriracha
- 2 tsp lemon juice
- 1 tsp Dijon mustard
- 1/4 cup mayonnaise

Directions

1. Add all ingredients except butter in a large bowl and mix until well combined.
2. Preheat the oven to 350 f.
3. Heat butter in a pan over medium-high heat.
4. Make crab cake from mixture and place in the pan and cook for 5 min.
5. Transfer pan in preheated oven and bake for 10 min.
6. Servings: and enjoy.

Nutrition Calories 251 Fat 16 g Carbohydrates 7.4 g Sugar 0.9 g Protein 15 g Cholesterol 97 mg

499. Shrimp & Broccoli

Preparation time: 10 min
Cooking time: 7 min
Servings: 2

Ingredients

- 1/2 lb. Shrimp
- 1 tsp fresh lemon juice
- 2 tbsp butter
- 2 garlic cloves, minced
- 1 cup broccoli florets
- Salt

Directions

1. Melt butter in a pan over medium heat.
2. Add garlic and broccoli to pan and cook for 3-4 min.
3. Add shrimp and cook for 3-4 min.
4. Add lemon juice and salt and stir well.
5. Servings: and enjoy.

Nutrition Calories 257 Fat 13 g Carbohydrates 6 g Sugar 0.9 g Protein 27 g Cholesterol 269 mg

500. Chocolate-Peanut Butter French Toast

Preparation time: 25 min
Cooking time: 0 min
Servings: 1

Ingredients

- 1/3 - cup liquid egg whites
- 2 - teaspoons unsweetened cocoa powder
- ½ - teaspoon vanilla extract
- Salt
- 2 - slices Eggplant
- 1 - tablespoon peanut butter
- 2/3 - cup fresh raspberries

Directions

1. In a shallow dish or bowl, whisk collectively egg whites, cocoa powder, vanilla, and a touch of salt. Absorb Eggplant egg blend, each reduce in flip, until all the egg is ingested.
2. In a giant, nonstick skillet blanketed with cooking time splash over medium warmth, consist of Eggplant cuts and cook dinner till underside is dim brilliant darker, round 3min. Flip and cook until terrific darkish colored and marginally firm, round 3min greater.
3. Spread nutty unfold on French toast. Top with raspberries.

Nutrition: Calories 404 Carbs 52g Protein 21g

501. Watermelon Quinoa Parfait

Preparation time: 15 min
Cooking time: 20 min
Servings: 1

Ingredients

- 1 - cup watermelon, cut into bite-sized pieces ½ - cup cooked quinoa
- 1 - tablespoon fresh mint, chopped
- ½ - cup plain 2-percent-fat Greek yogurt
- 20 - almonds, chopped

Directions

1. In a bowl, mix together watermelon, quinoa, and mint.
2. In a container or bowl, layer watermelon-quinoa blend with yogurt. Top with almonds.

Nutrition: Calories 411 Fat 17g Carbs 42g Sugar 17g Protein 25g

502. Carrot Cake Oatmeal

Preparation time: 5 min
Cooking time: 50 min
Servings: 1

Ingredients

- ½ - cup unsweetened almond milk
- 1 - small carrot, peeled and finely grated
- 1/3 - cup rolled oats
- 1 - tablespoon raisins
- 1 - teaspoon honey
- ¼ - teaspoon vanilla extract
- 1 - pinch cinnamon
- 1 - pinch salt
- 1 ½ - tablespoons peanut butter
- 1/3 - cup low-fat cottage cheese

Directions

1. In a bit pot, be part of almond milk, half cup water, carrot, oats, raisins, nectar, vanilla, cinnamon, and salt. Heat to the factor of boiling, at that point, reduce to stew and cook, mixing sporadically, until thick and oats are stout, 5 to 7min.
2. Blend inside the nutty unfold and take out from the heat.
3. Top cereal with curds and extra cinnamon.

Nutrition Calories 423 Fat 17g Carbs 51g Protein 21g

503. Coconut Cranberry Protein Bars

Preparation time: 20 min
Cooking time: 0 min
Servings: 1

Ingredients

- ¼ - cup unsweetened shredded coconut flakes ¼ - cup organic dried cranberries
- ¼ - cup almond butter
- 2 - tbsp almond meal
- 2 - tbsp flax meal
- 3 - tbsp coconut oil
- 1 - tbsp raw honey
- 2 - eggs
- 6 - scoops she coconut fuel protein
- Dash Himalayan sea salt
- Optional: 1/4 organic dark chocolate chunks/enjoy life's chocolate chips

Directions

1. Preheat stove to 350
2. Come to all fixings in a bowl and blend until a batter-like consistency Line an 8x8 preparation time ring dish with material paper Take off batter into a level and even square Preparation time for 15 to 20 min or until somewhat solidified Let cool and cut into squares

Nutrition Calories 214 Fat 12.2g Carb 8.2g Sugars 3.1g Protein 20g

504. Egg White Oatmeal and Strawberries with Peanut Butter

Preparation time: 5 min
Cooking time: 10 min
Servings: 1

Ingredients

- ½ - cup rolled oats

- ½ - cup unsweetened almond milk
- 6 - large fresh (or frozen, thawed) strawberries, cored and chopped 2 - teaspoons honey
- ½ - teaspoon vanilla extract
- 1 - pinch salt
- 1/3 - cup liquid egg whites
- 1 - tablespoon peanut butter

Directions

1. In a little pot, heat oats, 1/2 cup almond milk, 1/3 cup water, strawberries, nectar, vanilla, and salt. Heat to the point of boiling, at that point decrease to stew and cook, blending once in a while, until the blend is thick, and oats are full, 5 to 7min. Expel from warm.
2. In a bowl, whisk egg whites until somewhat bubbly. Add cooked cereal to egg whites a spoonful at once, rushing between every option, until oats are completely joined.
3. Pour blend once more into the pot and cook over low heat, mixing always, until oats are thick, 2 to 3min. Be mindful so as not to turn the warmth excessively high so eggs don't scramble.
4. Top cereal with nutty spread.

Nutrition: Calories 412 Carbs 51g Sugar 17g Protein 20g

505. Low Carb Cottage Cheese Pancakes

Preparation time: 5 min
Cooking time: 5 min
servings: 1

Ingredients

- ½ - cup low-fat cottage cheese
- ¼ - cup oats
- ⅓ - cup egg whites (2 egg whites)
- 1 - tsp. Vanilla extract
- 1 - tbsp. Stevia in the raw

Directions

1. Pour curds and egg whites into the blender first, at that point include oats, vanilla concentrate, and a little stevia.
2. Mix to a smooth consistency.
3. Put a container with a bit of cooking time shower on medium warmth and fry every hotcake until brilliant on the two sides.
4. Present with berries, without sugar jam or nutty spread.

Nutrition: Calories 205 Fat 1.5g Carb 19g Sugar 5.5g Protein 24.5g

506. Thai Chopped Chicken Salad With Peanut Vinaigrette

Preparation time: 20 min
Cooking time: 0 min
Servings: 2

Ingredients

Salad:

- 2 - heads romaine lettuce
- 2 - bell peppers, any color, thinly sliced
- 1 - mango, sliced
- 1 - cup shredded carrots
- ½ - cup roasted and unsalted peanuts
- 2 - cups cooked shredded chicken

Spicy peanut dressing:

- 4 - tbsp Thai peanut sauce
- 2 - tbsp olive oil
- 2 - tsp honey
- 2 - tsp rice vinegar
- 2 - tsp lime juice

Directions

1. Finely hack the lettuce and cut peppers and mango into slight strips. Toss lettuce, peppers, mango, carrots, peanuts, and chicken.
2. Make the dressing by whisking together shelled nut sauce, oil, nectar, vinegar and lime juice. Taste and change in accordance with your inclination, including more nectar on the off chance that you'd like it all the sweeter or lime juice on the off chance that you'd like it progressively tart.
3. Just before servings, add a large portion of the dressing to the plate of mixed greens and hurl well. Servings: a plate of mixed greens with staying half of dressing as an afterthought and add to your inclination.

Nutrition: Calories: 351 Carb: 36g Protein: 19g Fat: 18g Sugar: 23g

507. California Steak Salad With Chimichurri Dressing

Preparation time: 5 min
Cooking time: 20 min
Servings: 2

Ingredients

- 1.25lb. Flank steak
- 1 - tablespoon olive oil
- Salt & pepper to season
- 8 oz. Fresh arugula
- 1 - red onion, sliced into 1" rings
- 1lb. - asparagus, trimmed
- 1 - pint of assorted cherry tomatoes, halved 1 - avocado, sliced

Chimichurri dressing:

- 1 - garlic clove
- 1 - cup fresh cilantro
- 2 - tablespoon red wine vinegar
- 1 - tablespoon lime juice
- 3 - tablespoons olive oil
- ¼ - teaspoon smoked paprika
- ½ - teaspoon red pepper flakes
- Salt & pepper to taste

Directions

1. Preheat barbeque to medium-excessive heat.
2. Season asparagus and onion jewelry with olive oil and salt.
3. Set asparagus and onion earrings at the fish fry. Barbecue the asparagus for 5 min. Flame broil the onion rings for 5 min on every facet until scorch imprints show up. Take out and mounted a at ease spot.
4. Add 1 tablespoon of olive to flank steak, rub into every element. Season the two aspects with salt and pepper.
5. Spot flank steak at the barbeque. Flame broil every factor for 3 to 5 min. Let relaxation for 5 min earlier than reducing.
6. While the steak is resting add the accompanying to a chunk sustenance processor: a garlic clove, new cilantro, purple wine vinegar, olive oil, lime juice, smoked paprika, red pepper quantities, salt, and pepper. Mix till clean and resembles a dressing.
7. Collect the Servings: of blended veggies, embody crisp arugula, flame-broiled red onion cuts, asparagus, cherry tomatoes, cut avocado, and reduce flank steak to a big Servings: platter. Present with chimichurri dressing as an afterthought! Topping with a lime.

Nutrition Calories: 452 Sugar: 6g Fat: 32g Carb: 16g Protein: 36g

508. Egg salad

Preparation time: 25 min
Cooking time: 20 min
Servings: 2

Ingredients:

- 6 hardboiled eggs
- 1/3 cup low-fat mayonnaise
- 1/3 cup chopped fresh chives
- ½ teaspoon paprika
- ½ teaspoon pepper
- ½ teaspoon Dijon mustard
- ¼ teaspoon pink salt

Directions

1. Cut up 4 or the eggs into chunks
2. Take out the eggs of the remaining 2 eggs and cut up only the whites Mix all ingredients together

Nutrition: 100 calories; 5.8 g fat; 3.1 g carbohydrates; 8.1 g protein; 212 mg cholesterol; 388 mg sodium

509. Turkey salad

Preparation time: 25 minutes
Cooking time: 10 minutes
Servings: 2

Ingredients:

- 6 cups mixed salad greens
- 3 tablespoons dried cranberries
- 3 cups chopped cooked turkey
- 3 tablespoons olive oil
- ½ cup leftover wheat Eggplant stuffing
- ½ cup of protein powder
- ¼ cup cranberry sauce
- 1 tablespoon cider vinegar
- 1 teaspoon grated orange zest
- 1 cup roasted brussels sprouts
- ¼ teaspoon salt
- ¼ teaspoon black pepper

Directions

1. Place skillet with olive oil on medium heat Pour in wheat Eggplant stuffing and stir
2. Pour in protein powder
3. Stir for 3-5 min
4. Pour in cranberry sauce
5. Our in orange zest and stir for a minute
6. Put in vinegar and stir
7. Put in salt and pepper to taste
8. Put in turkey, vegetables and cranberries

Nutrition 417 calories; 19.8 g total fat; 3.2 g saturated fat; 70 mg cholesterol; 467 mg sodium. 892 mg potassium; 29.7 g carbohydrates; 2.6 g fiber; 13 g sugar;

Conclusion

Bariatric sleeve surgery, formally known as Nissen fundoplication, is a surgical procedure performed by bariatric surgeons that reduces the size of the stomach to about the size of a banana. The gastric sleeve gastrectomy is also considered a restrictive procedure because it restricts the amount of food one can eat at one time.

If you just had gastric sleeve surgery or are considering having it in the near future, this collection of healthy meal plans and tasty recipes will be an invaluable resource when it comes to how to lose weight after gastric sleeve surgery.

It is also important to note that surgical weight loss is not a quick fix but rather a long-term solution. During this process, you should concentrate on eating right, exercising regularly, and monitoring your progress every week.

Gastric Sleeve Bariatric Cookbook Advice on what to eat and how to stay healthy during weight loss surgery

After gastric sleeve surgery, you will be eating much smaller portions of food. You will need to work on adjusting your eating habits as well as your cooking techniques. With the gastric sleeve diet, you still get to enjoy meals such as frittatas, stir-fry, and baked fish dishes. As with any other surgery, it is important that you pay attention to liquids and drink plenty of water. This will help prevent dehydration, which can happen easily if you are not careful. It is also important that you avoid eating large meals or drinking a lot of fluids at once since they can create digestive problems in your stomach and intestines.

The gastric sleeve diet has been called the South Beach Diet 2.0 because it is low in Carbs: and helps you shed weight quickly. One of the better things about this new diet is that you do not have to starve yourself to lose weight as with other diets. As you follow the gastric sleeve diet plan, it will become easy to adjust your lifestyle and adopt a healthier way of eating that will help keep your weight down for good.

Once you have had gastric sleeve surgery, it will be easier for you to make the healthy eating changes necessary to stay on track and continue losing weight over time

The gastric sleeve diet has gained quite a bit of popularity because it is considered safe for most people and causes them to lose weight quickly. As long as you are willing to make some healthy changes to your diet, follow a regular exercise plan and set long-term goals, it is very likely that you will be able to shed pounds after having had the surgery in just a few months.

. The gastric sleeve cookbook is filled with recipes that have been created to help you keep your weight in check for good. These tasty and nutritious meals will not only give you the energy you need to get through the day, but they will also go a long way towards helping you lose weight and maintain a healthy lifestyle.

Index

Printed in Great Britain
by Amazon